Liberal Reform and Industrial Relations: J.H. Whitley (1866–1935), Halifax Radical and Speaker of the House of Commons

J.H. Whitley came from an established business family in Halifax, where he engaged in youth work and municipal politics before becoming MP for Halifax from 1900 to 1928. He was a Liberal Radical who worked with Labour, gave his name to the industrial councils of the First World War and was Speaker of the House of Commons 1921–28, presiding over the debates at the time of the General Strike of 1926. In 1929–31 he toured India as chairman of the Royal Commission on Indian Labour and he was chairman of the BBC between 1930 and 1935.

He was thus a vitally important political figure who was active at the rise of Labour and the decline of Liberalism, involved in the Liberal reforms of the Edwardian age, and deeply concerned about industrial relations in early twentieth-century Britain and beyond.

This volume brings together leading academics and provides new information and analysis on the life, work and times of J.H. Whitley, offering a study of his career in British politics and society, focusing particularly on the last decade of the nineteenth century and the first three decades of the twentieth century.

John A. Hargreaves is an Associate of the Leeds Centre for Victorian Studies, and is a Fellow of the Royal Historical Society, a Fellow of the Historical Association and a Fellow of the Society of Antiquaries. He has written extensively and co-edited *Slavery in Yorkshire: Richard Oastler and the campaign against child labour in the Industrial Revolution* (2012).

Keith Laybourn is the Diamond Jubilee Professor of the University of Huddersfield, a prolific writer on British labour history, and both President and Secretary of the Society for the Study of Labour History. He co-authored *Britain's First Labour Government* (Palgrave Macmillan, 2006, 2013) and has recently published *The Battle for the Roads of Britain: Police, Motorists and the Law c. 1890–1970* (2015).

Richard Toye is Professor of Modern History at the University of Exeter. He is widely published and his most recent book (co-written with Martin Thomas) is *Arguing about Empire: Imperial Rhetoric in Britain and France, 1882–1956* (2017).

Routledge Studies in Modern British History

https://www.routledge.com/history/series/RSMBH

Charles Pelham Villiers
Aristocratic Victorian Radical
Roger Swift

Women, Mission and Church in Uganda
Ethnographic encounters in an age of imperialism, 1895–1960s
Elizabeth Dimock

British Politics, Society and Empire, 1852–1945
Essays in Honour of Trevor O. Lloyd
David W. Gutzke

Deprivation, State Interventions and Urban Communities in Britain, 1968–79
Peter Shapely

Private Secretaries to the Prime Minister
Foreign Affairs from Churchill to Thatcher
Edited by Andrew Holt and Warren Dockter

Liberal Reform and Industrial Relations: J.H. Whitley (1866–1935), Halifax Radical and Speaker of the House of Commons
Edited by John A. Hargreaves, Keith Laybourn and Richard Toye

Liberal Reform and Industrial Relations: J.H. Whitley (1866–1935), Halifax Radical and Speaker of the House of Commons

Edited by John A. Hargreaves, Keith Laybourn and Richard Toye

LONDON AND NEW YORK

First published 2018
by Routledge

2 Park Square, Milton Park, Abingdon, Oxfordshire OX14 4RN
52 Vanderbilt Avenue, New York, NY 10017

Routledge is an imprint of the Taylor & Francis Group, an informa business

First issued in paperback 2019

Copyright © 2018 selection and editorial matter, John A. Hargreaves, Keith Laybourn and Richard Toye; individual chapters, the contributors

The right of John A. Hargreaves, Keith Laybourn and Richard Toye to be identified as the authors of the editorial material, and of the authors for their individual chapters, has been asserted in accordance with sections 77 and 78 of the Copyright, Designs and Patents Act 1988.

All rights reserved. No part of this book may be reprinted or reproduced or utilised in any form or by any electronic, mechanical, or other means, now known or hereafter invented, including photocopying and recording, or in any information storage or retrieval system, without permission in writing from the publishers.

Notice:
Product or corporate names may be trademarks or registered trademarks, and are used only for identification and explanation without intent to infringe.

British Library Cataloguing-in-Publication Data
A catalogue record for this book is available from the British Library

Library of Congress Cataloging-in-Publication Data
A catalog record for this book has been requested

ISBN: 978-1-138-29398-4 (hbk)
ISBN: 978-0-367-34883-0 (pbk)

Typeset in Bembo
by Apex CoVantage, LLC

 Printed in the United Kingdom by Henry Ling Limited

This collection is dedicated to the memory
of John Wilson Barrett
12 February 1963–2 October 2016
A Halifax man whose values inspired him to work
on a biography of J.H. Whitley

Contents

List of illustrations	ix
Notes on editors and contributors	x
Foreword by John Whitley (grandson)	xiv
Preface by John Bercow, Speaker of the House of Commons	xv
Acknowledgements	xvii
Abbreviations	xx
The Whitley Collection and J.H. Whitley Lectures,	
The University of Huddersfield	xxi
Timeline: John Henry Whitley 1866–1935	xxiii

1 **Introduction** 1
JOHN A. HARGREAVES, KEITH LAYBOURN AND RICHARD TOYE

2 **J.H. Whitley (1866–1935): a Speaker shaped by his Halifax roots** 7
JOHN A. HARGREAVES

3 **Clifton: inspiration and service** 30
C.S. KNIGHTON

4 **J.H. Whitley: a model for free churchmen** 50
CLYDE BINFIELD

5 **J.H. Whitley and Halifax politics between 1890 and 1906: the politics of social reform** 67
KEITH LAYBOURN

6 **Industrial relations and joint industrial councils: the UK and beyond 1916–39** 86
GREG PATMORE

7	J.H. Whitley as Speaker of the House of Commons, 1921–28 RICHARD TOYE	103
8	J.H. Whitley and St Stephen's Hall in the Palace of Westminster GRAHAM E. SEEL	113
9	J.H. Whitley and the Royal Commission on Labour in India 1929–31 AMERDEEP PANESAR, AMY STODDART, JAMES TURNER, PAUL WARD AND SARAH WELLS	129
10	J.H. Whitley at the BBC 1930–35 DAVID HENDY	143
11	'Equal partners in a great enterprise': experiencing radio in Yorkshire in the time of J.H. Whitley CHRISTINE VERGUSON	155
12	Self-government: J.H. Whitley's worlds in context KEITH ROBBINS	166
13	J.H. Whitley's 'first draft of history': a study of the obituaries and personal tributes JOHN BARRETT	183
	Index	197

Illustrations

Figures

Front cover: *John Henry Whitley, 1866–1935, Speaker,* Oil on canvas, by Glyn Warren Philpot, ©Parliamentary Art Collection, WOA 3226,

2.1	Undated photograph of Halifax Boys' Camp, Filey	14
2.2	The Hanson Lane Mills excursion to Blackpool 1919	21
3.1	The young Harry Whitley at Clifton College, Bristol	32
4.1	Park Congregational Church, Halifax	54
5.1	Portrait photograph of J.H. Whitley c. 1900 by Greaves & Co., Halifax	80
7.1	Punch Cartoon: Raven-Hill, Leonard. *The Referee's Farewell*	110
9.1	Indian Homes in Bengal	135
9.2	Women Workers in Burma	135
9.3	'Ready for the Mine'	136
9.4	Whitley and an elephant	137
9.5	Assam	137
10.1	BBC Photo: Whitley, J.H., Chairman of BBC ('August 1931')	144
10.2	Punch Cartoon: Partridge, Bernard *BBSecrecy*	151

Colour plates

1	Interior of St Stephen's Hall c. 1910 (looking East). Note the empty panels are dressed with red flock paper	112a
2	Interior of St Stephen's Hall as it appears today, showing the adornment sponsored by J.H. Whitley	112b

Table

5.1	General Election result, Halifax Constituency 1900	81

Editors and contributors

Editors

Dr John A. Hargreaves has taught extensively in secondary, higher and adult education, mainly in West Yorkshire. He obtained his first degree at the University of Southampton and later completed a master's degree and PhD part-time at the University of Huddersfield, where he is now a Visiting Research Fellow in History. He is also an Associate of the Leeds Centre of Victorian Studies, a Fellow of the Royal Historical Society, a Fellow of the Historical Association and a Fellow of the Society of Antiquaries. He is currently preparing a third edition of his history of Halifax and writing a bicentenary history of the Halifax Choral Society. He has written over forty articles for the *Oxford Dictionary of National Biography*, edited twenty-five volumes of the *Transactions of the Halifax Antiquarian Society* and a volume of nineteenth-century manorial court rolls published by the Yorkshire Archaeological Society. He co-edited *Slavery in Yorkshire. Richard Oastler and the campaign against child labour in the Industrial Revolution* for the University of Huddersfield Press in 2012 and reviews regularly for the Historical Association website.

Professor Keith Laybourn is the Diamond Jubilee Professor at the University of Huddersfield within the Division of History where he has also been Professor of Modern British History. He is a Fellow of the Royal Historical Society and an Honorary Fellow of the Historical Association. He edited the *Annual Bulletin of Historical Literature* for the Historical Association for eleven years and has written and edited more than forty books and written about eighty articles. He has written extensively on British Labour history, including a co-authored book on *Britain's First Labour Government* (Palgrave Macmillan, 2006, 2013) and has just published *The Battle for the Roads of Britain: Police, Motorists and the Law c.1890s–1970* (Palgrave Macmillan, 2015).

Professor Richard Toye is Professor of Modern History at the University of Exeter. He has published widely in the field of modern British History, including the history of parliamentary rhetoric and culture in the interwar years. He delivered the inaugural J.H. Whitley lecture at the University of Huddersfield. His most recent book is *The Roar of the Lion: The Untold Story of Churchill's World War II Speeches* (OUP, 2013)

Contributors

Dr John Barrett was an ex-police officer who undertook a PhD at the University of Huddersfield where he was supervised by Professor Keith Laybourn. He retired as a police officer and became involved in writing a book on the life of J.H. Whitley. Sadly he died on 2 October 2016. This collection of essays is dedicated to his memory.

Professor Clyde Binfield, OBE, FSA, and FRHist S, is Professor Emeritus in History, University of Sheffield. He was Head of Department 1988–91 overseeing the merger of the Departments of Ancient History, Economic and Social History, and Medieval and Modern History, to form the present Department of History. He served on the Council of the Royal Historical Society 1997–2001. The prime focus of his writing has been on the context of English Protestant Nonconformity, and he has written extensively, including his book *So Down to Prayers* (Rowman & Littlefield, 1977).

Professor David Hendy is Professor of Media and Communications at the University of Sussex. He is a media historian and regular broadcaster, and is currently researching and writing *The BBC: A Century of British Life* which will be published to coincide with the BBC's Centenary in 2022. He is the author of four books including *Life on Air: A History of Radio Four* (Oxford University Press, 2007) which won the Longman – History Today Book of the Year Award, and *Public Service Broadcasting* (Palgrave Macmillan, 2013) In 2011 the Media Ecology Association of North America awarded him the James W. Carey Award for Outstanding Journalism for his BBC 3 series on twentieth-century media history, *Rewiring the Mind*.

Dr C.S. Knighton is a graduate of Magdalene College, Cambridge and Magdalen College, Oxford. He was formerly an Editor of State Papers for the Public Record Office, responsible for volumes on the reign of Edward VI, Mary I and Anne. He has also written about Westminster Abbey and School in the sixteenth and seventeenth centuries. Since 2009 he has been Principal Assistant Keeper at Clifton College, and has edited a collection of documents from the College's early years for the Bristol Record Society. He is Fellow of the Royal Historical Society and the Society of Antiquaries.

Amerdeep Panesar obtained a BA degree in History and Politics at the University of Huddersfield in 2015 and completed an MA by Research at the University of Huddersfield in 2016. He is currently undertaking a PhD at the University of Leicester and, in connection with the Marylebone Cricket Club (MCC), into the history of minority in cricket.

Professor Greg Patmore is Professor of Business and Labour History at the University of Sydney, Australia. He has written extensively on industrial relations, business history, the co-operative movement and more broadly on international labour history. He has just published *Worker Voice: Employee Representation in the Workplace in Australia, Canada, Germany, the UK and the US 1914–1939* (Liverpool University Press, 2015).

Professor Keith Robbins, a Bristolian and an Oxford graduate, has held Chairs of History at Bangor and Glasgow Universities before becoming Vice-Chancellor of the University of Wales, Lampeter and also, for six years, Senior Vice-Chancellor of the Federal University of Wales. He has been editor of *History* and President of the Historical Association and of the Ecclesiastical History Society. He has lectured in North America, Australia, China and many European countries. He has written prolifically on many aspects of modern British, European and World History ranging from *Munich 1938* (Cassell, 1968) to *Transforming the World* (Palgrave Macmillan, 2013), with translations into German, Polish, Italian, Magyar, Latvian, Japanese, Russian, Spanish, Portuguese and Arabic. He has edited the series: *Profiles in Power, Turning Points, Religion, Society and Politics in Britain, Inventing the Nation, Britain and Europe, A History of the Contemporary World.* Pertinent books include *The Eclipse of a Great Power: Modern Britain 1870–1992* (Routledge, 1994), *Nineteenth-Century Britain: Integration and Diversity* (Clarendon Press, 1988), *History, Religion and Identity in Modern Britain* (Bloomsbury, 1993), *Great Britain: Identities, Institutions and the Idea of Britishness* (Routledge, 1998), *England, Ireland, Scotland, Wales: The Christian Church 1900–2000* (Oxford University Press, 2008). He holds honorary degrees from Wales and the West of England and is a Fellow of the Royal Society of Edinburgh and the Learned Society of Wales.

Graham E. Seel read History at St Andrews University before completing a Post-Graduate Certificate of Education (PGCE) at Cambridge University. He is Head of History at St Paul's School in London. He has published widely on British History. His most recent book is *King John, an underrated king* (Anthem Press, 2012).

Amy Stoddart has just completed her History degree at the University of Huddersfield (as of April 2017) and is hoping to take a Masters by Research degree at the University of Huddersfield from the autumn of 2017.

James Turner is a History student, currently in his third year at the University of Huddersfield.

Dr Christine Verguson began her career in the Local Studies and Archives department of Huddersfield Central Library before spending thirty years at the BBC in Leeds as librarian, researcher and finally journalist before leaving to become a full-time research student at the University of Huddersfield. She successfully completed her doctorate dissertation, '"Opting Out"? Nation, Region and Locality: The BBC in Yorkshire 1945–1990' in 2014. Since then she has started to develop some of the research which was only touched upon in her dissertation – in 2015 she received a 'special award' from the Yorkshire Society for her essay on the broadcasts of William Holt. While continuing to research the part Yorkshire played in the early development of broadcasting, she is actively pursuing her interests in local and urban history. She is Publicity Officer for Huddersfield Local History Society.

Professor Paul Ward is Professor of Modern British History at the University of Huddersfield. He is author of four books including *Britishness since 1870* (Routledge, 2004) and *Huw T. Edwards: British Labour and Welsh Socialism* (University of Wales Press, 2011). He is currently experimenting with the co-production of historical research with community groups and students to explore new ways of understanding the past in conversation with the present. Students on the first-year module Twentieth-Century Britain have conducted some of the research, interpretation of sources and writing of the chapter.

Sarah Jane Wells undertook a BA (Hons) in Textile Practice (Craft & Art) at the University of Huddersfield. Sarah is now involved in Contemporary Practice teaching and co-ordinating with communities on heritage projects.

Foreword by John Whitley (grandson)

Harry (J.H.) Whitley died five years before any of his grandchildren were born. We, the five children of his younger son Oliver, gradually discovered as we grew up that our grandfather had been a notable person – a Speaker of the House of Commons, who had given his name to 'Whitley Councils', recipient of the letters framed on our mantelpiece from PM Campbell-Bannerman and King George V. Only in later years did we (and our own children on visits to their ageing grandparents) begin to dip into the JHW scrapbooks and other family papers, fascinated by a Visitors' Book with signatures ranging from Crown Prince Hirohito to Mohandas K. Gandhi.

It fell to me on the deaths of my parents to find a suitable home for my grandfather's small archive which, reflecting both deep family roots in Halifax and a many-faceted career, would interest some historians. The family chose Huddersfield, as the local university for Halifax, with its excellent archive facilities and record of research on themes relevant to my grandfather's life.

This choice has resulted in the annual J.H. Whitley Lectures, a growing body of research and the 2016 Conference whose papers form the basis of this book. We are grateful to all who have contributed to this process, notably Professor Paul Ward, as overseer of the archive and organiser of the conference, and particularly Professor Keith Laybourn as overseer and chief editor of the book. Special thanks are also due to Professor Richard Toye and Dr John A. Hargreaves, not only as joint editors of the book but also as initiators of the whole project.

I must also pay warm tribute to the late Dr John Barrett, author of this book's final chapter, to whom the book is dedicated. In 2012, after completing, as a mature student, a doctorate on poverty in nineteenth-century Huddersfield, his interest in J.H. Whitley was aroused by Richard Toye's inaugural lecture. This led him to explore the Whitley Collection and carry out research more widely towards a biography – research sadly cut short by his untimely death in October 2016. I am delighted that his diligent work is now being picked up by John A. Hargreaves, so that the present volume will eventually be complemented by a full biography.

John Whitley, Cumbria

Preface by John Bercow, Speaker of the House of Commons

The official portrait of John Henry Whitley hangs in the dining room, in the State Rooms of Speaker's House. The style of the age decrees that his depiction – dressed in the robes of his office, holding a scroll at the entrance of Central Lobby – does little to mark him out from the other Speakers of a similar period whose portraits flank the walls.

Yet J.H. Whitley was a remarkable man. He was a Member of Parliament, government Minister, Senior Deputy Speaker, Speaker and, in later life, an outspoken advocate for the poor in India. His modest upbringing and background in the cotton industry was unusual in a House of Commons that was then primarily comprised of country gentlemen or members of the legal profession. Unbeknown to him or, indeed, anyone else at the time, he was also the last Liberal Speaker, and the only Speaker to refuse a peerage since the practice established in 1789 that one was offered on retirement from the chair.

By longstanding convention, the Speaker must be independent of political party. However, whilst Whitley was to be beset by the periodic accusations of partiality which are also a matter of longstanding (if unofficial) convention, this fascinating account of his life gives a flavour of how the philosophy, rather than the politics, of liberalism had a profound effect on his outlook and decision-making.

His 'loose-rein' approach to the behaviour of new Members was treated with a certain amount of hostility by their more established counterparts. All Speakers, myself included, would probably consider themselves to have served during testing times, and we would all probably be right to a greater or lesser extent. Whitley's Speakership was forged in the rise of the Labour movement, and the beginning of the end of the Liberal one, with all the consequent turmoil and uncertainty that such sea-changes bring. As Speaker, Whitley had to negotiate what the party's detractors referred to as the 'Labour rowdyism' – similarly deprecated by their leader Ramsay MacDonald – without losing the respect of the Chamber for either excessive indulgence to the demonstrations, or for over-proscriptive censure against them. By all accounts, he negotiated this tightrope – which is well recognised in all its manifestations by those who have occupied the Speaker's chair – with humour and self-deprecation. Whilst only a side-note in the histories of the Labour Party, it is interesting to reflect how his style as the chairman of the proceedings, praised as fair and gentle without being lax, actively assisted in transforming them into Her Majesty's Official Opposition.

This book is an intriguing account of an unconventional man, whose quiet impact at the time continues to have resonance many years after his death. In the words of a 1927 newspaper article on his Speakership, 'He is eminently reasonable without expecting in other people an equal grasp of the principles of reason, yet with a profound faith in the essential reasonableness of the human species.'

Rt Hon John Bercow MP
Speaker

Acknowledgements

All publications, and particularly collections of essays, owe a debt to the kindness and help of others. This is especially the case in this collection which derives from the interest of John P. Whitley and the Whitley family in depositing the J.H. Whitley collection (JHW) into the archives at the Heritage Quay at the University of Huddersfield. This provided the basic source for many of the contributions to this volume. From the depositing of this archive has arisen an annual J.H. Whitley Lecture, the first one of which (2012) has given rise to the essay by Professor Richard Toye, and the third of which (2015) was given by Dr. John A. Hargreaves, and became the basis of his essay on the life of J.H. Whitley, a Speaker shaped by his Halifax roots. In September 2016 many of the contributors to this volume spoke about their work at the J.H. Whitley Conference held at the University of Huddersfield. Organised by Professor Paul Ward, this conference was the opportunity for the contributors to display their research and interests. The idea for this book led to the idea of holding a conference, though the conference also partly shaped the book.

In producing this book we have to thank many people. John P. Whitley, and the Whitley family, allowed us to quote from that collection and allowed us to use some of the photographs from J.H. Whitley's private collection, which are indicated later in the introductory information on the illustrations. He has also allowed Clyde Binfield to quote from the unpublished manuscript of Oliver Whitley. In addition the Heritage Quay at the University of Huddersfield provided us with easy access to the J.H. Whitley collection. Daniel Sudron and the West Yorkshire Archives Calderdale provided access to archive sources and illustrations. Martin Hughes, Senior Archivist at the Bodleian Library, the University of Oxford, allowed us to use material from the Bodleian, most obviously the Harcourt collection. We would also like to thank Colin Harris at the Bodleian Library for organising permission to be granted through Martin Hughes and on behalf of Dr Chris Fletcher, Keeper of the Special Collection on the basis of 'non-exclusive right' for documents held in the Bodleian Library. Claire Batley, Senior Archivist (Public Services and Outreach) of the Parliamentary Archives, House of Commons approved the use of short quotes from Parliamentary Archives. Some material was gathered from The National

Archives at Kew, which gave permission to draw from their document collection under the Government Open Licence arrangements whose essential requirement is proper attribution. In addition we would like to thank the Controller of Her Majesty's Stationary Office (HMSO) (Norwich) for permission to quote from Crown Copyright material. For both The National Archives and the HMSO one simply has to observe the guidelines of the information sheet on the rules of Government Open Licence.

We were grateful to several bodies, families and organisations for the right to reproduce photographic and illustrative material. We have already acknowledged John Whitley and the Whitley family permitting us to use photographs from the J.H. Whitley Archive at the University of Huddersfield, and these appear in the article on Whitley's Halifax roots written by John A. Hargreaves and in that collectively written by Amerdeep Panesar, Amy Stoddard, James Turner, Paul Ward and Sarah Wells on the Royal Commission on Indian Labour. The front cover, a photograph of the official portrait of Speaker Whitley, is produced with the permission of Therese Crawley of the Palace of Westminster Curator's Office. Permission to use the photograph of Halifax Boys' Camp, Filey was given by Daniel Sudron, Archivist, on behalf of West Yorkshire Archives Service, Calderdale, Central Library, Northgate House, Northgate, Halifax, HX1 1UN. The photograph of the young J.H. Whitley at Clifton was supplied by Dr. C.S. Knighton who is the Principal Assistant Archivist at Clifton College, Bristol. The BBC allowed us to use the photograph of J.H. Whitley giving the inaugural Empire Service broadcast in 1932. This photograph is also reproduced within the volume. *Punch* permitted us to use Leonard Raven-Hill's cartoon *The Referee's Farewell*. They also permitted the publication of the Bernard Partridge cartoon *Secrecy*. Professor Clyde Binfield supplied the atmospheric print of Park Congregational Church, Halifax taken from the *Congregational Year Book, 1870*, London, Congregational Union, 1870, p. 372. The unknown illustrator is clearly dead and the illustration is clearly out of copyright and the *Congregational Year Book* ceased publication in 1972, but general permission was given to use this by the United Reformed Church (URC), by Louise Ault on behalf of John Proctor, the General Secretary of the URC. The photograph of St Stephen's Hall (East interior shot) is taken from the USA http://hdl.loc.gov/loc.pnp/pp.print and ppmsc 08561 http://hdl.loc.gov.pnp/ppmsc.08561 and permission has been given subject to the reproduction number being published with the credit to the Library as 'Library of Congress, LC-USXZ62–13459. Reproduced with credit to the Library of Congress Prints and Photographs Division, Washington DC, photographic number LD-DIG-ppmsc-08561 (digital file from the original) digital ID'. The image of St Stephen's Hall (looking west) is located on flickr at the address https:/www.flickr.com/photos/uk parliament/2700369675/in/album-72157606364297627/.

Finally, our thanks also go to Robert Langham and Michael Bourne and the Routledge editorial team for their perceptive and friendly guidance in preparing this collection of essays. They have added greatly to the final outcome.

As is obvious from the statements above, every effort has been made to trace copyright holders and to avoid any infringement of copyright. However, we apologise unreservedly to any copyright holders whose permission we may have inadvertently overlooked. We will certainly include such omissions in any further edition of the book.

Abbreviations

AFL	American Federation of Labour
AJICIRC	Association of Joint Industrial Council and Industrial Relations Committee
ASE	Amalgamated Society of Engineers
ASLEF	Associated Society of Locomotive Engineers and Firemen
BBC	British Broadcasting Corporation
CMA	Canadian Manufacturers' Association
CYB	Congregational Year Book
ERP	Employer Representation Plan
FBI	Federation of British Industry
ILO	International Labour Organisation
ILP	Independent Labour Party
JIC	Joint Industrial Council
JP	Justice of the Peace
JURCHS	*Journal of the United Reform Church History Society*
MBA	Master Builders' Association
MRC	Modern Records Office (Warwick University)
NA	National Arichives
NUR	National Union of Railwaymen
ODNB	*Oxford Dictionary of National Biography*
TUC	Trades Union Congress
UK	United Kingdom
UMFC	United Methodist Free Church
WMA	Wesleyan Methodist Association
YCYB	*Yorkshire Congregational Year Book*
YMCA	Young Men's Christian Association

The Whitley Collection and J.H. Whitley Lectures, The University of Huddersfield

In October 2011 the Whitley family deposited the papers of J.H. Whitley in the University of Huddersfield's Archives and Special Collections. As part of the deposit it was agreed to establish an annual J.H. Whitley Lecture relating to politics in the early twentieth century.

The Whitley Collection at Heritage Quay

The J.H. Whitley Papers, collected by his family, form the basis of a collection, which is being supplemented by papers relating to other members of his family.

This collection is being used for school visits, undergraduate and postgraduate research and can be consulted at heritagequay.org/archives.

The J.H. Whitley Lectures

The series so far:

2012

Punch and Judy Politics 1920s style: The House of Commons in the era of Speaker Whitley
   Professor Richard Toye, Exeter University

2013

Speaker Whitley's Britain: Parliament, Politics and Industrial Relations in the 1920s
   Professor John Shepherd, University of Huddersfield

2014

Can an old parliament be relevant to young people?
   The Rt Hon John Bercow, MP, Speaker of the House of Commons

xxii   *The Whitley Collection and J.H. Whitley Lectures*

2015

J.H. Whitley (1866–1935): a Speaker shaped by his Halifax roots
  Dr John A. Hargreaves, author of a history of *Halifax*

2016

The future of Trade Unions
  Sir Alistair Graham, Chairman of Committee on Standards in Public Life

2017

The myths and lessons of the 1924 Labour Government
  Michael Meadowcroft

Timeline

John Henry (Harry) Whitley 1866–1935

1866	Born in Halifax to Nathan Whitley and Sarah, née Rinder (d. 1869)
1878–84	Pupil at Clifton College, Bristol
1884	Began work for S. Whitley & Co, Cotton Spinners on death of his uncle. (Became senior partner in 1889 on death of his father.)
1884–85	External BA degree, London University
1892	Married Margherita (known as Margaret), daughter of Giulio Marchetti & Anne, nee Crossley
1893	Elected to Halifax Borough Council (Liberal)
1898	Replaced by his brother Alfred as senior partner, S. Whitley & Co.
1900–28	Liberal MP for Halifax
1907–10	Junior Treasury Minister & Liberal Whip
1910–11	Deputy Chairman of Ways & Means (Deputy Deputy Speaker)
1911	Sworn of Privy Council
1911–21	Chairman of Ways & Means and Deputy Speaker
1916–19	Chairman, Committee on 'Relations of Employers & Employees'
1921–28	Speaker of House of Commons
1925	Death of first wife
1928	Married Helen Clarke
1929–31	Chairman, Royal Commission on Labour in India
1930–35	Chairman, British Broadcasting Corporation
1935	Died in London. Ashes interred at Warley. (Memorial at Lister Lane Cemetery, Halifax.)

John Henry Whitley was never known by his first name. To family and close friends and in his early political career in Halifax, he was known as Harry. Otherwise he was simply known by his initials as (Mr) J.H. Whitley.

1 Introduction

John A. Hargreaves, Keith Laybourn and Richard Toye

J.H. Whitley, famously Speaker of the House of Commons in the 1920s, was a vitally important figure in many other areas of politics and civic, urban and religious life in the late nineteenth and early twentieth centuries. Born into a mill-owning family he became an employer before entering local and civic politics in Halifax, and then representing Halifax as an MP from 1900 until 1928 before rising to national recognition as Speaker of the House of Commons. Even after his retirement as Speaker, on grounds of bad health, Whitley remained in the public eye, being drawn into Indian and Empire affairs in the early 1930s and involved in governing the BBC. His life and achievements form the basis of this book. This is not a biography of him, however, although there is much on his life, but a reflection of the developments and changes in the world in which he lived and how he influenced them. Acting the role of businessman, philanthropist, Victorian politician, Edwardian Progressive, though not New, Liberal, industrial conciliator, politician, statesman and arbiter of the age of changing communications he in many ways reflected the changing face of British society from the 1890s to the 1930s. The essays in this collection aim to reveal the diversity of his work and experiences and the way in which he captured the mood of a changing world.

Whitley was born in 1866, during the final premiership of Earl Russell. The following year, Earl Derby's Conservative government (in which Benjamin Disraeli was the leading light) passed the Second Reform Act, which radically extended the parliamentary franchise. The year 1868 was when first Disraeli and then W.E. Gladstone each became Prime Minister for the first time. Whitley's lifetime also witnessed the Third Reform Act (1884), the Representation of the People Act (1918) and the Representation of the People (Equal Franchise) Act (1928). The latter measure was introduced during Whitley's Speakership and became law a month after he had retired. Thereby was completed the process by which a polity based on a restricted, property-based, franchise for men became one in which all men and women over the age of twenty-one were allowed to vote. We must, however, be cautious about relating these events as the completion of a Whiggish narrative of progressive reform, not only because of the subsequent persistence of anomalies such as university seats but also because of the problem of the House of Lords, which to this day has never been solved.[1] It is easy to forget, moreover, that constitutional change was not as peaceable as British national mythology suggests. The South of Ireland established itself as a Free State in 1922 through violent confrontation, following decades in which successive efforts to achieve Home Rule through parliamentary methods had failed.

Undeniably, what was left of the United Kingdom was a more democratic society at the end of Whitley's life than at the beginning. Yet it was also, to a considerable extent, a deferential and hierarchical one.

Another important political theme of Whitley's era was the decline of the Liberal Party and the (incomplete) rise of Labour. These phenomena were of course related to the extension of the franchise, although the relationship was not as straightforward as historians once believed.[2] Furthermore, the Liberal trajectory was not all downhill. After 1886, Gladstone's ascendancy was replaced by that of Lord Salisbury, which appeared confirmed by the Boer War and the 'Khaki election' of 1900.[3] Yet the war's troubled end and aftermath helped set the scene for a Liberal revival that was dramatically assisted by two major Unionist own goals. The first was the 1902 'Balfour' Education Act, which raised Nonconformist ire by funding Church of England and Catholic schools. The second was Joseph Chamberlain's 1903 proposals for protectionism (or 'Tariff Reform'), which blew apart the existing consensus in favour of Free Trade and united the normally fractious Liberals in defence of the status quo. Liberal culture was thus revealed to be very vibrant and dynamic, although, after the party returned to office in 1905, its pursuit of issues such as Home Rule also generated considerable popular hostility.[4]

As Peter Clarke has recently argued, the Gladstonian mindset remained 'a potent force' that shaped how Britain reacted to the First World War.[5] Indeed, the achievement for which Whitley himself is now chiefly remembered – the proposal for Joint Industrial Councils – was based on the classical Gladstonian belief that capital and labour shared fundamental interests, and that their conflicts were susceptible to resolution through processes of rational conciliation. This core assumption also underwrote the Liberal commitment to the 'progressive alliance' with the youthful Labour Party, of which Whitley was an advocate, but which broke down at the end of the war. Notwithstanding brief, partial revivals in 1923 and 1929, the Liberal Party was increasingly divided and, by 1931, was all but finished as an electoral force. How Whitley regarded this state of affairs was unclear because, as Speaker, he was debarred from controversial political pronouncements, which he seems to have eschewed in private too. But it is conceivable that that he looked upon it with a degree of equanimity: for although the Liberal Party was at death's door, many of the Liberal values he held dear retained a degree of currency. Stanley Baldwin, the dominant political figure of the age, was regarded by many as 'a sort of honorary Liberal' and as such had considerable appeal to Nonconformist opinion.[6] In the House of Commons in 1925 Baldwin made his famous plea for industrial harmony: 'Give peace in our time, O Lord'.[7] Given Baldwin's subsequent record, some might see this remark as a masterpiece of political humbug. However, we may imagine that at the time Mr Speaker Whitley, witnessing the scene from the chair, regarded it as sincere and gave it his silent endorsement.

The essays in this book capture the changes in British society and politics through the medium of the life of J.H. Whitley. John Hargreaves reflects upon how Whitley was shaped by his Halifax roots throughout his political life and outlines his career from social reformer, to municipal councillor and MP and eventually to Speaker of the House of Commons. Religion and education were important in his life but, above all, this essay emphasises the centrality of his association with his Halifax roots, the lynchpin of his life and career. C.S. Knighton examines the educational upbringing of Whitley at Clifton College, Bristol, a college which has tolerated varied and individual opinions and has encouraged outreach work into communities. J.H. Whitley was educated there and it encouraged within him a life-long commitment to social reform and tolerance. It was an association which he did not forget and which tied him to Clifton throughout his life. Clyde Binfield enforces this commitment in his life, noting that he became the first Free Church man and the first man from an industrial background to become Speaker of the House of Commons. His upbringing as a Congregationalist ensured that his thinking and actions throughout life were cemented in religious connection, education and familial Congregationalism.

J.H. Whitley's political career began in the radical politics of Halifax in the early 1890s when he was not yet thirty years of age. Keith Laybourn suggests that he was an unusual unifying political figure in Halifax politics and was returned as one of the two MPs for Halifax in 1900 largely because he combined his commitment to social reform with a range of Old Liberal and New Liberal values. He was from a well-established industrial family, supported Home Rule and the taxation of land values, but combined this with a fervent commitment to social welfare and a recognition of the right of trade unions and workers. These varied policies allowed him to draw support from a deeply divided Halifax Liberal Party and to also gain support from the emergent trade unions and Independent Labour Party, which meant that he was able to win a Halifax seat in the 1900 General Election and to share parliamentary representation with James Parker, the Labour MP, from 1906, in a constituency which was one of the centres of the emergent political Labour movement.

Reflecting upon the long-held Liberal belief that capital and labour were not necessarily in conflict and could be reconciled J.H. Whitley was closely associated with industrial conciliation throughout his life and particularly with a movement referred to as 'Whitleyism', which led to the formation of Joint Industrial Councils to facilitate industrial conciliation, and which emerged from the Whitley Report of 1917 and 1918. 'Whitleyism' peculiarly arose to deal with the problem of industrial conflict in Britain during the First World War and Whitley committees established themselves in the woollen and worsted textile industry, amongst civil servants, and in a small number of other industries. Nevertheless, 'Whitleyism' never really caught on in Britain though it did gather some limited interest in Australia, Germany, and particularly in the United States where the American Federation of Labour favoured it because it believed that it meant the legitimisation of trade unionism.

Whitley was an active MP, became a Liberal whip and rose up the political hierarchy to become Speaker of the House of Commons. Richard Toye considers him to have been at least a competent and possibly a good Speaker of the House of Commons in the 1920s, which was a period of major political upheaval and industrial conflict. This was the period which saw the emergence of the Labour Party as the party of government and Whitley chose to allow its inexperienced MPs flexibility in the House of Commons and 'to drive them with a loose rein'. He also kept business going as usual in the House of Commons during the bitterly fought General Strike of 1926. He emerged from these events and developments as an emollient, cooperative and consensual figure who believed in progress without being a 'hot gospeller'. Indeed, in many respects he brought many old Edwardian Liberal values to the Speakership and personally reflects the strange survival of Liberal England.

As Speaker of the House of Commons, Whitley was responsible for substantial schemes for the adornment in St. Stephen's Hall in the Palace of Westminster. He took close personal responsibility for the commissioning of the new panels of historical events, helping to raise the money through personal contacts and through negotiating on the imperial and Whiggish British historical scenes that were depicted by the panels. Always involved, making many appeals for support, to some he was seen 'as the greatest living patron of British pictorial art'.

From his early years as an advanced Liberal Whitley believed in the running of Empire by consent, arguing that it would not be otherwise feasible without the approval of the native peoples. He was given his opportunity to test his belief when he was appointed Chairman of the Royal Commission on Labour in India in 1929. From his India scrapbook we see him deeply involved in addressing poor factory conditions and industrial relations. The Commission he chaired made 357 recommendations to reduce factory hours and improve conditions for men, women and children largely from rural backgrounds and unused to factory conditions. These recommendations essentially depended upon the consent of Indian industrialists and Whitley, in his role, acted as a liberal imperialist leaving the destiny of India as 'our responsibility' rather than to the Indian people in their own name.

Despite his declining health, Whitley also became Chairman of the BBC in 1930. David Hendy reveals how this relatively new broadcasting medium benefited from his close relationship with John Reith who ran the BBC in its early years. The protection from political interference which Whitley offered allowed Reith to develop his firm control over the direction of BBC broadcasting. He certainly influenced the expansion of the BBC internationally (through the Empire Service), nationally and locally throughout the regions of Britain. Christine Verguson's essay, reflecting upon the last of these spheres of influence, examines the expansion of the BBC in Yorkshire up to Whitley's death in 1935 – arguing that its pragmatic expansion into music and light entertainment, which he partly encouraged, challenged his hope that people would restrict their listening in favour of other leisure activities

J.H. Whitley's lifetime corresponded almost exactly with the period when legislation saw Britain move from constitutional government to democracy, provoking within the United Kingdom and the Empire notions of self-government and self-regulation. In his essay, Keith Robbins argues that these developments mean that J. H. Whitley had to grapple with the issues of Home Rule for Ireland, of which he was deeply supportive, and of examining the future government of India through his chairmanship of the Royal Commission on Indian Labour. His precise work was marginal to Indian independence but did impinge on the issue of what self-government, popular government, commonwealth, Empire status, and Dominion status actually meant.

The late John Barrett offers a fitting conclusion of J.H. Whitley's life through an analysis of his obituaries – taking as his theme the view that obituaries should reflect the life rather than create myths. What he demonstrates is that the obituaries offer different levels of reflection and that, whilst local obituaries focus upon the man they knew, national obituaries often broadly related Whitley to his national activities and reflect more the man that locals did not know. What emerges is the picture of a much respected and modest man deeply steeped in his late Victorian and Edwardian upbringing trying to operate in the challenging environment of the early twentieth century.

In the final analysis, this collection of essays serves two main purposes. First, it establishes the changing political landscape of late nineteenth- and early twentieth-century politics at the local, national and international levels, raising issues about the move from constitutional government to democracy, imperialism to independence, industrial conflict to conciliation, and about developments in modernity. Secondly, it establishes the centrally important role that Speaker Whitley had in these events. Hostile to, and disdainful of, title and privilege, and deeply involved in the reshaping of the political, economic and social structure of Britain he was never able to escape fully from his Gladstonian upbringing in an age of imperialism. Nevertheless, James Parker, the Labour MP who joined Whitley to represent Halifax in 1906, reflected ironically that Whitley had sought to be a 'true commoner'.[8] This is an appropriate epitaph to a man committed to democratic reform and social elevation in an age of imperialism.

Notes

1 'Introduction', in Julie V. Gottlieb and Richard Toye (eds), *The Aftermath of Suffrage: Women, Gender and Politics in Britain, 1918–1945*, Basingstoke, Palgrave Macmillan, 2013, pp. 1–18.
2 H.C.G. Matthew, R.I. McKibbin and J. Kay, 'The franchise factor in the rise of the Labour party', *English Historical Review*, 9 (1976), 723–52; P.F. Clarke,. 'Liberals, Labour and the franchise', *English Historical Review*, 92 (1977), 582–9; Duncan Tanner, 'The parliamentary electoral system, the "fourth" Reform Act and the rise of Labour', *Bulletin of the Institute of Historical Research*, 56 (1983), 205–19; Michael Dawson, 'Money and the real impact of the Fourth Reform Act', *Historical Journal*, 35 (1992), 369–81; David Thackeray, *Conservatism for the Democratic Age: Conservative Cultures and the Challenge of Mass Politics in Early Twentieth Century England*, Manchester, Manchester University Press, 2013, pp. 117–18.

3 Paul Readman, 'The Conservative Party, patriotism, and British politics: The case of the General Election of 1900', *Journal of British Studies*, 40 (2001), 107–45.
4 Frank Trentmann, *Free Trade Nation: Commerce, Consumption, and Civil Society in Modern Britain*, Oxford, Oxford University Press, 2008; Daniel M. Jackson, *Popular Opposition to Irish Home Rule in Edwardian Britain*, Liverpool, Liverpool University Press, 2009.
5 Peter Clarke, *The Locomotive of War: Money, Empire, Power and Guilt*, London, Bloomsbury, 2017, p. 27.
6 Philip Williamson, *Conservative leadership and national values*, Cambridge, Cambridge University Press, 1999, p. 353.
7 *Hansard*, Parliamentary Debates, House of Commons Debate, 6 March 1925, vol. 181 col. 841.
8 *The Halifax Courier and Guardian*, 9 February 1935.

2 J.H. Whitley (1866–1935)
A Speaker shaped by his Halifax roots

John A. Hargreaves

Introduction

In Halifax Town Hall, the name of the Rt Hon. J.H. Whitley MP, who served as MP for Halifax from 1900 to 1928 and as Speaker of the House of Commons from 1921 to 1928, is inscribed in marble on both the rolls of honour of Halifax's former Members of Parliament and of those who received the Honorary Freedom of the County Borough of Halifax, which he was awarded in 1919. Moreover, J.H. Whitley is not the only member of the Whitley family who is similarly commemorated. His father Nathan's name appears no fewer than three times on the list of Mayors for 1876–77, 1881–82 and 1882–83; his uncle John, Nathan's brother, is also recorded as having been awarded the Freedom of the County Borough in 1907, whilst his elder son Percival's name is also displayed as Mayor of Halifax for 1941, identifying a family connection with the County Borough of Halifax spanning three generations. Indeed, J.H. Whitley's younger son, Oliver, speaking in Halifax in 1988, declared that 'family characteristics' such as the Whitley family's deep commitment to education in Halifax, depended 'on roots' which 'can be understood only by digging down into the past'.[1] The aim of this chapter is to enquire how far J.H. Whitley's ancestral and family roots, his education and upbringing, his experience of industrial relations, municipal politics and philanthropy in Halifax helped shape the remarkable parliamentary career of this son of Halifax who, on his retirement from the office of Speaker of the House of Commons in 1928, commented that he came to the Palace of Westminster 'rather reluctantly' since he had previously found fulfilment in local voluntary work with socially deprived youths 'in the rough and tumble of comradeship amongst the boys of a great industrial town'. Indeed, he maintained that these boys 'were my university, from whom . . . I learnt most of what I know, and a great piece of my heart is with them still'. He also sincerely and pointedly thanked his constituents 'whose forbearance had made it possible for the representative of an industrial constituency to occupy the Speakership'.[2]

Harry Whitley, as he was known within the family and locally, was born in 1866 at 9, Park Road, Halifax, an imposing Victorian mansion with commanding western views of Sir Francis Crossley's People's Park, designed by Joseph

Paxton and opened in 1857, with its serpentine lakes, classical statuary, Italianate pavilion and terraced promenades, where workers might take a recuperative stroll after a hard day's work and admire the distant views of the moorland encompassing the town. Indeed, the lofty mansions on Park Road, built on land acquired by Crossley, were expressly designed to obscure views from the park of the less salubrious housing of industrial Halifax in the valley beyond. This would have been a constant reminder to the family of the urban squalor within a mile of Whitley's home, as would the densely packed mills and terraces to the west of the park in the vicinity of King Cross. As a councillor for West Ward, Whitley purposefully continued to identify closely with this area, which encompassed his birthplace, his first home after his marriage, the Crossley model housing development at Westhill Park and the Lister Lane Cemetery, where the last Chartist demonstration in Halifax had taken place in 1853 at the funeral of the radical handloom weaver Ben Rushton and where his mother and father were later buried. Whitley's distinguished municipal and parliamentary career culminated in his election as Speaker of the House of Commons in 1921, serving for seven years until he retired on health grounds in 1928 during a turbulent era, which saw the formation of the first Labour minority government in 1924 and the General Strike in 1926. Before he became Speaker his name had already secured a place in history through his role in the establishment of Joint Industrial Councils as part of the process of reconstruction resulting from the First World War. After relinquishing the office of Speaker he chaired the Board of Governors of the BBC, in which capacity he spoke the very first words in the inaugural BBC radio broadcast across the British Empire, an unprecedented and unique distinction for someone born and bred in Halifax, and also chaired the Labour Commission in India, which added a global dimension to his reputation. Although Whitley retained a home in Halifax throughout his parliamentary career, he died in a London nursing home following surgery after suffering from pleurisy in February 1935.[3]

Whitley's service as Speaker of the House of Commons was significant in a number of respects. He was the first Nonconformist Speaker and the only Speaker representative of religious dissent since the Restoration, thereby setting a precedent for other Nonconformist Speakers to follow. He was the first Speaker to be engaged in manufacturing, since speakers before him were drawn chiefly from the landed gentry and the law. Indeed, northerners have been relatively rare amongst those holding the office of Speaker and Yorkshire incumbents even rarer. Before Whitley was called to the Speaker's chair over a century had elapsed since the previous Yorkshire Speaker, Charles Manners Sutton, had occupied it from 1817 to 1835. Both he and his Tudor predecessor Sir Thomas Gargrave (1495–1579) represented north Yorkshire constituencies as Members for Scarborough and York respectively. By contrast, Whitley was the first Speaker of the House to represent a northern industrial constituency and his only Yorkshire successor was Betty Boothroyd, MP for Dewsbury. He was also the first Speaker since the Municipal Corporations Act of 1835 with extensive experience in municipal politics. Uniquely, he was the very first Speaker who engaged in innovative voluntary philanthropy amongst the poor through the Halifax Guild of Help and with underprivileged young people in Halifax through his Recreative Evening School Gymnasium and annual Poor Boys' Camps. Also unusually, but like his immediate predecessor, the Conservative Speaker James Lowther, later Viscount Ullswater, he was elected Speaker after serving previously as Chairman of the Committee of Ways and Means and Deputy Speaker. Whilst his Speakership, curtailed by ill health, was relatively short, his effective chairmanship of committees of the House since 1910, capably dealing with such complex and contentious issues as Irish Home Rule, significantly extended his impact and service in these roles. If his progression to the chair was somewhat unusual, his lack of progression to the House of Lords in retirement was astonishing to many of his contemporaries in that he declined, for personal reasons linked with his own and his son Percival's involvement in social work in Halifax, the accustomed offer of the hereditary viscountcy which had become the expected reward for service as Speaker since 1789. Like so many of his decisions, it derived from his Halifax roots.

Other formative influences

There were other significant formative influences including his hitherto unexplored maternal ancestry in Leeds, which connected both Harry Whitley and his father Nathan with an acrimonious radical secession from Wesleyan Methodism in 1827. Nathan's first wife, Sarah Rinder (1830–69), J.H. Whitley's mother, was born in Leeds, the daughter of William Rinder, a woollen merchant of Gledhow Grove and Anne (née Briggs) born c. 1806. William Rinder (1800–75), Sarah's father, the son of John Rinder, was born at the Shambles and baptised at St Peter's Church, Leeds on 11 April 1800. He appears to have been a successful merchant, who is listed in the 1841 and 1851 censuses as a salesman and in the 1861 census as a woollen cloth merchant. Both his son William and his daughter Sarah were baptised at St Peter's, Leeds. By 1851, William and Ann were living with their sons, William, aged twenty-three and Thomas, aged seven, at 2, Roundhay Terrace, whilst their daughter Sarah, clearly developing her independence, was listed as a visitor at a household in Boston Spa. William died aged seventy-five, his wife having pre-deceased him and is last listed in the 1871 census as a widower living in Leeds Road, Potternewton. Indeed, Nathan and Sarah Whitley named their eldest child, born on 8 February 1865, Ada Rinder Whitley and she was educated at the North London Collegiate School under Miss Frances Mary Buss, the English pioneer of women's education, before proceeding to Girton College, Cambridge, revealing the family's commitment to widening both male and female educational opportunity. Their younger son, Harry's younger brother, Samuel Rinder Whitley, with his elder brothers Alfred and Harry, were educated at Clifton College, Bristol, a progressive public school in the south-west, which may also have been a consequence of the need to support the boys' educational development following the tragic loss of their mother in childhood.

Clifton must also be acknowledged as a significant influence, particularly upon the career of Harry, who maintained the strongest links with the school after he left, since the priority of managing the family business denied him the opportunity of a higher education away from the nerve centre of the family business in Halifax. However, to a remarkable extent the distinctive character of Whitley's seven-year tenure of the prestigious office of Speaker reflected supremely his Halifax upbringing and values, especially the formative influence of his family upbringing within a vibrant radical nonconformity, his hands-on experience of business and industrial relations and the 'rough and tumble' of his innovatory social work amongst poor boys in Halifax, which provided insights and skills as relevant to the political arena, together with his extensive experience of municipal politics in Halifax, which generated the concerns for so many of the issues which he raised most consistently as a Member of Parliament.

Ancestry

Although Whitley was Halifax born and bred, his ancestry was more geographically diffuse. Indeed, Huddersfield features as significantly in his paternal ancestry as did Leeds in his maternal ancestry. He was descended from Nathan Whitley (1724–66) of Warley township in the parish of Halifax who married Elizabeth Bancroft at Halifax Parish Church in 1754, both of whom perished in a pestilential fever in the summer of 1766 and were buried at the Warley Independent Chapel. Their youngest son, Nathan (1764–1829), was born in Warley and married at Heptonstall in 1788 to Mary Lord of Langfield township in the parish of Halifax. However, after residing for a few years at Holroyd in Langfield township he moved to Huddersfield, where he died (in 1829), followed by his wife a year later (in 1830) and both were buried at Highfield Independent Chapel, Huddersfield. Their son, John, born on 29 July 1789 at Holroyd in Langfield became a fancy cloth merchant and commission agent in Huddersfield and later manager of the Huddersfield branch of the Halifax and Huddersfield Union Bank. He married on 10 April 1820, Susanna (Susey) Whiteley who was born on 8 November 1794, daughter of John Whitley of Windhill Lane, Halifax, the founder in 1791 of the firm of John Whiteley and Sons, cardmakers, later of Brunswick Mills, Halifax. John and Susey Whitley, lived in Huddersfield at Newhouse, Halifax Road, but John, in his will dated 4 January 1843, bequeathed properties in Halifax to his sons, John, Nathan (1830–89), and Samuel and died on 20 April 1844. However, Nathan, the father of J.H. Whitley, though born in Huddersfield on 23 February 1830 and educated at Huddersfield College, subsequently moved to Halifax, where he became a clerk at the Halifax and Huddersfield Union Bank in George Street, combining the role unusually with induction into the technique of card-making by his uncles Joseph and George Whiteley, who succeeded their father John Whiteley in the family card-making business. Later, long after his family had moved from Huddersfield to Halifax, J.H. Whitley engaged extensively in work with Junior Liberal Associations and exerted a huge impact on recruitment into the party. Indeed, it was recalled in

1935 that Whitley had spoken nearly every year up to 1914 at the Saturday political evenings promoted by the Huddersfield Junior Liberal Association, which at its peak numbered over one thousand members.[4]

Radical nonconformity

The paternal roots of Whitley's radical nonconformity derived from Congregational approbation of the Protectorate of Oliver Cromwell. His son, Oliver Whitley, revealed in Halifax in 1988 that his own forename was derived from his father's admiration of Oliver Cromwell 'the first great Congregationalist' who 'showed Europe that it was possible for the establishment to be defeated by a determined and principled minority', which 'led to a strong social conscience among dissenters', particularly in the late nineteenth and early twentieth centuries.[5] These historic roots were reinforced by an increasingly active personal acquaintance with and involvement in a lively radical nonconformity in Halifax. Whitley's father was Sunday School Superintendent at Range Bank Congregational Sunday School, a deacon at Park Congregational Church and a trustee of the new Heath Congregational Church, a secession from the Square Congregational Church, which he supported liberally.[6] His son Harry was also a long serving and deeply committed Sunday School teacher at Park gaining his first experience of teaching children and young people which he acknowledged proved invaluable for his later voluntary work with socially deprived youths in Halifax.[7] Harry's radicalism was also no doubt shaped from an awareness of polemical Nonconformist issues mediated by passionate and lively Halifax preachers such as the Revd Dr Enoch Mellor (1823–81), a vociferous platform orator and strenuous opponent of church rates; the renowned Revd Dr J.H. Jowett (1863–1923), the Halifax born popular Congregationalist preacher who later espoused pacifism, and the Revd Bryan Dale (1832–1907), a champion of the building society movement.[8] Whitley's radical nonconformity also derived from his own identification with Nonconformist issues relating to education and most notably opposition to the terms of the 1902 Education Act, which were strongly opposed within Halifax and the Calder Valley through passive resistance.

The influence of his maternal ancestors is more difficult to determine, especially given the loss of his mother whilst Harry was only three years of age, but the close association of his father with the Rinder family reveals at the very least a propensity for marriage into a family with a strong reputation for radical nonconformity. Nathan (1830–89) married on 7 January 1864, his first wife Sarah, daughter of William and Ann Rinder of Leeds at Lady Lane United Methodist Free Church Chapel, Leeds.[9] J.H. Whitley's mother, is perhaps the most neglected figure in the Whitley narrative and receives no mention at all in at least one otherwise wide-ranging overview of her son's life.[10] Sarah's miniscule, indecipherable handwriting has been regarded as an orthographic challenge and it remains a mystery how the couple actually met. Other details of her life are also obscure, apart from references to her baptism at St Peter's Church, Leeds on

27 April 1831, and census data which reveals that by 1851 at the age of twenty she was staying with the household of Hannah Hessel, annuitant, and her two daughters, at Clifford cum Boston. However, her poignant death in childbirth over five years later on 6 November 1869, aged thirty-eight years, is recorded in two brief family announcements in the same edition of the *Halifax Courier* in 1869, recording in the birth notices the birth of their fifth child and in the death notices Sarah's death on the same day. The tragedy was a grievous blow to her husband and young family and may possibly have influenced the decision to send Harry to a residential school in Bristol.[11] Sarah was brought up as a Protestant Methodist until 1835 and then as a member of the Wesleyan Methodist Association and finally, after 1857, as a member of the United Methodist Free Church within a congregation which constituted the largest centre of free Methodism east of the Pennines. In 1827 Whitley's maternal grandfather, William Rinder (1800–75), had been one of the three leading radical Methodist signatories of a polemical address, placing him at the centre of a bitter Methodist secession in Leeds which rocked the Wesleyan Connexion, costing the Brunswick church at least 1,000 full members who, although 'wholly loyal to Methodist doctrine', felt compelled to leave 'a church where freedom seemed of small account and in whose governance the great mass of lay members counted for so little' as the chapel historian and Liberal MP Richard S. Wainwright observed, explaining the impetus behind the secession.[12]

William Rinder, listed as a woollen manufacturer residing at Park Place, later became a trustee of Park and Lady Lane Wesleyan Methodist Association (WMA) Chapel in 1840 and in 1866 of Lady Lane United Methodist Free Church (UMFC). He held a succession of other appointments during this period, including membership of the WMA Connexional Committee from 1844 until 1856; membership of the WMA Ministerial Superannuation and Benefit Fund Committee, from 1847 to 1849; membership of the WMA Connexional Chapel Fund from 1845 to 1849 and 1853 to 1854; and of the UMFC Foreign Missionary Committee in 1860.[13] Matthew Johnson with James Sigston, another schoolmaster, allied the Leeds Protestant Methodists with the Warrenite Associationists at Manchester in 1835 to form the WMA in their commitment to secure stronger lay delegation, serving as Secretary from 1829 to 1844 and President of the Annual Assembly in 1832. He was active in the Dissenters' successful campaign to take control of the Leeds Vestry where he had served as a Liberal overseer from 1819 to 1844 and served as Secretary of the West Riding Protection Society from 1848 until his death.[14] However, William's daughter Sarah, after her marriage in 1864 to Nathan Whitley worshipped at Park Congregational Chapel, which her husband's family had been instrumental in planting in Halifax's expanding western suburbs and which represented a liberal strand of Congregational churchmanship.

Moreover, this transition from new (Methodism) to old dissent (Congregationalism) was reinforced by the strongly Congregationalist East Anglian roots of his step-mother Lucy Delf. It had also been strengthened by Harry's first marriage into the Crossley family, one of the leading Congregational manufacturing families in Halifax, at Square Chapel on 29 June 1892. His bride was exotically named Margherita Virginia Marchetti (1872–1925), whose swashbuckling father Giulio had fought alongside Garibaldi in his struggle for Italian unification and whose mother Ann was the only daughter of John Crossley of Manor Heath. J.H Whitley's first wife (known as Margaret) was invariably at his side when campaigning and played a significant role in her own right as President of the Halifax Women's Liberal Association and as a leading District Organiser during the First World War. As President of the Women's Liberal Association she also sent a letter of support to a meeting calling for the formation of a Civic Council for International Friendship which her husband also supported held at Halifax Town Hall.[15] Following her death in 1925 he remarried Helen, daughter of J.A. Clarke of Hunstanton and Fransham, who also maintained a strongly supportive constituency role, for example attending the annual meetings of the Crossley Schools.[16]

Following J.H. Whitley's retirement as Speaker, the London correspondent of the *Yorkshire Post* maintained that 'his qualities had compelled respect deeply tinged with affection' and recalled the prolonged individual leave taking with MPs before he departed from the chamber, which revealed the deep personal respect in which the Speaker was held by many individual MPs, including those considered potentially the most disruptive, notably those returned from Clydeside.[17] The individual attention he demonstrated here was a product of his experience as a Sunday School and evening class teacher combined with the mentoring skills he had developed in the work place and the 'rough and tumble' of his voluntary youth activities.

Progressive education

Whitley and his three brothers were also profoundly inspired by their privileged progressive education at Clifton College in Bristol. Indeed, he subsequently used the office of Speaker to mount a major fund raising campaign to equip the school with state-of-the-art science laboratories and obtained the services of the heir to the throne to perform the opening ceremony in 1926, which coincidentally was the year in which the Prince of Wales visited Halifax. Moreover, Whitley remained deeply attached to Clifton, succeeding Earl Haig as President of the College and paid fulsome tribute to his former teacher Canon Wilson at Clifton, whose ministry in a neighbouring industrial parish at Rochdale he had encouraged, and at a memorial service for him at Steep near Petersfield.[18] Indeed, following his own funeral a memorial service was held for him in the chapel of Clifton College of which he had remained President up to the time of his death.[19]

Extraordinarily, Whitley effectively introduced his Clifton contacts to his social work in Halifax through invitations to visit his Poor Boys' Camps on the East coast, an unusual reversal of roles for a public-school-educated alumnus (Figure 2.1).[20] However, arguably his practical engagement with educational issues and voluntary social work amongst the poor and underprivileged young

Figure 2.1 Undated photograph of Halifax Boys' Camp, Filey. (Permission of West Yorkshire Archives, Calderdale, HAS B: 7/2.)

people of Halifax derived as much from his family's passionate engagement with the Halifax School Board as his own recognition as an employer of the limitations of educational opportunity for so many of the adolescents whose education had been constrained under the half-time system which remained deeply rooted in Halifax until it was phased out in the 1920s under the Fisher Act of 1918. Moreover, the adoption by Clifton College of an annual camp for the disadvantaged was itself modelled upon a visit to the established Halifax camp at Filey by representatives from the college. Unlike his younger brother Alfred, who proceeded from Clifton to Trinity College, Cambridge, the death of their uncle Samuel necessitated Harry's return to Halifax to engage in the management of the firm, and the completion of his university degree externally. Thus without the residential experience of a metropolitan university in London, it was hands-on local experience in Halifax which continued to shape his attitudes, not least his first-hand experience of industrial management to which he refers frequently in his parliamentary speeches and his experience of a progressive municipal Liberalism seeking to contend with the rising tide of Labour during a particularly turbulent period of industrial and political strife. His parliamentary interests reflected his constituency concerns, especially education and land reform, tempered by his experience as an assiduous backbencher, junior whip and committee chairman.

Municipal politics

It was the electoral experience provided by Halifax School Board that launched the Whitleys into Halifax politics. Harry's father Nathan was elected to the first Halifax School Board in 1871 and polled the second highest number of votes (10,117) when he stood for a further term in 1874 and was one of only two members re-elected. Two cases, which he brought forward for the remission of fees, were typical of the issues affecting individual disadvantaged families which Nathan pursued, one where 25s.6d. was the total weekly income for a family of eight and another where a mere 15s.0d. supported a family of five. Indeed, the Whitleys, with the Crossleys, supported the Range Bank Congregational School where 30 per cent of the children were half-timers, a proportionately more numerous total in Halifax than in adjacent towns. Nathan also supported the establishment of the Higher Board School, a secondary school built and opened in 1882 for children who had passed the third standard, which he viewed as 'putting the headstone on the edifice'. Following his death in 1889, his second wife Lucy became the first female member of the School Board, underlining the family's strong commitment to education and related concerns such as living conditions.[21]

Nathan first entered Halifax Town Council in 1873 when, as finance chairman with his bank training, he was credited with helping to place the town's faltering finances on a sounder basis, which undoubtedly won him future electoral support. Indeed, it was reported, that hitherto the municipal accounts had been presented so unsatisfactorily that no ratepayer could judge from them 'how the town stood in regard to its liabilities and assets' until Nathan Whitley and John Scarborough published the annual statement 'in such a form that a man of average business intelligence could easily understand from it how the borough stood financially'.[22] He served as Mayor in 1877 subsequently retiring from the Council but then returning to restore harmony in the Council by serving a second two-year term as Mayor from 1882 to 1884. He became an Alderman for a second time in 1883 but in October 1884 he resigned when his brother Samuel died and he had to take over the management of the Hanson Lane Mills. He was impressed with how much longer children in Germany stayed at school than they did in England and felt that Britain would suffer commercially on this account. He served as a governor of both the Crossley and Porter Orphanage, the largest institution of its kind in northern England caring for 500 children of both sexes, and Heath Grammar School, as did his son later, helping to guarantee the school financially after its re-opening in 1887 and founding a scholarship at a cost of over £304 shortly before his death. He also took a leading role in founding the Halifax High School for Girls, became a director of the Halifax Mechanics Institute in 1862 and later served as chairman of the Halifax School Board. He was appointed a magistrate in 1878 and for several years was treasurer of the Halifax Infirmary. He was also one of the secretaries of the committee appointed in February 1862 to plan the commemorative equestrian statue to the Prince Consort, who was greatly admired by Halifax businessmen for his role in promoting the Great Exhibition. He also advised the Halifax Industrial Society to invest its surplus capital in workmen's dwellings.[23]

Harry Whitley dutifully continued his father's wide-ranging interest in education, finance and his support for the building society movement. He became a governor of both the Crossley and Porter Orphanage and Heath Grammar Schools, helping to rescue Heath when 'it quietly died away' between 1883 and 1887, and a member of the Committee appointed in 1893 to plan the construction of the Halifax Technical College. Nathan Whitley had served as a trustee of both the Halifax Permanent and the Halifax Equitable Building Societies and J.H. Whitley, as Speaker of the House of Commons, was invited to open the extensions to the London Offices of the Halifax Permanent Benefit Building Society in Charing Cross Road. Harry Whitley followed his father Nathan into municipal politics and maintained his father's distaste for caucus politics. His father's reputation undoubtedly assisted his son's successful entry into municipal politics. One contemporary, writing before his son achieved distinction as Speaker of the House of Commons, described Nathan Whitley as 'one of the Borough's truest and most worthy citizens' on account of his 'thoroughly disinterested' approach to public service where 'he tried with a pure purpose to benefit the town and people about him, and [add] his tone and character to any cause with which he was associated'.[24] Indeed whilst performing his civic duties he suffered a severe cold after the mayoral party was drenched returning from the opening of a new reservoir at Widdop in August 1888 from which he never fully recovered and died convalescing in Bath in November 1889.[25]

Harry, like his father, represented West Ward, where both addressed large gatherings in the ward in its capacious Liberal Club, and declared that it moved him very deeply that he stood where his father had stood so many years ago.[26] Learning from his father's experience, after he eventually acceded to pressure upon him to stand as a ward councillor he made it clear to his constituents that he should be 'free to use his own judgment in all matters' and not be subject to 'caucus meetings of any kind' but felt that 'he owed it to the town in which he was brought up not to shirk his share of responsibility'. However, whilst he lacked a business partner he insisted that he continue to give 'deep consideration' to his business affairs 'upon which such a large number of working people depended'. Gratitude was also expressed to the new Councillor 'for the personal sacrifices he has made' for 'the mental, physical and moral improvement of their children'.[27] This included in West Ward his Presidency of the King Cross Cricket Club, viewing cricket as a contributory factor to a healthy and disciplined workforce. Whitley urged that the secret of the future success of Liberalism lay in 'enlisting young men in the cause and his attention to local issues resulted in a growth of Liberalism in the ward'.[28]

J.H. Whitley was convinced after visiting the continent that an electric overhead tramway system could be worked with advantage in Halifax. He also visited the USA at his own expense to consider how trams might best be extended into the suburbs.[29] His detailed involvement, for example, in the planning of routes undoubtedly contributed to the popularity and success of the trams, and one election poster in 1899 proclaimed 'Vote for Whitley if you value the trams'. He argued that the trams had given better access to the countryside and enabled Halifax people to become acquainted with the outside districts which some of them he feared had known as little about 'as the centre of New Zealand'. They had even contributed to the extension of electric light into the suburbs.[30] Their success, notwithstanding a strike over conditions of work and wage levels, enhanced his electoral reputation since, as with gas workers, he had sought to enhance wages and protect the rights 'of any body of men' if they wished to combine.[31] Harry Whitley entered Halifax Town Council in 1893 at the age of twenty-seven, winning the seat with a large majority. In 1899 he secured the highest individual ward majority with 1,214 votes out of 1,900 voters and in the Billiard Room of the West Ward Liberal Club there was a great celebration of his 'notable triumph'.[32] On completing a three-year term he was elected unopposed, retaining his seat on the Council until he had completed his term after his election to Parliament.[33] Municipal politics provided him with the experience of committee work by which he was to make his name in the House of Commons and developed his expertise in education and finance.[34] Moreover, his municipal electoral success considerably enhanced his prospects for election as MP for the Halifax constituency.

Parliamentary politics

Harry's effective service as a councillor and the strong electoral support base he developed provided the foundation for his bid to represent Halifax in Parliament, though he initially resisted repeated attempts by Liberals to nominate him as parliamentary candidate primarily on account of his business commitments until he knew that the family firm could be managed in his absence by his brother Alfred.[35] He was finally persuaded somewhat reluctantly to seek election to Parliament in response to party pressures and local political circumstances, which demanded a strong Liberal candidate in order to secure the seat. However, in the event it was primarily educational issues which drew him to seek election to Parliament. In a speech in February 1897 he maintained that the forthcoming election 'would be to a large extent on the Education Bill', and his son Oliver's memoir of his father made it clear that he made his mark in Parliament by supporting the voluntaryist opposition to the 1902 Education Bill and by raising the issue of standards in order to safeguard evening schools which appeared threatened by intended legislation. He expressed his opposition to the Bill in his maiden speech in 1901 referring to his fifteen-year experience 'in the management of some of the most successful evening schools in Halifax' and later through his assiduous committee work, for which he was already making his mark.[36]

After a few weeks in the House of Commons he criticised the 'un-business like methods of the Government' and the Leader of the House for giving 'an unnecessarily long holiday to the Members of the House' and declared that 'there are some of us who think that the discharge of public business is of more importance than shooting grouse'. His persistence in scrutinising public expenditure gained him a parliamentary reputation particularly in committee work.[37] For example, he challenged a salary increase of £2,500 for the Director of Public Prosecutions; urged the need to check the expenses of Sheriffs in connection with judges' lodgings; and criticised Charity Commissioners' investments and an increase in salary for Clerk of Council. But characteristically he also noticed the proposal to reduce the weekly payment of the charwoman from 12s.0d. to 10s.6d., which provoked laughter. Undeterred, he added, revealing the thoroughness of his preparation, that 'he thought the wages of charwomen might have been left as they were while two messengers have been removed and their salaries of £100 each saved by the Treasury'.[38]

At the General Election of 1906 Whitley was the sole Liberal nominated and, from 1918, the solitary member for Halifax when Halifax became a single member constituency. His ministerial career commenced on 28 February 1907 with his appointment as Junior Lord of the Treasury and he was later appointed Whip with an annual salary of £1,000.[39] Besides his unwavering scrutiny of financial accounts Whitley was a prominent campaigner for land tax reform, which he regarded as the imperative facilitator of urban expansion and commended Harcourt's 'splendid reform extending death duties to landowners as well as property owners'. In 1909 Lloyd George's budget included four new land taxes. Whitley commended Glasgow Town Council for having under consideration the taxation of land values in the Burghs of Scotland.[40] He also regarded the drink problem as a 'very serious' constraint on national prosperity. He preferred fixed salaries for publicans unrelated to the quantity of drink sold and expressed the hope to see in his lifetime England become 'the soberest country on the face of the earth'.[41] He regarded Irish Home Rule as 'a deep political grievance' and having accepted self-government for Canada and Australia protested 'how could they on a matter of principle give Home Rule to the most distant relatives and withhold it from a brother by their side', which won him the electoral support of the Halifax branch of the United Irish League.[42] Moreover, as Speaker Whitley made a landmark ruling on 3 May 1923 with regard to the Stormont Parliament stipulating that 'with regard to those subjects which have been delegated to the government of Northern Ireland, questions must be asked of Ministers in Northern Ireland and not in this House' except for the policy of voting money in aid of Irish services.[43] Parliamentary reform for J.H. Whitley included primarily reform of the House of Lords, payment of MPs and registration reform. He argued that it remained almost as difficult for 'a poor man to enter Parliament as it was for a rich man to enter the kingdom of Heaven' and that the only thorough reform of the House of Lords was 'to make a clean sweep of them'.[44] Married to a daughter of Giulio Marchetti, who had fought with Garibaldi's redshirts, Whitley had also expressed support for international liberalism, recalling that 'men of Halifax stood by James Stansfeld when he was hounded out of government because he was a friend of Mazzini' and he expressed concern that Crete, Greece and Armenia suffered under 'the terrible yoke of Turkey' and hoped that the Boer War might speedily be concluded.[45]

Pat Dawson has argued that the Halifax election of 1906 'marked a profound change in local politics' as Labour slowly began to replace Liberalism as the party of the working class, successfully returning its first Labour MP running in tandem with Whitley in Halifax's first 'progressive alliance' in the two-member constituency of Halifax, where electors possessed a dual vote. Squeezed by a locally robust Conservative Party, though divided on the issue of tariff reform, and a resurgent Labour Party, fuelled by a wave of industrial strife, the Liberals embraced the opportunity to defeat the Conservatives after what their opponents regarded as 'ten years of Tory misrule'. However, Dawson has also emphasised the chemistry between the prospective Liberal and Labour candidates and the instrumental role of Whitley, who persuaded the Liberal Party to break with its usual practice and field only one candidate, thereby facilitating the alliance. Whitley perceived the need to make a concession to the growing trade union interest in Halifax but appears also to have developed a good working relationship with James Parker, the Labour candidate, declaring that 'on all the immediate questions of the day Councillor Parker and myself are agreed', their strong mutual respect deriving from their respective Nonconformist associations. J.H. Whitley was returned at the head of the poll with 9,354 votes closely followed by James Parker with 8,937 and Tory candidate Sir Savile Brinton Crossley trailing with 5,041 votes.[46]

Reacting to Savile Crossley's Tory candidacy Whitley had told a constituency meeting that he hoped that the sight of a Crossley on a Tory platform would rouse the men of Halifax to show that they had not forgotten their traditions or they had not gone backwards in their politics since Sir Francis Crossley was previously their esteemed and respected Liberal member. He confessed that 'he preferred to be called a Radical, believing that it was a name to be proud of since a Radical instead of tinkering with a job at the top went to the root to remove any obstacles or evils'.[47] However, introducing a lecture on the future of Liberalism by J.M. Robertson at Halifax Mechanics Institute, Whitley affirmed that 'as long as there was suffering around them to be remedied, as long as there were unjust privileges to be removed Liberalism could not die. As long as there was left in men's hearts some of that divine discontent which made men ever strive to better the lot of their fellow men, there Liberalism was, and there the Liberalism of the future would find its enthusiasm and its faiths.' He also commended the great benefit of local work well done and his experience of close contact with people and his Liberal convictions as a preparation for a parliamentary career.[48] Whitley contributed significantly to the growth of Liberalism in Halifax through energetic, extensive and innovative campaigning, and emphasising the need to recruit young men in the cause. He received a hearty reception touring the constituency ward by ward to report on his representation of the constituency at Westminster.[49] He remained an effective constituency MP for nearly twenty-eight years and for nearly twenty-one years was continuously in office. His sudden retirement in 1928 was taken on medical advice and also coincided with his re-marriage to Helen, daughter of J.A. Clarke of Hunstanton and Fransham following the loss of his first wife in 1925.[50]

As Speaker he faced the extraordinary challenges of the first Labour Government and the 1926 General Strike, where he declared his determination to continue if necessary by candlelight. He was noted for his 'quiet tact, confident yet tolerant firmness and utter impartiality' during a period when 'more and more MPs wished to take an active part in debates' and when 'legislation became more complicated'.[51] On his retirement on 18 June 1928 the Prime Minister Stanley Baldwin praised 'the zeal, ability and impartiality with which he has discharged the duties of his high office during a period of unusual labour, difficulty and anxiety and the judgments and firmness with which he has maintained the dignities and privileges of the House', whilst Ramsay MacDonald the Labour leader and Lloyd George the Liberal leader both expressed regret that he was retiring, the former praising his approachability and helpfulness. Moreover, this was endorsed by Mr Saklatvala, the solitary remaining communist MP, whilst Halifax Labour MP James Parker recalled that 'no man in Parliament knew parliamentary procedure better and he did not suffer fools gladly. I have seen him "call" recalcitrant members to order and then an hour or two later seen and heard him coaching that same member in the art of saying the things he wished to say and still keep within the rules of debate', thus deploying counselling skills developed through his youth work in Halifax. The *Huddersfield Examiner*, whilst grudgingly asserting that Whitley had not been 'a great Speaker', acknowledged that he 'certainly has been a thoroughly human one and gained the affection of members by his kindly humour and gentleness', only rarely speaking sternly and even then 'with a note of sorrow'.[52]

Industrial relations

Whitley also followed his father into the family business and gave it priority over developing his political career at least until his election as MP for Halifax. Following his father's death in 1889 he helped to ensure that industrial relations remained 'of a cordial character' because the Whitleys 'accepted the combination of workmen as a right' and never imposed any restriction on trade unions 'being employed there'. The firm also developed a co-partnership scheme and when they had traded well voluntarily distributed to their employees a share of the extra profits earned in the form of a substantial bonus. His thirty-five years' experience of industrial relations not only proved invaluable in his relations with a growth of new Labour MPs in the House of Commons during his Speakership, but also provided the springboard for his involvement in the Whitley Councils and the Royal Commission on Indian Labour. The centenary of the related family business of John Whiteley and Sons, Brunswick Mills, Halifax was commemorated in July 1891 and, in the construction of a terrace of superior spacious workers' housing close to the Brunswick Mills in the Boulevards, followed the example of the model housing schemes associated with Edward Akroyd at Copley and Akroydon, and the Crossleys at West Hill, for which Nathan Whitley acted as a trustee. In 1919 S. Whitley & Co. enjoyed a threefold celebration for 450 workers of Hanson Lane Mills and their friends, in the form of a day trip to Blackpool at the invitation of 'the Rt Hon J. H. Whitley, M.P.' (see Figure 2.2). The event marked the coming of age of his son Percival, the celebration of which had been deferred since 1914 owing to the First World War. It also marked the golden jubilee of the establishment of the Hanson Lane Mills in 1869 and the entry into the business of Mr Percival Whitley and Miss Phyllis Whitley, infusing 'youth and energy' into the business. Speaking at the Blackpool trip J.H. Whitley declared 'Youth deserved its opportunity and indeed it was better for the world that youth should have an opportunity while it was full of vigour and spirit'. Whitley's speech also looked back nearly thirty-five years to the time when he went to work at Hanson Lane Mills and, when he looked round, 'there were still a very substantial number of men and women who were there at the mill before he was and were still going apparently as strong as ever'. This, he believed, sprang from 'a kind of affection between the firm and the workers'. Typically displaying concern for the individual, he proceeded to mention several by name and acknowledged his debt to his brother Alfred 'a faithful ally throughout all the years'. The *Halifax Courier* concluded that since the First World War Whitley's name had been 'on the tongue of all' on account

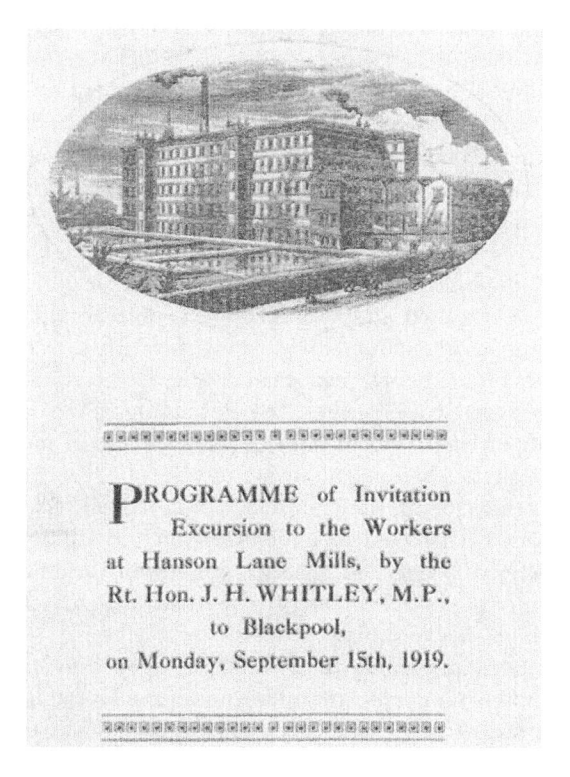

Figure 2.2 The Hanson Lane Mills excursion to Blackpool 1919. (© J.H. Whitley Archive, Heritage Quay, University of Huddersfield, and Whitley Family.)

Philanthropy and voluntary social work

Harry Whitley continued his innovatory voluntary social work alongside his municipal and later parliamentary duties together with his brothers, Alfred, Samuel and Edward, and other younger members of the family. Recreative Evening School (RES) classes first operated in Halifax from the winter of 1886–87. They were open to girls as well as boys over the age of thirteen, offering a refund of fees for 100 per cent attendance and later included gymnastic classes. As an active sportsman himself, enjoying cricket, tennis, fives and cycling, Whitley was keen that Halifax should have a gymnasium where the youth of the town would have facilities for keeping fit. At a meeting of the Halifax School Board he expressed concern about the proposed reduction to the grants supplied by the Education Department to evening schools for physical exercise, and indeed this may have convinced him of the need to offer himself as a Liberal parliamentary candidate.[54] The annual Filey Poor Boys' Camp was conceived as a summer supplement to the winter evening classes and was designed to enhance recruitment. Whitley convened a meeting of teachers to plan the first camp which, supported by public subscriptions, became an annual event until the outbreak of the Second World War. He viewed the RES especially as a means by which socially and culturally deprived young men might improve their physical well-being, and raise their self-esteem through competitive sport, compensating them for the limited educational opportunities resulting from the half-time system. Initially, temporary accommodation was obtained at the Drill Hall and at Heath School, but later premises in the former British and Foreign School on Great Albion Street were acquired. In October 1889 it was reported that 'in Halifax gymnastic teaching has been found to be a great draw'. By the third winter there were 1,200 names on the books, more than double the previous total, with ages ranging from thirteen to twenty-eight. 'We are training up the rising generation' he declared 'with a lower standard both of physique and of intellect than that which obtains in all the chief neighbouring towns; laying the basis for hardship and lack of prosperity', hence the importance of developing Evening Continuation Schools carrying on to sixteen or eighteen since education so often ceased at thirteen. It offered 'bright and cheerful training of the mind, healthy and vigorous training of the body' rivalling the alternative attractions of the 'flaring gaslights' and 'rough street roaming'.[55]

He was also motivated by the new emphasis upon muscular Christianity derived both from his Nonconformist upbringing and his public school education. Like other local Congregationalists, notably Sir Francis Crossley and Sir Titus Salt, he was a strong supporter of the YMCA serving as President of the Halifax Young Men's Christian Association at Clare Hall. He also encouraged membership of the Boys' Brigade and TOC H. At the Halifax Poor Boys' Camps he ensured that there was compulsory Sunday observance with the provision of worship and alternative activities to Sunday games.[56] He recruited 'chiefly half-timers and members of the Recreative Evening Classes' but also included 'poor orphans and others who have never gazed on the sea and it is really amazing how many little fellows there are in Halifax with this latter qualification'.[57] Whitley was recognised as 'one of the pioneers of this scheme . . . for whom many a poor, ragged lad holds as much respect as he almost does for his own brother'. He often took personal charge of both camps, returning almost immediately to Filey with the second contingent after having arrived home on the previous night with the first contingent and seemed as 'proud as Punch' to have that honour. He experienced the full rigours of camp life, including the legendary nocturnal intrusion of a wandering and inquisitive cow 'with unwarrantable disregard of discipline' seeking 'to effect entrance to the captain's tent rousing him from his slumbers' and causing mayhem when, chased by the camp dog, it charged another tent, got entangled in the ropes, snapped the pole and brought the tent down on the heads of the sleeping boys', generating much hilarity whenever the episode was graphically recalled. The camps continued from 1889 until 1938 and were only abandoned with the approach of war in 1939, later resuming for a few years after the war under the leadership of Percival Whitley.[58] The impact of the week at the seaside was epitomised by the '100 brown faces and merry hearts scattered among the homes of Halifax' and by the 'boys would have wished the week to be a month'. For many it was the first glimpse of the sea by lads whose only experience of water 'had probably been formed from the Calder and Hebble Navigation and the Hebble Brook'. His influence was recognised across the religious denominations. When he opened the new St Bernard's Catholic Association Recreation Rooms, Father Quinlan affirmed that 'no man in Halifax took more interest in the training of youth than did J.H. Whitley'.[59]

Keith Laybourn has examined how J.H. Whitley and the Whitley family supported the formation of the Halifax Citizens' Guild of Help in 1905.[60] With other guilds it was later part of the National Council of Social Service, of which Whitley became the first national President in 1919. With his brother Alfred and other members of the Whitley family he offered energetic leadership to this extraordinary attempt within the voluntary sector to deal with the extremes of poverty and unemployment experienced in Halifax in the decade before the outbreak of the First World War. He convened at his residence Brantwood a private meeting of Halifax clergy, ministers and laymen with his brother Alfred, who was to play a key role in the development of the guild both locally and nationally as Secretary and Vice-president of the National Association of Guild of Help, to consider how to respond to the growing problem of poverty in Halifax. The meeting invited a Bradford speaker to address a conference in Halifax sharing the vision of the Bradford Guild, which had been inspired by continental initiatives in Elberfeld, Leipzig and Berlin, which enabled an enthusiastic public launch of the Halifax Citizens' Guild of Help to take place within a year on 12 December 1905. Here the Revd G.J. Williams emphasised the importance of providing 'moral influence' together with the provision of clothing and coal and money for house rent. The Halifax Citizens' Guild was organised by a Central Board supported by a general Representative Committee and from 1910 by Group Head Meetings. Divided into twenty-four districts, by 1909 each district was headed by a Captain who worked with voluntary helpers, with names appropriated from the organisation of the Halifax Poor Boys' Camps, who would take on cases and give advice and help to the poor. There were at least 280 helpers in Halifax by 1911 when Halifax Citizens' Guild was the fifth largest of the eighty or so Citizens' Guilds operating nationally. Keith Laybourn has concluded that the leadership in Halifax appeared predominantly middle class, with no surviving evidence of working-class Captains or Helpers, but with distinctly more women in Halifax acting as helpers and lady health visitors than elsewhere, including a strong representation of Whitley women, notably the second Mrs Nathan Whitley, Mrs Edward Whitley, Miss Whitley and Mrs Marchetti. The Halifax Citizens' Guild encouraged the local authority to appoint health visitors, contributed to the provision and distribution of school meals and operated a Children's Welfare League, maternity classes, a small workshop for unemployed men and allotment gardens for the poor to grow their own food using spare municipal land. Whitley was a generous contributor with other members of his family, including Alfred and S.R. Whitley and some 200 other Halifax donors to the Emergency Fund.[61]

Independently of this philanthropic beneficence, he initiated grants to enable students to go to university, in what was referred to as 'the Big Brother Scheme' examined in some detail by Clyde Binfield. He provided accommodation at Spring Hall, which he purchased and adapted for young professional men requiring temporary accommodation whilst taking up employment in Halifax during the period up to 1931. Under the terms of the Town Planning Act, he persuaded the Town Council to engage in urban improvement, instituting design awards for architectural excellence after 1911. He provided playing fields in the grounds of Spring Hall Mansion in 1919 and other sports facilities at Spring Hall, Heath and Crossley and Porter Schools. He later bequeathed £3,000 to secure the continued use of the Spring Hall grounds for recreative purposes and to benefit young people in other ways, and after his death the trust acquired playing fields at Nursery Lane, Ovenden and built the Whitley Memorial Sports Hall, opened in 1959. He also endowed a campsite at Jerusalem Farm in the Luddenden Valley and commenced a scheme to restore vegetation to Beacon Hill which proved abortive but served to highlight the impact of pollution on the natural environment close to the town centre.[62] J.H. Whitley had thus pursued a remarkable career in social and philanthropic duties alongside his major contribution to municipal and parliamentary politics.

Declining the burden of a peerage

Although Whitley had made it a condition of accepting the Speakership that he would not be required to accept a title on retirement, the realisation of his wish was still greeted with astonishment by many of his contemporaries. However, like so many other facets of his public life this decision strongly reflects his Halifax roots. It was ultimately taken after consultation with his family and particularly his eldest son, who testified that he was never more proud of his father than in his decision to decline the viscountcy. His opposition to the House of Lords as a radical Liberal in Halifax was well known. He had been applauded at a Halifax constituency meeting for declaring that 'he was not a Second Chamber Man' and believed in 'removing the House of Lords altogether'. He once proclaimed that 'the Liberal Party would come quickly to see that it would be no good patching or mending or bothering with the House of Lords at all'. 'Let them stand on their merits and not on their titles', he continued, 'Let them come down from their gilded chamber' and stand for election 'on equality with other men'. No Speaker of the House of Commons had made such uncompromising attacks on the House of Lords since the Commonwealth period, which was the inspiration for Whitley's iconoclastic radicalism mediated through an enduring Puritan tradition in Halifax. In 1895 in a lecture at the West Ward Liberal Club before a 'good audience' he proclaimed that 'each human life was of equal value to the state and that when an added value existed it was worth of character not titles or blue blood, it was ability of work, not riches and possessions' that made the difference, which was endorsed with cries of 'hear, hear'.[63]

In other respects, however, Whitley sought to maintain the traditions of his office, even to the extent of accepting the advice of his brothers at the time of his election as Speaker to petition the Earl Marshall for a Grant of Arms so that, notwithstanding his own indifference to heraldry, his armorial bearings could be permanently displayed with those of previous Speakers in the Speaker's official residence at Westminster. His decision to eschew the customary honour of a hereditary peerage on his retirement as Speaker was nonetheless sensational and broke a 120-year precedent, yet, for him, acceptance would have been incongruous with his association, and that of his son Percival, with the Halifax youths whose perception of them both might have been very different with the title an hereditary peerage would have conferred.[64]

Conclusion

J.H. Whitley never allowed the extension of his public work into the national sphere to extinguish his interest in and devotion to his native Halifax and the constituents he represented for so long as a municipal councillor and Member of Parliament. In concluding his retirement speech, by giving 'special thanks to his constituents, whose forbearance made it possible for the representative of an industrial constituency to occupy the Speakership' he was acknowledging concerns which had emerged within a minority of his constituents who considered themselves effectively disfranchised because of the tradition of not opposing the Speaker at general elections. Whitley answered such criticisms by pointing out the enhanced influence he carried at Westminster in pursuing the interests of his constituents through other channels deriving from the relationships fostered by his parliamentary office.[65]

His youngest son, Oliver, observed that his father declined Asquith's invitation to him to serve as Chief Whip in 1915 because he saw himself as essentially 'a business man, a cotton spinner from the industrial North, a conciliator, a fervent believer in participation, consultation, delegated and shared discipline, who had practised these precepts in his boys' camp and in co-partnership schemes in his mill'. Viscount Halifax, former Viceroy of India, also attributed the success of Whitley's later chairmanship of the Indian Labour Commission to 'his early experience of human needs in his native town of Halifax'. Whitley remained profoundly indebted to his formative engagement with Halifax young people through his Sunday School teaching at Park and Range Bank, the Halifax RES and Poor Boys' Camp, for his ability to handle difficult situations calmly as Speaker. Relations with Labour in Halifax also helped him to respond positively to the challenge of Labour representation in House of Commons, whilst his involvement in Halifax industrial relations enabled him to make the distinctive contribution nationally through the Whitley Councils. Above all, the values of Halifax Nonconformity shaped his political attitudes especially in relation to educational issues, making him the most radical Speaker since the Protectorate.

His educational legacy was recognised by the incorporation of his name into the J.H. Whitley Secondary Modern School opened by a successor as Speaker, Viscount Ruffside, on 15 May 1953, though the name regretfully disappeared with subsequent amalgamations. Drawing on his mildly self-deprecating sense of humour whilst opening the London branch of the Halifax Permanent Benefit Building Society in 1924, Whitley memorably reminded his audience that 'twenty-four years ago Halifax got rid of him to London – now Halifax came to London itself and came offering to the less fortunate Londoners great benefits built on Yorkshire thrift, on Yorkshire security'. However, he thought that 'London people would learn to know the value of thrift' and he was 'fairly confident' that the branch he was opening would 'prove too small for the Society's operations', requiring 'migration to larger premises'. The Speaker proved accurate in his prognostications. The Charing Cross Road premises proved too small and in 1934 Halifax House, the great building in the Strand was completed though Whitley was not present at the opening ceremony. He was on a visit to South America where he was stricken with an illness that proved fatal the following year.[66]

Throughout the twenty-eight years of his life J.H. Whitley spent at Westminster, there is a very real sense in which he consciously sought to import the values of his Halifax upbringing into his parliamentary responsibilities. The combined influences on his parliamentary career of his Halifax ancestry, his business interests, his nonconformity, his engagement with municipal politics, his hands-on experience of industrial relations and his innovative educational and voluntary social work within the town of his birth, evidenced both in his own testimony as well as the observations of contemporaries, provide sufficient evidence to conclude that his character and vocation were recognisably shaped to a considerable extent by his Halifax roots. His legacy was reinforced by his son Percival's continuing involvement in municipal politics, education and social work in Halifax, and a sports hall at Spring Hall and countryside centre at Jerusalem Farm still enhance the educational opportunities of children and young people in Halifax over eight decades after his death, whilst the deposit of the Whitley Archive at the University of Huddersfield offers the opportunity to both young and mature students to discover more about the influences which shaped his remarkable career.

Notes

1 Whitley Archive, University of Huddersfield, Press Cuttings, JHW 2/1/49; R. Bretton, 'The Whitleys of Halifax', T[ransactions] [of the] H[alifax] A[ntiquarian] S[ociety], 1963, 63–76; O. Whitley, 'Percival Whitley and his forbears: and their concern for education', The First Percival Whitley Lecture, Calderdale College, Halifax, 28 June 1988, p. 1. I am grateful to John P. Whitley for his comments on a draft version of this chapter.
2 *Halifax Courier and Guardian*, 4 February 1935. Also *Hansard*, 28 June 1928.
3 JHW 2/8/91; B. Harris, *The Origins of the British Welfare State. Social Welfare in England and Wales 1800–1945*, Basingstoke, Palgrave Macmillan, 2004, p. 176; 'J.H. Whitley' *Oxford Dictionary of National Biography*, Oxford, Oxford University Press, revised 2004.
4 Bretton, 'The Whitleys of Halifax', 52–3, 58–9, 65–6; J. Wild, 'Some Local People of Note 2', *THAS*, 1977, 75; the affinity of Italian nationalists with Victorian liberals and radicals including the Halifax MP James Stansfeld, has been surveyed most recently by Marcella Pellegrino Sutcliffe, *Victorian Radicals and Italian Democrats*, Martelsham, Royal Historical Society, Boydell Press, 2014; *Huddersfield Daily Examiner*, 5 February 1935.
5 Whitley, 'Percival Whitley and his forbears', pp. 1–2.
6 *Halifax Courier*, 30 November 1889.
7 Ibid., 28 June 2009, 2 July 2009.
8 J.A. Hargreaves, 'Baptists and Congregationalists in Halifax 1852–1914', *THAS*, n.s., 10, 2002, 96–125; C. Binfield and J. Taylor (eds), *Who They Were in the Reformed Churches of England and Wales, 1901–2000*, Donnington, Shaun Tyas, United Reformed Church History Society, 2007, pp. 121–2; N. Arnold, *et al.*, *Gold Under the Hammer, Passive Resistance in Cornholme, 1902–14*, Todmorden, WEA, 1982.
9 Bretton, 'The Whitleys of Halifax', 63.
10 Wild, 'Some Local People of Note', 75–6.
11 *Halifax Weekly Courier*, 13 November 1869.
12 R.S. Wainwright, *Lady Lane 1840–1940*, Leeds, J. and S. Ltd, 1940, p. 3; W.R. Ward, *Religion and Society in England 1790–1850*, London, Batsford, 1972, pp. 146–7, 315; D.A. Gowland, *Methodist Secessions*, Manchester, Chetham Society, 1979, pp. 6–13, *passim*, and M.R. Watts, *The Dissenters, Vol. II. The Expansion of Evangelical Nonconformity 1791–1859*, Oxford, Clarendon Press, 1995, pp. 414–16; *Address of the Wesleyan Methodist Nonconformist Leaders, Local Preachers and Members of the Methodist Preachers assembled in Conference in London*, Briggate, Leeds, John Barr, 1828, pp. 3–8.
13 I am grateful to D.C. Dews for details of Rinder's Methodist offices extracted from Lady Lane UMFC circuit preachers' minutes, 1857–96, Lady Lane UMFC trust minutes 1839–71 and Sunday School minutes 1877–1927 and to M. Meadowcroft for supplying documentation relating to the Rinder family.
14 *UMFC Magazine*, 1864; O.A. Beckerlegge, in J.A. Vickers (ed.), *Dictionary of Methodism in Great Britain and Ireland*, Peterborough, Epworth Press, 2000, p. 385.
15 *Halifax Courier*, 11 July 2014.
16 Wild, 'Some Local People of Note', 75; *Halifax Courier*, July 1931.
17 *Huddersfield Examiner*, 4 February 1935.
18 JHW 2/1/27.

19 *Huddersfield Examiner*, 6 February 1935.
20 JHW 2/1/21; 2/1/25; JHW/21/1/31; 2/8/83; 2/8/84; 2/8/85. See Chapter 3 of this volume for C.S. Knighton's essay on J.H. Whitley at Clifton.
21 E. Webster, 'Halifax Schools 1870–1970', *THAS*, 1970, 11, 16, 18, 21.
22 *Halifax Courier*, 30 November 1889.
23 Bretton, 'The Whitleys of Halifax', 63–4; *Halifax Courier*, 30 November 1889.
24 J.W. Alderson and A.E. Ogden, *The Halifax Equitable Benefit Building Society, 1871–1921*, Halifax, Halifax Equitable Benefit Building Society, 1921, p. 55.
25 *Halifax Courier*, 30 November 1889.
26 JHW 2/1/13; *Halifax Courier*, 30 November 1889.
27 JHW 2/1/13.
28 JHW 2/1/49.
29 JHW 2/1/36; JHW 2/1/84; JHW 2/1/85.
30 JHW 2/1/65; JHW 2/1/83; JHW 2/1/85.
31 JHW 2/1/83; JHW 2/3/5.
32 JHW 2/1/65.
33 Wild, 'The Whitleys of Halifax', p. 75.
34 JHW 2/1/65.
35 Alfred Whitley had previously worked at John Whiteley & Sons, cardmakers, before moving to the family firm of S. Whitley & Co, Cotton Spinners, thus releasing J.H. Whitley to pursue his parliamentary career.
36 JHW 2/1/13; JHW 1/1/4; JHW 2/1/58; JHW 21/1/29.
37 *Halifax Equitable Benefit Building Society Jubilee 1921*, pp. 12–14, 33.
38 JHW 2/3/19; JHW 2/3/21; JHW 2/3/22; JHW 2/3/32; JHW 2/3/23; JHW 2/3/27; JHW 2/3/36; JHW 2/3/37.
39 JHW 2/1/43; Wild, 'The Whitleys of Halifax', p. 75.
40 G.R. Searle, *A New England? Peace and War 1886–1918*, Oxford, Clarendon Press, 2004, pp. 410–11; JHW 2/1/49; JHW 2/1/64; JHW 2/1/75; JHW 2/1/86; JHW 2/2/1; JHW 2/3/17; Pat Thane, *Cassell's Companion to Twentieth Century Britain*, London, Cassell, 2001, pp. 227–8; JHW 2/1/17.
41 JHW 2/1/68; JHW 2/2/9.
42 Chapter 3 refers to him debating Home Rule and Clifton and Chapter 5 indicates in more detail his connection with the United Irish League.
43 JHW 2/1/64; JHW 2/1/93; JHW 2/2/20; JHW 2/3/2; on Whitley's landmark ruling of 3 May 1923 see M. Laban, *Mr Speaker. The Office and the Individuals since 1945*, London, Biteback Publishing, 2013, p. 17.
44 JHW 2/1/44; JHW 2/1/68; JHW 2/2/6; JHW 2/1/45.
45 JHW 2/1.58; Sutcliffe, *Victorian Radicals and Italian Democrats*, pp. 18, 20, 51, 74, 91, 98, 101, 111, 129, 134, 137, 141, 158, 160; JHW 2/1/49; JHW 2/2/7.
46 P.A. Dawson, 'Liberalism and the challenge of Labour: the 1906 progressive election in Halifax', *THAS*, 2 n.s., 1994, 107–24.
47 JHW 2/1/44; JHW 2/1/40; JHW 2/1/68.
48 JHW 2/1/46.
49 *Lancaster Guardian*, 9 November 1901, JHW 2/3/18.
50 Wild, 'The Whitleys of Halifax', 75.
51 Ibid., 75; *Huddersfield Daily Examiner*, 18 June 1928.
52 *Huddersfield Daily Examiner*, 18 June, 19 June, 20 June 1928; *Halifax Courier and Guardian* 4 February 1935.
53 *Halifax Courier*, 30 November 1889; 22 September 1900; JHW 2/2/12; lithographic illustration for the centenary of John Whitely and Sons, Brunswick Mills, Halifax, 1791–1891, W(est) Y(orkshire) A(rchive) S(ervice), C(alderdale) D(istrict) A(rchives), WT; 2/3; Bretton, 'The Whitleys of Halifax', 62–4, 70; *Halifax Weekly Guardian* 20 September 1919; JHW 2/6/67; JHW 2/6/71.

54 Webster, 'Halifax Schools 1870–1970', 19; JHW 2/1/22; JHW 2/1/28; *Daily Chronicle*, 31 July 1901, JHW 2/3/15; JHW 2/3/16.
55 Wild, 'The Whitleys of Halifax', 75; JHW2/1/56; *The Satchell*, 1914–18; JHW 2/1/11; JHW 2/1/8; JHW 2/1/18; JHW 21/1/31.
56 C. Binfield, *George Williams and the YMCA. A Study in Victorian Social Attitudes*, London, Heinemann, 1973, p. 237.
57 JHW 2/1/41.
58 JHW 2/1/41; JHW 21/1/31; WYAS Calderdale, Halifax Boys' and Girls' Camp, records 1893–1938, HAS/B:7/2.
59 *Daily Chronicle*, 31 July 1901, JHW 2/1/31,; 2/1/39; 2/1/41; JHW 2/3/15.
60 K. Laybourn, 'The New Philanthropy of the Edwardian Age: the Guild of Help and the Halifax Citizen's Guild, 1905–18', *THAS*, ns, 23, 2015, 73–94.
61 Ibid.
62 Bretton, 'The Whitleys of Halifax', 68; JHW 2/6/104; Wild, 'Some Local People of Note', 76.
63 JHW 2/1/53.
64 Bretton, 'The Whitleys of Halifax', 56–7; Wild, 'Some Local People of Note', 76; JHW 2/1/44; JHW 2/1/45; JHW 2/1/53.
65 *Huddersfield Daily Examiner*, 20 June 1928, JHW 1/1/4; Whitley, 'Percival Whitley and his forbears', pp. 1–2; JHW 2/6/108; The Rt Hon. Viscount Halifax 'John Henry Whitley', *The Listener*, 13 February 1935.
66 Bretton, 'The Whitleys of Halifax', 51; O. R. Hobson, *A Hundred Years of the Halifax*, London, Batsford, 1953, p. 93.

3 Clifton

Inspiration and service

C.S. Knighton

Nathan Whitley chose Clifton for his sons because he understood it to be a school 'in which differences of opinion were tolerated and a boy had to make his way by character and industry'.[1] How these credentials reached Halifax remains a mystery. Clifton certainly advertised itself in the north, as in all other parts of the kingdom. No parent, however, would despatch offspring to a distant school on such slender basis, so there must have been some personal testimony or recommendation.

Clifton was a new school, one of many which sprang up in imitation of Arnold's Rugby.[2] Arnold's reputation has been progressively pruned since Lytton Strachey first laid an axe to it. What remains is his core concept of the school as a regulated Christian community.[3] It matters not whether Rugby really achieved this status; such was the public perception, and so Rugby became the template. Clifton was founded by a group of local professionals, wanting a Rugby-type school for their stately suburb high above the city of Bristol.[4] So they asked Arnold's successor, Frederick Temple, to nominate their first Head Master, and he gave them one of his junior assistants, John Percival. Hard work and determination had taken Percival from lowly origins in Westmorland to the highest honours in Oxford's schools. Though still young and untried, Temple saw that the force was with him, within a few years Percival had put his school in the major league. He imported a quantity of Rugby terminology and traditions to give the new institution some ballast; more significantly he brought the spirit of Arnold, reincarnated in his own person.[5]

Percival left in 1879 to become President of Trinity College, Oxford.[6] His place at Clifton was taken by James Wilson, another import from Rugby. Wilson was a more amiable character than Percival, though no less driven, and likewise combining religious ardour with radical politics. He had been Senior Wrangler at Cambridge and mathematics remained his subject, though as Head Master he felt obliged to teach classics to the Sixth.[7] At Rugby he had done his best to develop science, for which Clifton provided larger opportunity; this alone set him apart from other head masters and made him a national figure.[8] His *Morality in Public Schools and its Relation to Religion* (1882) also brought him celebrity in the campaign against vice. His solution, apart from prayer, was regimented and exhausting athleticism. This notion had not been part of Arnold's system, and Percival was not obsessed with it; but Wilson spoke for a cause which in his time would become the dominant ethos of the public school.[9] Percival and Wilson endowed Clifton with a high sense of mission and a grinding dedication to public service. The downside was some shortage of imagination and humour; Whitley once told his old schoolfellows that he found no fault in them 'except an undue graveness of temper'.[10]

Such was the school which Whitley entered in May 1878, at the age of twelve. After a year in the junior department he moved up into Wiseman's House, which became virtually a family residence.[11] Harry would be joined there by his brothers Alfred (1881–86) and Samuel (1882–88). The fourth brother Edward followed later (1887–92) and would be joined by both relatives and friends. Among Edward's contemporaries in the House was Ernest Marchetti (1887–92), son of Crossleys' manager and destined to be Harry's brother-in-law. In due course Wiseman's was home to Harry's younger son Oliver (1925–30) and then to *his* four sons (1954–68).[12] The first Whitleys were charges of the founding House Master, H.J. Wiseman, a portly cleric known as 'Buffer'. He liked cricket and St Paul, and had some skill in music.[13] Wiseman was popular in a general way, and was remembered for his 'freedom from self-assertion, and wholesome manly temper'.[14] He was, however, not among the great characters celebrated in a volume which Whitley introduced, saluting 'the remarkable men – so much more than mere schoolmasters – who helped to make Clifton what she is'.[15]

One reason for Clifton's rapid rise to prominence was the excellence of the staff which Percival recruited.[16] Early masters included Evelyn Abbott (Jowett's colleague and co-biographer), H.G. Dakyns (tutor to Tennyson's boys), and the Manx poet T.E. Brown. Of the last Whitley wrote, albeit on a partial occasion: 'the poet who can keep alive our daily life is a greater man, to my mind, than any other'.[17] Though classics still had pride of place in the curriculum, modern languages were taught from the start. So too was science, which in Whitley's time was directed by W.A. Shenstone, known for pioneering work on silica, and W.A. Tilden. Both were elected Fellows of the Royal Society while on the staff, and Tilden was later knighted. For a short period, while posts in the universities were few, those schools which took science seriously were able to engage men of such calibre.[18]

Under this powerful tutelage Whitley made solid though not spectacular progress. His first term's report was: 'Excellent. No prodigy, but a good sensible boy, making the most of himself', though later in the year he was 'a little overpressed'. By his first summer he was 'getting on nicely' and 'needs no pressing'. There is a dip in the middle when he 'lacks attention' and stands seventh out of twenty in Vγ, the bottom stream of the Classical Fifth. 'Is he doing his best?' is the sole comment one term (surely the last time this question was asked of J.H. Whitley). A couple of months later he is 'much improved', and the final assessment is 'quite satisfactory'. He rose to be Head of the House.[19]

Alongside Whitley in Wiseman's were a future Governor of Malta (Sir David Campbell), General Officer in Command (GOC) in Malaya (Sir Leopold Oldfield), envoy to Serbia (Sir Charles Young), Irish High Court Judge (G. FitzGibbon), Conservative MP (W.E. Pease), Treasury mandarin (Sir Thomas Heath), connoisseur (Sir Robert Witt) and Cambridge philosopher (J.M.E. McTaggart). Contemporaries elsewhere in the school included Field Marshals Earl Haig and Lord Birdwood; Vice-Admiral John Luce; Sir Francis Younghusband, explorer and scourge of the lamas; Sir Lee Stack, Governor-General of Sudan; Sir John Clauson, High Commissioner in Cyprus; Sir Louis Mallet, Ambassador to the Sublime Porte; his brother Sir Bernard, Registrar-General; two bishops,[20] six more MPs,[21] two Oxford heads of house,[22] physicist Sir Richard Threlfall, astronomer H.H. Turner, archaeologist B.P. Grenfell, literary scholar F.S. Boas, historian A.H. Thompson, poets Sir Henry Newbolt and Sir Arthur Quiller-Couch, writers Elliott O'Donnell and Robert Hichens, artists Roger Fry and Henry Tonks, and singer Harry Plunket Greene. A mighty band, but the Speaker of the House of Commons would outrank them all (Figure 3.1).

When he reached the Fifth Form Whitley's chief mentor was S.T. Irwin, a classicist who later chose *Spiritus intus alit* for Clifton's motto.[23] Whitley took

Figure 3.1 The young Harry Whitley at Clifton College, Bristol. (Dr C.S. Knighton, Principal Assistant Keeper to the Archives at Clifton College, Bristol.)

voluntary French and German lessons from a Frenchman, Eugène Pellissier. In the Sixth he continued German with Clovis Bévenot, another Frenchman, and one with an adventurous past and a distinguished future.[24] Whitley was in the first set for science, under Shenstone and H.B. Jupp. This was only class instruction; Whitley did no laboratory work, for which an extra charge was made.[25] He was evidently a keen but not an active scientist. Though on the Committee of the Scientific Society, he never gave a paper or made any recorded contribution to debate. The Society met weekly in the Michaelmas and Lent terms, attracting forty or so boys, by no means all intending science as a career. They shared the platform with the masters, because visiting speakers were rare. During 1884 members heard about the sun from Mr Jupp, about the flight of birds and insects from the Secretary (later Professor of Mathematics at Iowa), and from Roger Fry about moss. Other talks covered geology, climate, photography and ichthyology. At the last meeting of the year Shenstone expounded on the physical and chemical researches of Alexandre Dumas.[26]

In the summer Whitley would have played cricket, and in the Michaelmas term, football (for which Clifton had its own rules, derived from those of Rugby). In the spring, while the Close recovered from the rougher game, there were cross-country runs. Most gruelling was the ten-mile course to and from Penpole ridge above the Severn.[27] First place in the 'Long Penpole' ranked with a Balliol scholarship, and it was a distinction to 'come in', that is, to finish within a certain time of the winner. In his last year Whitley was the only competitor from Wiseman's, determined to come in for the honour of the House. Wilson had thought him unfit and tried to dissuade him from running, but would not forbid it. He did however take a cab down the course, and found a very weary Whitley plodding up Stoke Bishop Hill. For a while Wilson and another master ran alongside, and finally took hold of him. With his last wind Whitley politely punched the Head Master, crying 'you have no right, sir, to stop me', and then fainted. He was brought back to school unconscious, passed an anxious night and promptly recovered. Wilson gave this story to *The Times* when Whitley was elected Speaker, adding: 'He is a true sportsman, every inch of him.'[28]

Between them there developed an enduring bond of mutual regard. Like all headmasters of the heroic age, Wilson directed his school from the pulpit, and Whitley cherished the memory of his performances.[29] Wilson was also a keen promoter of the College mission. Many public schools set up such ventures in the East End of London. Clifton's aspirant social workers had urban squalor closer to hand, and adopted a tough area of north Bristol. This would eventually become the separate parish of St Agnes, with a new church and school; during Whitley's time a hall and a workmen's club were built. Among the boys who prospered there was the son of the College cobbler; Wilson found him a job as a laboratory assistant, on which foundation developed the notable career in science and socialism of Sir Richard Gregory, FRS.[30] The mission records do not survive from this period, but we can be sure that Whitley was much involved. Before long the master was learning from the pupil. Wilson heard about the successful camps which Whitley started at Filey, sent up observers, and then adapted the idea by bringing collegians and city lads together under canvas. The first annual St Agnes camp was held at Weston-super-Mare in the summer of 1890.[31]

By then Wilson had relinquished his charge. In a farewell sermon on 27 July, he paid a striking tribute to Whitley and his brothers. Referring to a recent claim by Archbishop Benson that 'no institution has done so much for true religion as the public schools', Wilson characterised Clifton as 'a community of vigorous, hearty, manly boys and masters . . . bound together by a community of purpose and the silken ties of honourable memories, traditions, and common ideals'. He hoped that those like him who were leaving might take that spirit of unity with them into other spheres: 'If you want to learn how, go to Halifax, and see what three Clifton boys have done there.'[32]

Best documented of Whitley's extra-curricular activities is the school Debating Society.[33] Like the Oxford and Cambridge Unions, this body affected parliamentary procedure, with government and opposition, honourable members, and a speaker attempting to keep order. Whitley made his front bench debut on 24 February 1883 supporting the motion 'That this House would approve of the acquisition by the state of the ownership of land'. This was lost by twenty-five votes to seven. That anyone voted for it at all reflects on Clifton's social mix. The Society rested during the summer. In September Whitley led the government in approving Lord Ripon's policy in India, and lost by thirty-two votes to seventeen. He led again in November, proposing 'That the continued exclusion of Mr. Bradlaugh from the House of Commons is unconstitutional and unjustifiable'. Charles Bradlaugh's long campaign to take his seat without swearing a religious oath was eventually conceded.[34] So although Whitley's government lost this debate (twenty-two to thirty-three) it accorded with progress, albeit of atheism. Rather more on home ground, Whitley next spoke for disestablishment of the Church, losing by just four votes. In February 1884 he championed the real government's bill for extending the franchise,[35] which was decisively rejected by Clifton's legislators. At his last attempt Whitley ended on the winning side, albeit by the narrowest margin of the Speaker's casting vote. The motion was: 'That this House approves of the political separation of Egypt and the Soudan'. The date was 15 March 1884: Gordon was in Khartoum, charged with enforcing that separation. Unknown to the debaters, the Mahdi's forces had just severed his last link with the outer world. The Sudan crisis split Liberal opinion, and the failure to save Gordon fatally weakened Gladstone's government. These events cast a longer shadow.[36]

In the Clifton debates Whitley mostly spoke alongside John McTaggart and Roger Fry, fellows in the forlorn promotion of radical causes. McTaggart and Fry rebelled against Clifton's code in different ways, and found comradeship in contrasting nonconformities.[37] The future lovers of a Cambridge don were nevertheless strange associates for someone of Whitley's background and strict principles.[38] Another contemporary recalled: 'I have never seen a boy who looked more high-minded than Whitley, and his nature did not belie his looks.'³⁹ It was meant as a compliment, richly redolent of its time. Fifty years earlier, in Keate's Eton, precocious moral elevation would have invited a flogging for 'conceit'.⁴⁰

A practical tribute came from Herbert Prentice, with whom Whitley shared a study.⁴¹ Prentice served round the Empire in the Royal Engineers, attaining a half-colonelcy in the First World War, and latterly worked for Firmin & Sons, prestigious military button-makers. In November 1932 he told Whitley of his wish to leave £2,500 to Clifton to found a 'Whitley-Prentice' scholarship in memory of their 'happy association in Wiseman's'. He reckoned this would provide £75 p.a. to support a boy chosen for aptitude in science and mathematics. Whitley approved the scheme, though putting Prentice's name first, and helped to revise it further on advice from the school. Scientific ability is not generally detectable in boys of thirteen, and a scholarship requires a specific examination: so it became the 'Prentice-Whitley Benefaction'. Prentice hoped to double the capital, but died in September 1933 before he could do so. Unfortunately he said nothing of this to his wife, who was distraught when the will was read. She appealed directly to Whitley, claiming that the legacy unfairly depleted the estate, leaving her son with no more than £40 p.a. This was virtually to accuse Whitley of pocketing the widow's mite. He nevertheless replied tactfully that Prentice had taken so much care over the matter that 'there can be no doubt about his wishes'. He explained that the College now had a legal trusteeship, and doubted if it could be renounced.⁴² This evidently did the trick, because nothing more was heard from the lady for five years, by which time she had remarried; she then merely asked for details of the boys who had held the award.⁴³

Less complicated was the bequest of £100 from Whitley's brother Samuel, who died in 1933. No purpose was specified, but JHW was adamant that the money should '*not* be lost in the general accounts'. He eventually approved the endowment of a prize in history or English, to be known simply as the 'Whitley Prize': because, as he said, 'in our family we never differentiate between the brothers.⁴⁴

Whitley was the last man to flaunt his old school tie or to approve of those who did. Nevertheless, Clifton equipped him with an affinity extending well beyond his contemporaries, and into the upper reaches of many callings. When Whitley entered the Commons in 1900, he found eight other Old Cliftonians in the chamber, with a predictably large Conservative majority.⁴⁵ Of these, the most distinguished was Sydney Buxton, who had already been a junior minister under Gladstone and Rosebery, and who would be in the Cabinet from 1905 to 1914, before six years as Governor-General of South Africa. During Whitley's Speakership the Tories again predominated among Cliftonian MPs,⁴⁶ though the best known were Liberals. Edwin Montagu was Secretary of State for India in Lloyd George's government and, along with Lord Chelmsford, took a major step towards self-government. Leslie Hore-Belisha was a high-profile Minister of Transport, whose eponymous beacon still flashes round the world.⁴⁷ There were other Clifton connexions in the higher reaches of the Liberal Party, notably

W.W. Asquith, brother of the Prime Minister, a master from 1876 to 1910. Guy Morley (at school 1882–86) was the nephew and ward of one member of Asquith's Cabinet, while George and Alexander Grey (1881–83 and 1884–85) were brothers of another. Sir Edward Grey and Buxton were close friends, and belonged to an elite pressure group within the parliamentary party which looked to John Morley as their guide.[48]

Despite heavy public duties, Whitley was increasingly drawn into the affairs of his old school. In December 1914 he was among the first to endow an exhibition for the sons of Old Cliftonians killed in the war. Within two years seventeen such awards had been funded. The Commander-in-Chief commended efforts to give boys 'an education such as their fathers would have wished for them'.[49] In 1917 Whitley was President of the Old Cliftonian Society, and in that capacity chaired the first discussion about a war memorial.[50] In February 1920 he was elected to the Council, the school's governing body; later that year he was President of Clifton's annual Commemoration festival.[51] Whitley's election to the Speaker's chair was greeted by the formal congratulation (and self-congratulation) of the Council, to which he replied 'All that I can say is, Clifton did it.'[52] Birdwood, then in India as Commander-in-Chief, regretted that he would not be able to attend a celebration dinner being arranged by Sir Francis Newbolt. Regretting that Lord Chancellor Birkenhead was not an Old Cliftonian, Birdwood ventured to hope that the school might yet provide Whitley's 'opposite number' in the Lords.[53] Council business brought Whitley to Bristol from time to time. On one occasion he travelled down with Haig, Younghusband and Newbolt, and they entertained one another with good talk. Newbolt was 'moved . . . to admiration' when Whitley told how he had quieted 'the Wild Men' (i.e. Labour members) with lessons in constitutional law and practice.[54]

The Council decided that Clifton's war memorial should be an arch bearing the names of the 578 casualties. This was dedicated on 30 June 1922 in the presence of Earl Haig, who had recently become President of the College. The Council Chairman, Sir Herbert Warren, fussed characteristically with protocol: 'I suppose the Speaker and Mrs. Whitley, and Canon and Mrs. Wilson, ought to be put up very high on the list.'[55]

Whitley maintained close links with his old Head Master. On leaving Clifton, Wilson had been appointed Vicar of Rochdale and Archdeacon of Manchester, and then in 1905 a Canon of Worcester Cathedral. Whitley thought he deserved better, and shortly after becoming a government whip, he asked the Prime Minister if Wilson might have a bishopric. Campbell-Bannerman replied that this had already been offered, and declined because of age. Wilson was then seventy, two months younger than the Prime Minister.[56] In June 1926, with Wilson's ninetieth birthday approaching, Whitley hosted a reception and dinner at Speaker's House attended by Clifton's greatest and best. There was alarm at the start when Wilson fell and cut his head; but he had taken worse knocks.[57] The Speaker sat between Haig and Buxton, while the guest of honour opposite was flanked by Warren and Sir Thomas Inskip.[58] Haig responded to the toast to the school with which his name was coupled.[59] Longer speeches were not usual at Speaker's dinners, but by Whitley's particular request, Wilson paid a tribute to John Percival.[60] In what seems to have been the final message between them, Wilson wrote warmly to Whitley on the eve of his departure to India: 'this is the noblest act of a noble life; the most self sacrificing and the most truly Christian'.[61] Wilson died in his ninety-fifth year, and Whitley spoke at the memorial service in Clifton Chapel on 3 May 1931. His address consisted chiefly in construing a familiar aphorism of the father of medicine: ἢν γὰρ παρῇ φιλανθρωπίη, πάρεστι καὶ φιλοτεχνίη ('where there is a love of man, there is also a love of your calling'). Harnessed to the Christian gospel, this meant that 'to those who had the special fortune to enjoy a Public School life there was a call to give from what they had gained to the less fortunate'.[62]

In the 1920s Clifton envisaged a major extension of science facilities, and though current revenue was buoyant, this alone was not enough. Whitley resolved the matter by undertaking to raise the funds from Old Cliftonians, and he did just that. The Council was thus able to commission a wholly new building.[63] Whitley personally wrote hundreds of letters appealing for contributions, acknowledging them and passing on the cheques. Anticipating modern practice, donors were invited to fund particular aspects of the project. Rooms were named after cherished figures, Canon Wilson among them.[64] Armigerous donors, including Whitley himself, were suitably commemorated.[65] Newbolt helped to furnish the walls with artistic depictions of scientific advance.[66] Three days before the official opening, Whitley reported that the target of £40,000 had been reached by the offer of a blank cheque to top up the receipts to that figure.[67] The fund remained open, because fittings and equipment would bring the total cost to about £50,000.[68] This was duly passed, enabling better provision for the Science Library.

On 2 June 1927 the new building was opened by the Prince of Wales, who had been Warren's unappreciative pupil at Oxford.[69] Haig presided, having approved Whitley's draft programme as having 'not too much formality about it', Whitley having advised against a 'guard of honour' of which HRH 'must be sick'.[70] On the day, the Prince contrived graceful tributes to the Clifton eminences who sat beside him. In Whitley he claimed to have discerned 'what the exercise of tact, patience and fair-mindedness can achieve'.[71]

Norman Whatley, appointed Head Master two years earlier, recalled Whitley as the sharpest of his interviewers, and the most forceful presence at subsequent Council meetings. There was, however, an awkwardness. In June 1926 Whitley presented the prizes at Commemoration.[72] His son Oliver was now in the school, and Whitley asked if they could both take communion at the preceding service. However, the senior chaplain, E.I.A. Phillips, insisted that only confirmed Anglicans might approach his altar. Appeal was made first to the Head Master and then to the Bishop of Bristol, the latter answering with some reluctance that the chaplain was within his rights. This produced what Whatley called 'a short period of strain', on which he later commented 'I don't think Whitley realized that by its statutes Clifton was a

Church of England School'. For his part Whitley stayed away from subsequent Commemorations.[73]

Whitley had urged the new Head Master to preach regularly as his predecessors had done. Whatley did as he was bidden, though with no illusions about his impact.[74] With the same notion of regenerating the spiritual life of the school, Haig and Younghusband proposed a morale-boosting manifesto, to be endorsed by a few select names. The drafting was committed to Newbolt, though the prevailing voice is Younghusband's intergalactic mysticism.[75] The message was that 'no kind of life can make the world intelligible or give us any lasting satisfaction, unless there enters into it the element which is called Religion'; this was distanced from any specific creed, and drifted airily away in the assurance that man's life 'progresses by conformity with a Universal Spirit and divine beauty of character.' To this Whitley put his name, along with those of Haig, Warren, Newbolt and Younghusband. The collection of signatures was halted when Haig died suddenly on 29 January 1928, and the letter was published as part of his Clifton obituary.[76]

Within a week of Haig's death, Warren started the process of finding Clifton a new President. His first instinct was to call for a list of Old Cliftonians in the House of Lords, though he was also prepared to consider any local magnate, or even Birdwood (as yet a mere baronet).[77] Seniority prevailed, and on 28 March the Council nominated Earl Buxton for election by the Governors. If he would not stand, the Speaker was to be asked.[78] Buxton declined. He had limited regard for his old school, and with some reason: a leg injury on the Clifton football field developed into a lifelong disability, eventually requiring amputation.[79] So Warren was not surprised by the reply, and at once informed Whitley that he was now the chosen son. In response, Whitley hoped that another name might yet be found. Failing that, because Clifton had done so much for him, he would serve 'on the principle of fielding where you are told'.[80] He was duly elected President by the Governors on 16 May.[81]

Congratulations from other Clifton grandees were coupled with tributes to Whitley's Speakership, which he resigned in the following month. Birdwood averred that Whitley had 'fully carried out all Cliftonian traditions', though he regretted that he would not be transferring to the Upper House. When news of the new appointment reached Simla, Birdwood felt confident that all Clifton's 'old traditions [sic] and interests' were in safe hands.[82] Newbolt as ever painted a broader canvas: Whitley's deft control of a fractious House had been 'the true glory of our times, a great chapter in the History of England'.[83]

With the Speaker's retirement in prospect, Warren doubtless trusted that Clifton would at least have a viscount as its figurehead. In this he was to be disappointed, but Whitley had a more immediate surprise for him. In accepting the presidency, he asked if he might continue to attend the Council 'as a Speaker can sit and vote in a Committee as a private member'. This notion was not welcome to Sir Herbert Warren. The relative roles of President and Chairman had not been clearly defined; the College Charter implied that a Chairman acted only in the President's absence.[84] Nevertheless during the long reign of the first President, Lord Ducie (1860–1921), the post faded into the background. The Chairman assumed command, emphatically so after Percival's appointment in 1895. Warren had inherited this shogunate in 1917, and was not minded to share power with a reactivated emperor.

Warren cited his experience as Vice-Chancellor at Oxford when Curzon, the Chancellor, sometimes chaired the Hebdomadal Council.[85] This was irregular but, if the Chancellor exercises his right to attend, he must take charge. On the other hand a Visitor, though *in extremis* wielding greater power, does not ordinarily displace a Head of House. At Clifton the Bishop was originally Visitor, but the post lapsed after the departure of its first holder.[86] Warren argued that the President now supplied that role of residual umpire, and so should not participate in routine business. Illness freed Warren from the awkwardness of confronting Whitley directly, and he deputed Newbolt to sound out the other Councillors.[87] Only two saw no difficulty in Whitley's continued presence at the board.[88] The majority supported Warren's view that the President had an appellate jurisdiction obliging him to keep his distance, 'above any suspicion of bias or party'.[89] All stressed their personal regard for Whitley; two had actually opposed his election because they did not want to lose his valued counsel.[90] Newbolt met Whitley on 17 January and, without disclosing individual opinions, reported the Council's verdict. This Whitley allegedly received 'with the clear judgment and consideration natural to him'.[91] Yet one senses his frustration at being relegated to the dignified part of the constitution. On receiving the papers for the next AGM, Whitley said he would not come unless specifically invited by the Chairman or the Head Master. He merely suggested that the latter's house could be brightened with a few window-boxes.[92] He attended only six subsequent Council meetings, including those following Warren's death and the resignation of his successor, when he took take the chair.[93]

Although Whitley was only seen occasionally in the flesh as President, in 1930 he became a fixture in oils. At that year's Commemoration the Old Cliftonian Society presented a copy by H.J. Haley of the Philpot portrait lately made for the Palace of Westminster.[94] In 1932 Whitley escorted Lady Alexandra Haig at the unveiling of a statue of her father overlooking the playing fields where (as Whitley recalled) the Chief's earliest battles were fought and won.[95] Appropriate as these words for the occasion were, the ideology they expressed was already in decline.[96] There was another big fund-raising operation, this time for a new preparatory school, built just north of the College. This was opened by the Duchess of Atholl, already known to Whitley as a Unionist MP and a junior minister in Baldwin's second government. It was Whitley's last great occasion at Clifton. The Council marked his death with a tribute to his 'long and eminent service to the School'.[97] Of this there was one final instance; he bequeathed £1,000 to the general purposes of the College; and that stipulation was precisely followed.[98].

Appendix: index of persons, places and statutes associated with Clifton

Persons

Abbot, Charles Hardcastle, Clifton councillor
Abbott, Evelyn, Clifton master
Allen, Percy Stafford, President of Corpus Christi College, Oxford
Arnold, Thomas, Headmaster of Rugby
Asquith, Henry Herbert, Earl of Oxford and Asquith, Prime Minister
    William Wynans (brother of HH), Clifton master
Atholl, Duchess of *see* Stewart-Murray
Badcock, Gerald Eliot, Clifton bursar [*occ. 1938*]
Baker, Richard Philip, mathematician
Baldwin, Stanley, Earl Baldwin of Bewdley (1937), Prime Minister
Barking, Bishop of *see* Inskip
Belisha *see* Hore-Belisha
Benn, Sir Arthur Shirley, Baron Glenravel of Kensington (1936)
Benson, Edward White, Archbishop of Canterbury
Bévenot, Clovis Maurice Camille, Clifton master
Birdwood, Sir William Riddell, Bt, Baron Birdwood of ANZAC and Totnes (1938)
Birkenhead, Earl of *see* Smith
Boas, Frederick Samuel, literary scholar
Bradlaugh, Charles, MP
Bristol, Bishop of *see* Nickson
Bristol and Gloucester, Bishop of *see* Thomson
Brown, Thomas Edward, Clifton master
Browne, Alfred Murray [*J.M. Wilson's assailant*]
    Arthur Howe, Marquess of Sligo
Butler, Sir George Geoffrey Gilbert, MP
Buxton, Sydney Charles, Viscount Buxton (1914), Earl Buxton (1920)
Caldecote, Viscount *see* Inskip
Campbell, Sir David Graham Muschet, Governor of Malta
Campbell-Bannerman, Sir Henry, Prime Minister
Chelmsford, Viscount *see* Thesiger
Christie, Octavius Francis
Clauson, Sir John Eugene, High Commissioner in Cyprus
Coles, Hugh Thomas, Clifton councillor
Cooper, Sir Richard Ashmole, Bt, MP
Craig, Charles Curtis, MP
Culverwell, Cyril Tom, MP
Curzon, George Nathaniel, Marquess Curzon of Kedleston
Dacre of Glanton, Lady *see* Haig
Dakyns, Henry Graham, Clifton master
Dickinson, Goldsworthy Lowes, classicist
Ducie, Earl of *see* Reynolds-Moreton

Dumas, Alexandre (père), writer
Eberle, Victor Fuller, Clifton councillor
Edward, Prince of Wales (later Edward VIII)
FitzGibbon, Gerald. Judge of the High Court, Irish Free State
Fry, Roger Eliot, poet and critic
Garibaldi, Giuseppe, Italian nationalist leader
George V, King
Gladstone, William Ewart, Prime Minister
Glenravel, Lord *see* Benn
Gordon, Charles George, Major-General
Goulding, Sir Edward Alfred, Bt (1915), Baron Wargrave (1922)
Greene, Harry Plunket, singer
Grenfell, Bernard Pine, archaeologist
Grey, Alexander (son of Edward)
    Sir Edward, Bt, Viscount Grey of Falloden (1916)
    George (son of Edward)
Haddock, George Bahr, MP
Haig, Lady Alexandra Henrietta Louisa (daughter of Douglas), Baroness Dacre of Glanton (1979)
    Sir Douglas, Earl Haig (1919)
Haley, Henry James, artist
Hay, Thomas William, MP
Heath, Arthur Howard, MP
    Sir James, Bt (1904), MP
    Sir Thomas Little, Treasury official
Hereford, Bishop of *see* Percival
Hermon-Hodge, Sir Robert Trotter, Bt (1902), Baron Wyfold of Accrington (1919)
Hewett, Walter Pearse, Old Cliftonian Secretary
Hichens, Robert Smythe, novelist
Hill, Hilda *see* Prentice
Hippocrates, physician
Hore-Belisha, (Isaac) Leslie, Baron Hore-Belisha (1954), Minister of Transport
Hutchinson, Arthur, Master of Pembroke College, Oxford
Inskip, James Theodore (brother of TWH), Bishop of Barking
    Sir Thomas Walter Hobart, Viscount Caldecote (1939), Lord Chancellor
Irwin, Sidney Thomas, Clifton master
Jex-Blake, Thomas William, Head Master of Rugby
Jowett, Benjamin, Master of Balliol College, Oxford
Jupp, Herbert Basil, Clifton master
Keate, John, Head Master of Eton
Leo XIII, Pope
Lewis, Herbert Clark, Baron Merthyr of Senghenydd
    W.J. Clifton College Secretary
Lloyd George, David, Earl Lloyd George of Dwyfor (1945), Prime Minister

Luce, John, Vice-Admiral
    Sir Richard Harman (brother of John), MP
Macfadyen, Sir Eric, MP
McTaggart, John McTaggart Ellis, philosopher
Mallet, Sir Bernard, Registrar-General
    Sir Louis Du Pan (brother of Bernard), Ambassador to the Sublime Porte
Manchester, Archdeacon of [*J.M. Wilson*]
Marchetti, Ernest, JHW's brother-in-law
    Giulio (father of Ernest)
    Marguerita Virginia *see* Whitley
Mendl, Sir Sigismund Ferdinand, MP
Merthyr, Lord *see* Lewis
Montagu, Edwin Samuel, Secretary of State for India
Morley, Guy Estell (nephew of John)
    John, Viscount Morley of Blackburn (1908), Cabinet Minister
Morris, Sir Harold Spencer, MP
Muhammad Ahmad bin Abd Allah, called the Mahdi
Murchison, Sir Charles Kenneth, MP
Newbolt, Sir Francis George (brother of HJ), author
    Sir Henry John, poet and author
Nickson, George, Bishop of Bristol [*occ. 1926*]
O'Donnell, Elliott, writer
Oxford and Asquith, Earl of *see* Asquith
Pease, William Edwin, MP
Pellissier, Eugène, Clifton master
Percival, Arthur Jex-Blake (son of John)
    John, Head Master of Clifton, Bishop of Hereford (1895)
    Lancelot Jefferson, KCVO (son of John), Deputy Clerk of the Closet
Phillips, Egbert Ivor Allen, Clifton chaplain
Philpot, Glyn Warren, artist
Pine, Duncan Vernon, MP
Prentice, Derek (son of Herbert)
    Herbert
    Hilda (wife of Herbert), later Mrs Hill
Primrose, Archibald Philip, Earl of Rosebery and Midlothian, Prime Minister
Quiller-Couch, Sir Arthur Thomas, poet
Rashleigh, Edward Stanhope
Reynolds-Moreton, Henry John, Earl of Ducie
Ridley, Samuel Forde, MP
Ripon, Marquess of *see* Robinson
Robinson, Sir Foster Gotch, Clifton councillor
    George Frederick Samuel, Marquess of Ripon, Viceroy of India
Rosebery and Midlothian, Earl of *see* Primrose
Schiller, Ferdinand Nassau, connoisseur
    (Ferdinand Philip) Maximilian (brother of FN), KC

Selby, Bishop of *see* Woolcombe
Shenstone, William Ashwell, Clifton master
Sligo, Marquess of *see* Browne
Smith, Frederick Edwin, Earl of Birkenhead, Lord Chancellor
Stack, Sir Lee Oliver Fitzmaurice, Governor-General of Sudan
Stewart-Murray, Katharine Marjory, Duchess of Atholl
Storr, Vernon Faithfull, Canon of Westminster
Strachey, (Giles) Lytton, author
Sumner, Bertram
Temple, Frederick, Headmaster of Rugby, Archbishop of Canterbury (1896)
    William (son of Frederick), Archbishop of Canterbury (1942)
Tennyson, Hallam, Baron Tennyson (1892)
    Lionel (brother of Hallam)
Thesiger, Frederic John Napier, Viscount Chelmsford, Viceroy of India
Thompson, Alexander Hamilton, ecclesiastical historian
Thomson, George, Bishop of Bristol and Gloucester, Archbishop of York (1862) [*as Clifton Visitor*]
Threlfall, Sir Richard, physicist
Tilden, Sir William Augustus, Clifton master
Tonks, Henry, artist
Trevor-Roper, Lady Alexandra *see* Haig
Turner, Herbert Hall, astronomer
Udal, Nicholas Robin, Clifton bursar [*occ. 1934–35*]
Wargrave, Lord *see* Goulding
Warren, Sir (Thomas) Herbert, President of Magdalen College, Oxford
Whatley, Norman, Head Master of Clifton
Whitby, Bishop of *see* Woolcombe
Whitehead, Sir George Hugh, Bt
    Sir Rowland Edward, Bt (brother of GH), MP
Whitley, Alfred William (brother of JH)
    Andrew Michael (grandson of JH)
    David Forrester (grandson of JH)
    Sir Edward Nathan (brother of JH)
    John Henry ('Harry'), Speaker of the House of Commons
    John Paton (grandson of JH)
    Marguerita Virginia, *née* Marchetti (first wife of JH)
    Nathan (father of JH)
    Oliver John (son of JH)
    Percival Nathan (son of JH)
    Richard Stephen (grandson of JH)
    Samuel Rinder (brother of JH)
Wilson, James Maurice, Head Master of Clifton
    Maurice Temple (son of JM)
Wiseman, Henry John, Clifton master

Witt, Sir Robert Clermont, art collector
Woolcombe, Henry St John Stirling, Bishop of Whitby then Selby
Wyfold, Lord *see* Hermon-Hodge
Young, Sir Charles Alban, Bt, envoy to Serbia
Younghusband, Sir Francis Edward, explorer

Places

Birmingham, Warwicks, University
Bristol
   Grammar School
   St Agnes, parish
   Stoke Bishop
   see also Clifton
Cambridge, University
Clifton, Bristol
Clifton College
Cyprus
Egypt
Filey, Yorks ER
Halifax, Yorks WR
India
Iowa, IA, University
Khartoum, Sudan
London, East End
Malaya
Malta
Man, Isle of
Oxford, University
   Balliol College
   Corpus Christi College
   Pembroke College
   Trinity College
Penpole, Glos
Rochdale, Lancs
Rugby, Warwicks, School
Serbia
Simla, Punjab
South Africa, Dominion
Sudan
Uppingham, Rut, School
Westminster, Middx, Abbey
   Palace
Weston-super-Mare, Soms
Worcester, Cathedral

Statutes

48 & 49 Vict. c. 3, Representation of the People (1884)
51 & 52 Vict. c. 46, Oaths (1888)
1 & 2 Geo. VI c. 45, Inheritance (Family Provision) (1938)

Notes

1 So asserted the Head Master (Norman Whatley) at JHW's memorial service in Clifton College Chapel, 7 February 1935: *The Cliftonian*, 33/11 (February 1935), 394.
2 The principal narratives are O.F. Christie, *A History of Clifton College 1860–1934*, Bristol, Arrowsmith, 1935; D. Winterbottom, *Clifton after Percival: A Public School in the Twentieth Century*, Bristol, Redcliffe, 1990. Documentary collection: C.S. Knighton (ed.), *Clifton College: Foundation to Evacuation*, Bristol, Bristol Record Society, 65, 2012 [hereafter *CCFE*]. Biographies of masters and boys: J.A.O. Muirhead (ed.), *Clifton College Register, 1862 to 1947*, Bristol, Arrowsmith, 1948. For Clifton's place in the chronology of new foundations see B. Gardner, *The Public Schools: An Historical Survey*, London, Hamish Hamilton, 1973, pp. 159–201.
3 M.W. McCrum, *Thomas Arnold Head Master: A Reassessment*, Oxford, Oxford University Press, 1989, pp. 116–17.
4 The view from Clifton's chief local rival is that the college is 'in Bristol, if reluctantly, but not of Bristol': K. Robbins, *Pride of Place: A Modern History of Bristol Grammar School*, Andover, Phillimore, 2010, p. 16.
5 Percival's first biographer was his godson William Temple, whose *Life of Bishop Percival*, London, Macmillan, 1921, is appropriately devout. Balance is provided by A.C. Percival (no relation), 'Some Victorian Headmasters', in B. Simon and I. Bradley (eds), *The Victorian Public School: Studies in the Development of an Educational Institution*, Dublin, Gill and Macmillan, 1975, pp. 73–80; D. Winterbottom, *John Percival: The Great Educator*, Bristol, Historical Association, 1993; R.J. Potter, *Headmaster: The Life of John Percival, Radical Autocrat*, London, Constable, 1998.
6 After returning to Rugby as Headmaster (1887) he became Bishop of Hereford in 1895; in the same year he regained authority at Clifton as Chairman of the Council.
7 [A.T. Wilson and J.S. Wilson (eds)], *James M. Wilson: An Autobiography 1836–1931*, London, Sidgwick & Jackson, 1931.
8 T.W. Bamford, *Rise of the Public Schools: A Study of Boys' Public Boarding Schools in England and Wales from 1837 to the Present Day*, London, Nelson, 1967, pp. 88, 96, 109 and *passim*.
9 J.R. de S. Honey, *Tom Brown's Universe: The Development of the Victorian Public School*, London, Millington, 1977, pp. 178–80 and *passim*; J.A. Mangan, *Athleticism in the Victorian and Edwardian Public School: The Emergence and Consolidation of an Educational Ideology*, Cambridge, Cambridge University Press, 1981, p. 190 and *passim*.
10 Christie, *Clifton College*, p. 203. Cf. comments by Whatley shortly after becoming Head Master: *CCFE*, pp. 102–3.
11 Wiseman's occupied a building just west of the main site. In 2006 this property was sold, and the House moved to new quarters. In the process a board commemorating the Whitley dynasty was regrettably mislaid.
12 Percival Whitley went to Rugby. In calling his elder son after his old Head Master, JHW had some precedent: one of John Percival's own sons was named 'Jex-Blake' after a Rugby Headmaster, and J.M. Wilson gave the name 'Temple' to his youngest boy.
13 [Sir F.H. Newbolt], *Clifton College Twenty-Five Years Ago: The Diary of a Fag*, London, Robinson, 1904, p. 183; O.F. Christie, *Clifton School Days (1879–1885)*, London, Shaylor, 1930, pp. 44–5.
14 Unsigned obituary, *The Cliftonian*, 20/9 (October 1908), 357.
15 J.R. Mozley, *Clifton Memories*, Bristol, Arrowsmith, 1927, p. 5.

16 Potter, *Headmaster*, pp. 33–31.
17 D. Winterbottom, *T.E. Brown: His Life and Legacy*, Douglas, Manx Experience, 1997, p. 175.
18 A.B. Pippard, 'Schoolmaster-Fellows and the Campaign for Science Education', *Notes and Records of the Royal Society*, 56/1 (January 2002), 63–81.
19 Clifton College Archives [hereafter CCA], K2 (Record Sheets), 1884; copy in Huddersfield University Archives [hereafter HUA], JHW/10/1.
20 H. St. J.S. Woolcombe (Whitby then Selby); J.T. Inskip (Barking); better known were V.F. Storr, Canon of Westminster, and L.J. Percival (son of John), Domestic Chaplain to George V.
21 G.B. Haddock, Maj.-Gen. Sir R.H. Luce, S.F. Ridley; C.C. Craig; Sir S.F. Mendl, Sir R.E Whitehead.
22 P.S. Allen, classicist, President of Corpus; A. Hutchinson, mineralogist, Master of Pembroke.
23 CCA, M77. The phrase (*Aeneid*, 6, 726) was adopted when arms were granted in 1895.
24 Like JHW's future father-in-law, Bévenot had fought with Garibaldi; after Clifton he became Professor of French and Italian at Birmingham University.
25 CCA, School Lists (printed), 1881(2), pp. 23, 40; 1884(2), pp. 47, 52; 1884(3), p. 51.
26 CCA, Scientific Society Minute Book 2, pp. 75–113; largely printed in *Transactions of the Clifton College Scientific Society*, 2/4 (1887), 27–34.
27 Christie, *Clifton College*, pp. 293–303.
28 *The Times*, 30 April 1921, letter dated 24th; copied by *Western Daily Press*, 17 May (CCA, Truscott Album 13, p. 10). Christie, *Clifton College*, p. 302 n. 6, quotes a faulty recollection that this occurred in 1885, the year after JHW left. The story illustrates Clifton's benign regime: at Uppingham runners were pursued by bicycling praepostors armed with horse whips, to encourage the dawdling and lame: Mangan, *Athleticism*, p. 85.
29 CCA, HM6, memoir of N. Whatley (1961), p. 54. This document comprises separately paginated sections with no overall title; the pagination used here is archival.
30 W.H.G. Armytage, *Sir Richard Gregory: His Life and Work*, London, Macmillan, 1957, pp. 3, 7–9.
31 HUA, JHW/2/1, pp. 14–15 (unidentified newspaper cutting); Christie, *Clifton College*, pp. 122–9; Wilson, *Autobiography*, pp. 138–42.
32 J.M. Wilson, *Sermons: Second Series. Preached in Clifton College Chapel 1888–1890*, London, Macmillan, 1891, pp. 165–6.
33 CCA, Debating Society Minute Book 2 (unpaginated), 24 February, 29 September, 10 November, 7 December 1883; 2 February, 15 March 1884; reprinted in *The Cliftonian*, 7 (1881–83), 429; 8 (1883–85), 99, 136–7, 174–5, 214–15. The minutes do not report the substance of speeches.
34 51 & 52 Vict. c. 46.
35 Enacted as 48 & 49 Vict. c. 3.
36 On 9 December 1924, when Whitley stood at the Bar of the Lords to hear George V open Parliament, the first matter in the gracious speech was the murder of the Governor-General of the Sudan, Whitley's old schoolmate Sir Lee Stack: *Parliamentary Debates*, 5th ser., 60 (House of Lords, 1924–25, sess. 1), p. 6.
37 Potter, *Headmaster*, pp. 92–7.
38 D. Proctor (ed.), *The Autobiography of G. Lowes Dickinson*, London, Duckworth, 1973, pp. 92–3 and *passim*; pl. 7 shows Dickinson, Fry, McTaggart and the Clifton master W.W. Asquith at the Swiss home of the aesthete and collector Ferdinand Schiller (Clifton 1881–84) and his brother Maximilian (1882–86), both major contributors to Whitley's Science School appeal.
39 Christie, *Clifton School Days*, pp. 48–9.
40 J. Chandos, *Boys Together: English Public Schools 1800–1864*, London, Hutchinson, 1984, p. 270.

41 Prentice left at Christmas 1883, in Whitley's penultimate year.
42 Not until 1938 were the courts empowered to redistribute an estate in favour of dependants: 1 & 2 Geo. VI c. 45.
43 CCA, RB2/19 (file): principally Prentice to JHW, 10 and 20 November 1932; exchanges between JHW and Whatley, 22–24 November; Derek Prentice to JHW, 16 September 1933, reporting his father's death (and showing *he* knew and approved of the bequest); Mrs Prentice to JHW, 19 December and reply, 21 December; same (now Mrs Hill) to Bursar, 3 August 1938; Council Minute Book 10, pp. 159–60, 166; Book 11, pp. 12, 37; *The Times*, 15 November 1933.
44 CCA, RB4/12 (file): principally JHW to Bursar, 27 January 1934; to Whatley, 2 February 1934.
45 A.S. Benn, E.A. Goulding, A.H. Heath, J. Heath, R.T. Hermon-Hodge, S.F. Ridley; S.C. Buxton, D.V. Pine.
46 Sir G.G.G. Butler, Sir R.A. Cooper, C.T. Culverwell, T.W. Hay, Sir T.W.H. Inskip, Sir R.H. Luce, Sir C.K. Murchison, W.E. Pease; C.C. Craig; I.L.H. Belisha, Sir E. Macfadyen, E.S. Montagu, Sir H.S. Morris.
47 Like Whitley he learned his oratory at school: *The Cliftonian*, 41/2 (March 1957), 41–2.
48 D.A. Hamer, *John Morley: Liberal Intellectual in Politics*, Oxford, Oxford University Press, 1968, pp. 245–8; K. Robbins, *Sir Edward Grey: A Biography of Lord Grey of Falloden*, London, Cassell, 1971, pp. 29–30; D. Waley, *A Liberal Life: Sydney, Earl Buxton, 1853–1934*, Newtimber, Newtimber, 1999, pp. 99–100.
49 Christie, *Clifton College*, p. 191; CCA, P1981, Haig to Sir Francis Younghusband, 1 December 1916.
50 *The Cliftonian*, 25/4 (December 1917), 163–6.
51 F. Borwick (ed.), *Clifton College Annals and Register 1862–1925*, Bristol, Arrowsmith, 1925, pp. xxv, cvi.
52 CCA, Council Minute Book 7, pp. 253–4, 18 May 1921; HUA, JHW/4/1/36, copy sent, 21st.
53 HUA, JHW/4/1/37, 30 May. Birdwood's wish was granted in 1939 when T.W.H. Inskip (Clifton 1886–94) ascended the woolsack as Viscount Caldecote.
54 M. Newbolt (ed.), *The Later Life and Letters of Sir Henry Newbolt*, London, Faber, 1932, pp. 292–3; Potter, *Headmaster*, pp. 127–30.
55 CCA, K48, Warren to College Secretary, 24 June 1922 (*CCFE*, p. 382).
56 HUA, JHW/2/5, pp. 26–7, PM to JHW, 16 September 1907.
57 On his birthday in 1882 he had been stabbed by a deranged pupil: Wilson, *Autobiography*, pp. 117–21.
58 HUA, JHW/10/2, seating plan for dinner, 18 June 1926; *The Cliftonian*, 29/8 (July 1926), 205.
59 HUA, JHW/4/1/66, JHW/4/1/69, Haig to JHW, 16 March and 14 June 1926.
60 Wilson, *Autobiography*, pp. 160–4; speech also in Mozley, *Clifton Memories*, pp. 187–91.
61 HUA, JHW/4/1/93, 19 September 1929.
62 HUS, JHW/4/1/108, 3 May 1931.
63 CCA, HM6, Whatley memoir, pp. 21, 22; Science School papers, *passim*.
64 Ibid., JHW to Wilson, 18 May 1927, and reply, 21 May; to Head Master, 27 July; to College Secretary, 21 October 1926, 2 May 1927. The donors of the Wilson Room were revealed as F.P.M. Schiller (£1000), E.S. Rashleigh (£500), Lord Merthyr, Sir T.W.H. Inskip and B. Sumner.
65 Ibid., JHW to College Secretary, 21 October 1926.
66 Ibid., JHW to Whatley, 22 July 1927. Whitley and Newbolt were simultaneously collaborating over the decoration of St Stephen's Hall: see Chapter 8 of this volume, by Graham E. Seel, on 'J.H. Whitley and St. Stephen's Hall in the Palace of Westminster'.
67 CCA, Science School papers, JHW to same, 31 May 1927; the donor was Sir George Whitehead, who had been the first Old Cliftonia to support Whitley's appeal.

68 *The Cliftonian*, 30/2 (1927), 47, letter from JHW, 5 July.
69 HRH thought Warren 'an awful old man': P. Ziegler, *King Edward VIII*, London, Collins, 1990, p. 40.
70 HUA, JHW/4/1/73, Haig to JHW, 18 Februaray 1927; related papers in *CCFE*, pp. 348–53.
71 *The Cliftonian*, 30/1 (July 1927), 36.
72 Ibid., 29/8 (July 1926), 209.
73 CCA, HM6, Whatley memoir, pp. 46, 54–5. By 'statutes' Whatley meant the 1877 charter, which required as 'a fundamental condition of the constitution of the College' that its religious teaching should accord with that of the Church of England: *CCFE*, p. 60.
74 Ibid., p. 56. Whatley was the second lay Head Master.
75 P. French, *Younghusband: The Last Great Imperial Adventurer*, London, HarperCollins, 1994, pp. 131, 151–2 and *passim*. Haig envisaged 'a great Imperial Church' but remained personally loyal to his Presbyterian roots: G.S. Duncan, *Douglas Haig as I knew Him*, London, George Allen & Unwin, 1966, p. 130; N. Cave, 'Haig and Religion', in B. Bond and N. Cave (eds), *Haig: A Repappraisal 80 Years On*, Barnsley, Pen & Sword, 1999, pp. 246–57. Newbolt's religion was patriotism, though McTaggart's philosophy latterly persuaded him that the spirit was the sole reality: Newbolt, *Later Life*, pp. 322–4, 373–4. Warren's conventional Anglicanism was qualified only by a fawning regard for Leo XIII: L. Magnus, *Herbert Warren of Magdalen: President and Friend 1853–1930*, London, Murray, 1932, pp. 74–9.
76 *The Cliftonian*, 30/5 (February 1928), 179–80; reprinted in Newbolt, *Later Life*, pp. 410–12, with additional commendation by Haig, 31 August 1927; CCA, P1917, Newbolt to JHW, 21 March 1928, regretting that agreed alterations to the text had not been printed.
77 CCA, RB2/36 (file): Warren College Secretary, 8 February, 25 April 1928; JHW to Warren, 17 April 1928 (*CCFE*, pp. 75–7).
78 CCA, Council Minute Book 8, p. 275.
79 Waley, *Buxton*, p. 21.
80 CCA, RB2/36, JHW to Warren, 17 April 1928 (*CCFE*, p. 75).
81 CCA, Council Minute Book 8, p. 284.
82 HUA, JHW/4/1/84, 90, Birdwood to JHW, 4 June and 15 July 1928.
83 HUA, JHW/4/1/87, Newbolt to JHW, 22 June. See Chapter 8 by Graham E. Seel in this volume. Refer also to n. 94 below. A copy of the J.H. Whitley portrait as Speaker of the House of Commons appears on the front cover of this volume.
84 *CCFE*, pp. 63, 67.
85 CCA, RB2/38 (file): Warren to Newbolt, 12 November 1928. *Cf.* Magnus, *Warren*, pp. 136–46.
86 *CCFE*, p. 41 and n. 116.
87 CCA, RB2/38, circular from Newbolt, [7] November 1928, citing Council's resolution of 24 October (not in minutes of that meeting: Book 8, pp. 305–8).
88 CCA, RB2/38, Younghusband and Sir F.G. Robinson to Newbolt, 9 November 1928.
89 Ibid., C.H. Abbot to Newbolt, 9 November 1928.
90 Ibid., H.T. Coles and V. Fuller Eberle to Newbolt, 9 and 13 November 1928.
91 Ibid., Secretary to Council, 28 January 1929.
92 Ibid., JHW to Secretary, 19 March 1929.
93 CCA, Council Minute Books 8, p. 341; 9, pp. 7, 166; 10, pp. 42, 103; 11, p. 15.
94 CCA, RS2/46 (file): W.P. Hewett (Hon. Secretary of the Old Cliftonian Society) to the College Secretary, 10 March, 24 June 1930. The copy was a three-quarter length reduction, not for economy but to harmonise with existing portraits of Haig and Birdwood. Having languished for some years in a basement, it was rescued by the present writer and now hangs in the Archive Room.
95 *The Cliftonian*, 32/8 (July 1932), 308.

96 *Cf.* Mangan, *Athleticism*, pp. 207–18.
97 CCA, Council Minute Book 11, p. 78.
98 CCA, RB4/7 (file): Percival Whitley to College, 31 March 1935, enclosing cheque; Bursar to PNW, 4 June 1935, conveying the Council's decision (21 May) to keep the money on current account pending a decision on its use, on which further report was promised but never made.

4   J.H. Whitley
A model for free churchmen[1]

Clyde Binfield

What might be read into this?

> Family characteristics . . . don't just happen. They depend on roots and can be understood only by digging down into the past . . . Character is mostly an inheritance.
>
> My first name is Oliver because my father admired Cromwell. [My family] have tended to be Congregationalists. Oliver Cromwell was the first great Congregationalist and is still the greatest. He showed Europe that it was possible for the establishment to be defeated by a determined and principled minority. It has quite often happened since: it had very rarely happened before. He democratised an army. He declined the Crown of England . . . He found moderates among those opposed to him more congenial than some of his own more militant supporters. Courted eventually by the principalities of Europe, his relentless conscience prevented him from being otherwise than humble.
>
> He had no use for what we would now call class distinctions. Quality mattered, not lineage, wealth or popular support . . .[2]

I have been selective in my quotation but the style is spare, the interpretation Whig. Let the speaker continue (it might help to bear in mind that he is speaking in June 1988):

> [I]t is just when the clenched fists of dogma have the grace to relax a bit that new ways are most likely to be revealed for progress through conciliation. Some refer to the pathfinder as the Holy Spirit. But Glasnost will do . . .
>
> [T]his belief that dogma is the enemy of revelation . . . is wholly consistent with the quantum leap of realisation recently that we live in an indetermined world, where the concept of the unknowable is not intellectual cowardice, where powers of intuition are being released from scientific dogmatism and where among profound questions, affecting society, is doubt whether it is valid to equate the quality of life with ever rising material standards of living. The resultant revaluation of the spiritual and moral dimension of human existence can never be complete.[3]

That amounts to a creed although it must be apparent that creeds would be abhorrent to the turn of mind that has been revealed. It is the speaker's creed but he imputes it to his much older brother, born in 1893, and to their father, born in 1866. It is in their memory that he is speaking.

Who is this man? He is in his mid-seventies, speaking in Yorkshire's West Riding but long retired to Scotland's west coast. As outlined in *Who's Who* he belongs quietly but firmly to the establishment: Clifton College, New College Oxford, barrister-at-law, war service with the Navy (the Normandy landings and the Far East), and the BBC, latterly as chief assistant to the Director General and Managing Director of External Services.[4] His obituary in *The Times* would refer to him as 'the conscience of the BBC'.[5] Perhaps he was the best Director General the BBC never had. For my purposes, however, throughout his BBC years he was member, deacon, and then Secretary of a Congregational church, spiritually and architecturally distinctive, in the quieter part of Surrey.[6]

Now to the elder brother, about whom Oliver was speaking. His name, too, is significant: Percival. Neither Arthurian nor Wagnerian overtones should be read into this. Percival was named after one of Victorian England's great head-masters. Since that headmaster became head of an Oxford college and a bishop the establishment notes are inescapable: this young Percival was Rugby, New College Oxford, and then nearly forty years keeping the family firm afloat. He was a third generation master cotton spinner, councillor, alderman, mayor, Justice of the Peace (JP), Chairman of his borough's Education Committee, and of its Libraries and Museums Committee, and of the Bench, devoted to social service, the Young Men's Christian Association (YMCA), Boy Scouts (he became District Commissioner), boys' clubs, and camps. For my purposes, however, throughout his civic years he was member and deacon of a more conventionally distinctive Congregational church in his home town.[7]

Percival's war service was in the First World War. It illustrates the strenuous asceticism of a man who burned himself out in his mid-sixties. Only in retrospect might it be fitted into an establishment framework but it is not uncharacteristic of the mindset that I am constructing. Its nature might be suggested by two quotations. The first is from a war-time memoir. The second is from a letter to a provincial newspaper. The writer of the first is recalling YMCA Forces' work in Le Havre in 1916. Conscription had just been introduced. Consequently, out of a staff of less than a hundred, over half were women and the men were either over-age, obviously unfit, or exempt as ministers of religion. Of the rest:

> One outstanding hut leader . . . refused to attest: I had long known him to be a conscientious objector. We said goodbye to him with sincere regret and he went home to waste, I suppose, much valuable time in prison, alongside many willing Quakers, in ignominy which he did not deserve.[8]

That did not happen but after the war and back in the family firm that hut leader, who was Percival, stood for his Town Council. He was heckled about his war service; he had been the recipient of white feathers. It prompted a long letter in the local newspaper. Its tone, straightforward, manly, impassioned, and wholly of its time, should be noted:

> I was out in Salonika in 1918, and it was there that I first met [him]. For six weeks of my time in that country I worked under his direction, and frequently shared his tent with him. I have good reason, therefore, to know something about his work. No man out there considered his own comfort or health less than [he]. Whatever the job was – hard or easy, dirty or clean, mental or manual – he was in at it, and he seems to have a preference for the hard and dirty jobs. He was the most disreputable looking of all the Y.M.C.A. workers out there, and one little wonders. He would have needed a new uniform every week at least to look anything else. He seemed to defy the atrocious climate, and he certainly disregarded all the warnings of his friends, and he suffered for it. There was no sort of risk which he did not face. The wonder is that he ever lived to come back. He might have had a 'soft' job at the Y.M.C.A. headquarters at Salonika, but he preferred to be a pioneer worker. He followed the army as it advanced up country, and it was his business to found Y.M.C.A. centres in the service of the men. That was a very different matter from going to centres already established, and meant 'roughing it'.
> I wish he could be persuaded to tell the whole story himself . . .
> I have not been asked to write this letter . . . I am far from holding the opinions of a conscientious objector but . . . [m]y own feeling is that all . . . who, like myself, had sons in the fighting line, have reason to thank God that there were a few men who served our lads as [he] did. Would that there had been many more . . .[9]

The writer of that letter was new to the town whose newspaper he was addressing. He was a Congregational minister, on the cusp of fifty, coming to the defence of a church member, still in his twenties. Although of an older generation, he was a Congregational minister of a relatively new type: Lincoln College, Oxford (Modern History), Mansfield College, Oxford (Theology) – varied but promising, even superior, pastorates; a man of consequence in successive communities (Essex, Manchester, Aberdeen, and now the West Riding), for whom the First World War marked a defining chapter in contemporary citizenship.

This brings me to the father of Oliver and Percival, reared like them in the West Riding Congregational church whose minister wrote that letter. For some years, however, he had lived chiefly in London. This was because he had represented his West Riding town in Parliament since 1900. Indeed, in 1921, when his elder son entered its Town Council, he had become Speaker of the House of Commons. The establishment aspect of that is undeniable.

I have reached him through his sons because I want to suggest a sense of family and tradition that is as strong as any to be found in *Burke's Peerage*. Through such a tradition a family is congregating. Here gather individuals who are more than an aggregation of Independents.

J.H. Whitley, 'Harry' to friends and family, was Speaker of the House of Commons from 1921 to 1928.[10] It was a relatively short Speakership. His successor, Speaker Fitzroy, Eton and Sandhurst, died in office, having held it for fifteen years.[11] His predecessor, Speaker Lowther, Eton and Trinity, outlived them both, having been Speaker for sixteen years.[12] Speakers Lowther and Fitzroy were Conservatives, Speaker Whitley was a Liberal. It was a momentously fraught time: post-war reconstruction, political re-alignment, the emergence of Labour as official Opposition and therefore a party of Government, the steady retreat of Liberalism, industrial unrest, the General Strike.

Whitley's preparation for the post was consistent and cumulative, hardly easy but – if only in retrospect – inevitable. For his first seven years in Parliament, five of them in Opposition, he had been a backbencher, a usefully active coming man. For the next fourteen years he held office, first as a Junior Lord of the Treasury, then as Deputy Chairman and Chairman of Ways and Means: that is to say as a Government Whip, Deputy Deputy Speaker, and Deputy Speaker. These were not offices to seize the public eye but they presupposed in their holder administrative and executive grasp and authoritatively persuasive collegiality.

By Whitley's time the Speakership was studiedly non-partisan.[13] It was hardly non-political. The Speaker's judgment as to when and how to limit debate was critical; so was his role with regard to Private Members' Bills and the selection of amendments. Balance was the aim but not always the achievement. It was an ancient office. Its holder had evolved since the late fourteenth century as spokesman for the Commons in its dealings with the Crown. He took precedence after the Royal Family, the two Archbishops, the Lord Chancellor, Prime Minister, and Lord President of the Council, and he was rewarded accordingly: a ministerial salary, pension, a house in the Palace of Westminster, and the prospect of a peerage, usually a viscountcy. The Speaker represented parliamentary tradition. He was a representative national figure.

The Deputy Speaker was no less significant a figure. He did more than deputise for the Speaker when the latter was absent. Ways and Means was a Committee of the Whole House; its business was primarily financial – it scrutinised and determined the budget proposals, for example. Its Chairman, though proposed by the Prime Minister, was elected by his fellow MPs to hold office for the duration of a Parliament. Judicious independence was inseparable from his brief. The Deputy Speaker was not a national figure but he was a representative Commons man.

This Deputy Speaker had been a Government Whip. The Whip was exactly that. He held the whip hand – the analogy has to be fox hunting and horse riding – largely by virtue of what he had come to know (about his pack?) but quite as much by virtue of his credibility.

Harry Whitley's path to the Speakership was less smooth than it appeared.[14] His election was unopposed but it was marked by three Tory speeches of protest and it had been threatened by a Tory rebellion. No man of Whitley's type, indeed no Liberal of Whitley's type, had yet been Speaker. Many Tories had yet to forgive Whitley's supposed partiality while chairing a pre-war meeting of Ways and Means in so prolonging debate that a government defeat was averted. Their argument now was that Ways and Means should not be seen as a normal route to Speakership. That was disingenuous. Speaker Lowther had been Chairman of Ways and Means, Speaker Fitzroy would be Deputy Chairman of Ways and Means, and one of the three vocal Tories would himself become a long-serving Chairman of Ways and Means, although the Speakership eluded him.[15] Ways and Means was a sensible path to Speakership.

What then was Whitley's type as man and Liberal? He was the first avowed Free Church Speaker, reared since early childhood at Park, the Congregational church in Halifax in which members of his family were active from its formation in the 1860s to the 1950s, when they ceased to live in Halifax (Figure 4.1). He was also the first working industrialist to be Speaker. Whitleys had been cotton masters since 1844, first as cardmakers (their firm, John Whiteley & Sons, into which they had married, had been founded in 1791), then as spinners (their firm, S. Whitley & Co., had been founded in 1863).[16] Harry Whitley's career as master

Figure 4.1 Park Congregational Church, Halifax. (From the *Congregational Year Book, 1870*.)

cotton spinner was precipitated by the death of an uncle and the ailing health of his father. The family firm was not large – 200–300 workmen in the years of his Speakership – but the partners lived in substantial stone houses.[17] Harry Whitley's first Halifax house was a solid, detached, double-fronted villa, its central entrance flanked by generous bay windows. His second Halifax house was larger yet, built in the 1870s, with tennis and fives courts, and room for three houses in its grounds when the time came to build on them. Harry's houses, his sons' houses, a daughter's house, were all called Brantwood; Ruskin permeated these stones of Halifax as, later, the brick and render of Surrey's white highlands.

This first Free Church, industrial, Speaker was also the first Liberal Speaker of his type. In Tory eyes Whitley could be pigeon-holed as a Radical. It would be fairer to place him on the judicious if decided left of his party's centre. He perfectly represented for his generation a type of MP seen increasingly in Parliament from the 1830s and especially from the 1870s: men who had consolidated socially over several generations, who had accumulated commercial and industrial experience and were in a position to pay their own way, and whom urban and especially northern industrial constituencies found sympathetic. Such men were often Nonconformists. That could be an advantage, not least when their Nonconformity could be presented as the mark of proud underdogs or of resurgent Parliamentarians. Harry Whitley, Halifax cotton spinner, was to their manner born. His Nonconformity would have fitted Halifax admirably had he been a Baptist, a Unitarian, a Free, Primitive, or Wesleyan Methodist. His Congregationalism fitted his town particularly well.

These factors merit further exploration. If diehard Tories in 1900 saw the new junior member for Halifax as yet another representative of a new, indeed *nouveau*, type he was in fact markedly entrenched. His wife's grandfather sat for Halifax in the mid-1870s and her great-uncle in the 1850s, moving on to Yorkshire's West Riding in the 1860s.[18] His sister's father-in-law sat for Bolton in the 1850s, her sister-in-law's husband for Halifax in the 1890s, and his father in the 1880s.[19] If one turns from the cotton-spinning Whitleys to the card-making Whiteleys, Harry's first cousin Jessie had a brother-in-law who sat for Elland in the 1880s and 1890s, and his first cousin Annabella had a brother-in-law who sat for Monmouth in the 1890s and Central Hackney from 1906 to 1918.[20] Better yet, Harry Whitley had a first cousin who switched from the cotton-spinning Whitleys to the card-making Whiteleys and entered Parliament as MP for Skipton in the same year as Harry Whitley; and that cousin's son-in-law, the egregious Commander Kenworthy, represented Central Hull, first as a Liberal and then as a Labour MP throughout Harry Whitley's Speakership.[21]

In short, nobody could say that Speaker Whitley did not come from the parliamentary classes, nature's industrial baronets, knights of the Ridings, almost to a man. This last point is brought home by Whitley's first two Halifax elections.

1900 was the year of the Khaki Election. The Tory candidate, who was indeed a baronet, was Eton, Balliol, and over 3,000 Suffolk acres. He was also on active service in South Africa, serving with the Imperial Yeomanry: his wife, a general's daughter, fronted his campaign. He won convincingly.

Yet all was not quite what it seemed. That landed and gallant baronet was Savile Crossley whose family firm had carpeted innumerable middle-class houses and transformed the Halifax townscape.[22] His parents had been Congregationalists; that was then, but he was, even so, a first cousin-once-removed of young Mrs Harry Whitley, whose father was a director and soon to be Managing Director of the great Crossley firm and would succeed Sir Savile as its Chairman. The Tory victor was almost one of the family. Halifax at that time was a two member constituency. In 1900 Harry Whitley was the Liberal victor, unexpectedly beating Alfred Billson, the sitting Liberal since 1897. Harry was the youngest candidate, Billson was the oldest. Billson was a Liberal solicitor from Leicester but he was a bit better than a carpet bagger, if only because of his own Congregational and Baptist links.[23] And the fourth candidate? James Parker was the Labour candidate. He was a Methodist, educated at a Wesleyan school but worshipping with Free Methodists. His was a face of the future.[24]

1906 was the year of the Liberal landslide. Billson had bowed out of the Halifax scene, leaving Crossley, Parker and Whitley as candidates. This time Whitley and Parker were elected. Crossley and Parker, as types, exactly foreshadowed the types with whom Speaker Whitley would have to contend in the 1920s; and he had more in common with either than might have been imagined.

Thus Parliament; it remains to explore two more aspects, one political, the other social. Harry Whitley's political formation was municipal. In this he consolidated a family tradition. His wife's Crossley grandfather was Halifax's third mayor, a Crossley great-uncle was its second mayor, and a Crossley cousin followed suit as, on the Whitley side, did several more distant family connections, but it was Harry's father, Nathan Whitley, who was the first municipal Whitley: town councillor and alderman in the 1870s and, more briefly, the 1880s, Chairman of the Finance Committee and mayor three times (1877, 1882, 1883).[25] Harry followed him as a councillor from 1893, active on the Electricity and Tramways Committees, with a growing reputation as a progressive when it came to labour and trade union rights and considerably to the left of several of his politically active family connections.[26]

To the civic formation should be added a social dimension: it was the responsibility of the municipal classes to enable the achievement of their fellow citizens' potential. Harry Whitley's father, uncles and brothers were to the forefront of such work. His father, Nathan, focused on education: Chairman of the School Board, Governor of Heath Grammar School and the Crossley and Porter Orphanage Schools, a founder of the Girls' High School, a director of the Mechanics' Institute; he was also Treasurer of the Infirmary.[27] Harry's card-making uncle John focused on more obviously charitable work: Chairman of the Crossley and Porter Orphanage, Treasurer of the Infirmary, President of the Tradesmen's Benevolent Institution, trustee or governor of two sets of Crossley almshouses, Abbott's Ladies' Homes, Lancaster's Royal Albert Asylum, Somerscales and Bowcock's Charity; he was also a trustee of the Halifax Equitable Benefit Building Society.[28] This was much more than the small change, or even the sum of the small change, of social and civic responsibility; it was the capital which allowed for the refocusing of welfare, the enlargement of vision, to immediate practical effect.

The next generation confirmed this. Of Harry Whitley's younger brothers, Alfred was the one closest to him in Halifax life and work. He was a trustee of Balme's Charity, founded for the benefit of Yorkshire Congregationalists.[29] He chaired the Somerscales and Bowcock's Charity, inaugurated the district Nursing Association, and founded and presided over the Citizens' Guild of Help, looking boldly to Germany for its rationale. The Halifax Guild was founded on the Elberfeld System, that is to say on 'Principles of permanent value . . . as valid and good for English conditions as German conditions', most notably 'that the poor of a community were a proper charge on that community, and that the deserving poor ought to be able to obtain ready help, not so much by charity, but of right'.[30] The third brother, Samuel, who left card-making in Halifax for dairy farming in Surrey and Berkshire, turned his practical attention to Lingfield's Colony for Epileptics and Unemployables.[31] Even the youngest and longest-lived brother, Edward, a solicitor who was the most conventional of them all (Brigadier General Territorials, KCB, CMG, DSO, DL, JP,[32] President of the Yorkshire Agricultural Society), was a director, later President, of the Halifax Building Society.[33]

Their wives matched such commitment. The second Mrs Nathan Whitley had run a girls' boarding school in Essex.[34] In Halifax, now widowed, she was the first woman on the School Board and she promoted the Girls' High School and an Employment Society to help 'afflicted people in the Workhouse'. She was a woman 'who delighted to gather together representatives of different schools of thought, at her own home, for the exchange of views'; 'to waste time was to her abhorrent; and she sought to impress her views on others'.[35] Her daughter-in-law, Mrs Alfred Whitley, was cast in a similar mould: company director, JP, town councillor, regionally active in Girl Guides, St John Ambulance, District Nursing, Women's Voluntary Service (WVS), governor of a string of secondary schools.[36]

Harry Whitley compounded this active, practical, social citizenship.[37] There were the school governorships. There were the Recreative Evening Schools, several evenings a week each winter, with their emphasis on boys' gymnastic classes, which he started. There were the annual boys' camps at Filey, which he started and organised. Whitley brothers, sons, nephews, cousins were recruited to play their due part in running classes and camps alike. There was the Halifax YMCA, of which he was a founder and first President. If Alfred was President of the Guild of Help, Harry was active in that Guild's promotion and much later he was President of the National Council of Social Service, There was also an environmental concern. In the first decades of the Garden City movement, Whitley was inevitably called on, and in Halifax he promoted a Town Planning competition, adjudicated by Liverpool's Professor Adshead, for which he provided the prizes.[38] The First World War prevented its practical municipal implementation but it had provided a stimulus: the playing field, the neighbourhood park, the farm scheme, such an environment as might encourage local boys from elementary schools to aim for university scholarships, buttressed by a 'Big Brother Scheme' which, through local Rotarians, he engineered; bursaries to make up the difference between what a scholarship allowed for and what living expenses in fact required. Again, though perhaps small-scale, this was not small-change philanthropy. It was a logical extension and practical application of the Crossleys' Victorian largesse in Halifax and a commentary on W.H. Lever's contemporary largesse at Port Sunlight and in Bolton.[39] It coloured Whitley's positioning as a back-bench MP, vocal on education and licensing, one of a type indeed, yet perhaps too easily typecast. In the words of his younger son, 'he had no use for collectivism, socialism, Marxism. They were not the answer.' His was a consultative creed: employers and employed, citizens all, linked (in his son's words) 'in a framework of regular systematic consultation, of shared ideas and feelings, which can gradually build up mutuality and trust'.[40]

With that we return to Whitley's industrial aspiration and to what most accented his outlook: the nature of his family's prosperity and the question of its conservation; his generation's class and education; and his Congregationalism.

Every town had its Whitleys, flourishing most representatively between the 1860s and the 1930s: an interconnection of attitudes in business, politics and religion, bound by family relationships, frequently as dynastic as those of any peerage or principality, and marking those who reacted against their formation as much as those who conformed to it. For at least four generations Whitley men and women married into local industry and commerce: cotton spinners, card makers, carpet manufacturers, wool staplers, wire manufacturers, all in Halifax but with waves of commercial relationship rippling strategically out – card makers in Huddersfield, cotton spinners and bleachers in Bolton, wool merchants in Leeds and wool manufacturers in Alloa. This was the capital that sustained their service on the Bench, in the Town Council, in the Chamber of Commerce, and in Parliament.

For Harry Whitley's generation there was another sort of capital, also cemented by relationship: education. Whitley was not himself a university man, although he had a London external degree – family circumstances dictated that he go straight from school into the works – but two of his brothers went to Trinity College, Cambridge, and his sons were at New College, Oxford; his Bolton bleacher brother-in-law was at Balliol.[41] There was a further dimension: he had a sister at Girton and nieces at Newnham and Somerville. These people took women's education seriously. For them, as for their brothers, there were the presumed benefits of the Victorian public school revolution. For his sister that meant North London Collegiate School; for her nieces it meant Abbey School, Reading, and Wycombe Abbey.[42] For him, his brothers, one of his sons, a brother-in-law, and two of his wife's closer Crossley cousins, it meant a school founded the year before the Whitley cotton-spinning enterprise: Clifton College.

Clifton was new, eligible, accessible by rail, and informed by the spirit which had transformed Rugby. It had grown with American rapidity. It was educationally promising, even up-to-the-mark. It was attractive to northern industrial parents. In Harry Whitley's time one sharply notable assistant master, who had arrived two-and-a-half years earlier, was from a very similar background in all respects: W.W. Asquith.[43] Such a school was attractive for another reason: its pupils were effortlessly assimilated into an enlarged establishment. Whitley benefited from two headmasters, each of whom he revered: John Percival and James Maurice Wilson. Each exemplified that establishment, Percival as Fellow of Queen's, Oxford, Assistant Master at Rugby, later as President of Trinity, Oxford, Head Master of Rugby, and Bishop of Hereford; Wilson as Assistant Master at Rugby, Fellow of St John's, Cambridge, later as Vicar of Rochdale, Archdeacon of Manchester and Canon of Worcester.[44] They were remarkable men, fine head masters, and distinctive Churchmen.

With this we turn to the third accent, the familial Congregationalism. Clifton had one particular attraction: 'no boy was to be compelled to attend services to which his parents conscientiously objected'.[45] It had a small Jews' House and its pioneer historian (who was a contemporary of Whitley's) recalled that 'there must have been many boys who were Nonconformists or of Nonconformist stock; but I can't remember that any of them ever made a difficulty about attending Chapel'.[46] As for that Chapel:

> we never heard the significance of the Altar emphasized. Our religion was not Sacramental. Our Clergymen-Masters were not High Churchmen; their sermons were not expositions of dogma, but guides to conduct. Nor had they any evangelical fervour . . . Some boys had an inner religious life, but none ever talked about religion. There was no Anglo-Catholic group . . . I remember one boy, who was a fervent Evangelical; but he did not try to proselytize at Clifton . . .[47]

That boy became a Presbyterian missionary in India. He was younger than Harry Whitley, than whom 'I think I have never seen a boy who looked more high-minded . . . and his nature did not belie his looks'.[48]

Whitley was the first of his particular family connection to go to Clifton. One can see its value as a preparation for responsible civic life and for parliamentary life too; its religion would stand a Speaker in good stead should he feel it his duty to worship each Sunday morning (mattins not eucharist) at St Margaret's, Westminster; but for a Congregationalist . . .?

Whitleys had been Congregationalists at least from the mid-eighteenth century, their baptisms recorded at Warley Independent Chapel from 1755, their burials from 1759.[49] Their church membership had spread with Halifax: Square, Park, Heath, Stannary, Sion, but chiefly Square (the Crossley cathedral) and Park (its architect virtually the Crossleys' house architect).[50] They were members, office-holders, deacons, trustees. They were pillars of Yorkshire Congregationalism. John Whitley (1827–1912), Harry's uncle who was like a father to him after his own father's death in 1889, was lay preacher, deacon at Square for 50 years, was Treasurer of the Yorkshire United Theological College in Bradford and district treasurer of the Yorkshire Congregational Union. In the last year of his life he contributed generously to the Union's scheme for Church Extension in the South Yorkshire Coal Fields, and his unmarried daughters continued to subscribe annually to the Union and regularly to its occasional appeals.[51] So did Alfred Whitley and his nephew Percival Whitley of Park Church. On 25 September 1913, Alfred opened South Elmsall, one of the new South Yorkshire Coalfield churches.[52] In 1920 he gave £500 to the Ministerial Stipends Fund and in Spring 1923 he addressed the Yorkshire Congregational Union's Assembly on 'Distress in Germany'. He was repaying his debt to the Elberfeld System:

> The middle-class population in Germany were starving for lack of food, lack of clothing, and lack of education. He begged his audience to forget the past and allow their broad public spirit to have play, and to take up and hand on the tradition of their fathers in their sympathy for those who suffered.[53]

This commitment was replicated by the families into whom the Whitleys married – Smiths and Fisher-Smiths, Thomsons and Whitley-Thomsons, Spicers, Waymans, Pells, Crooks, Bowmans. Not all were Congregationalists. The card-making Sykeses of Lindley, Huddersfield, were Wesleyans, the wool-making Rinders of Leeds were Free Methodists, and down the line the Forrester-Patons of Alloa were United Free Church of Scotland. The Congregationalism, however, was energetic, social gospel, YMCA, youth club and Rotarian in flavour. Its aesthetics were Ruskinian. It was generally undogmatic. It was mission-conscious (Alfred was a Yorkshire Director of the London Missionary Society and Treasurer of its Halifax Auxiliary)[54] but it was not entangled in overseas-missionary families and it was surprisingly free of ministers. The Whitley daughter who married a Congregational minister found that he turned into an Anglican parson, and the Whitley son who had Congregational ministry in mind (and, like Harold Wilson, was married in Mansfield College Chapel) became a Quaker and turned to school-mastering.[55] This Congregationalism was persuasively traditional. It was instinctive but not flabby. It was exemplified in Speaker Whitley.

His Speakership was a blessing for Cliftonians and Congregationalists alike. He became Clifton's President, his presidency sandwiched between those of Earl Haig and Lord Birdwood, Old Cliftonian Field-Marshals both.[56] He was on call to appear on Congregational platforms. He was not allowed to forget earlier Halifax days as a teacher in Park's Sunday School. He subscribed annually to the Yorkshire Congregational Union. He too contributed to its church extension work in the South Yorkshire coalfields and to its other special appeals, and with his fellow Free Church or Liberal MPs he figured at Yorkshire Congregational events. On 14 March 1913 the Halifax Congregational Association held its Annual Meeting in the Victoria Hall. The star attraction was C.S. Horne, MP for Ipswich and minister of Whitefields Tabernacle in London's Tottenham

Court Road. Horne's 'magnificent address' was 'a help and inspiration for a long while to come', but Whitley, as the senior Member for Halifax and Deputy Speaker too, was also on hand with 'an encouraging address on the work and its importance of the Individual Church Member'.[57] He was not at the Yorkshire Congregational Union's Assembly the following month, when James Parker addressed an afternoon conference on 'The Churches and Industrial Unrest' and an evening 'Demonstration on Public Questions' when Parker spoke on 'Labour and Religion', nor was he at the 1919 Assembly when Parker ('informative and arresting') again spoke on 'Causes of Industrial Unrest', and Norman Rae, MP for Shipley, spoke on 'Industrial Councils', but as the progenitor of such councils, Whitley was there in spirit.[58] He was there in person for other occasions. In September 1914 he and his fellow Park Church member (and family connection), Sir George Fisher-Smith, laid foundation stones for the new Highroad Well Congregational Church; just over two months earlier, Mrs Alfred Whitley had cut the first sod.[59] In May 1917 he was at Holywell Green's golden jubilee celebrations, unveiling a tablet commemorating its benefactors and builders, three brothers, James, Thomas and Samuel Shaw, who had been at Holywell Green what Whitleys had been at Park.[60] Thirteen years later his name dignified another Yorkshire celebration and building scheme. Silcoates, the school near Wakefield for sons of northern Congregational ministers, planned a new chapel and assembly hall. As part of its strategy it instituted the office of Vice-President, thirteen men and one woman of northern clout. Nathan and Alfred Whitley had been generous to the school in earlier years; Harry was one of the new Vice-Presidents.[61]

He was on call beyond Yorkshire. In May 1913 the national Congregational Union's Spring Assembly included a Thanksgiving Demonstration at the Royal Albert Hall to celebrate the completion of the Union's Central Fund for Ministerial Support. A choir of a thousand voices rendered Gounod, Mendelsohn (*Elijah*) and Handel's Hallelujah Chorus. Two Congregational commercial princes moved resolutions of gratitude; three pulpit princes, one of them C.S. Horne, delivered addresses, and a fourth led in prayer. The whole was chaired by Deputy Speaker Whitley:

> It was a magnificent and inspiring gathering . . . an occasion when probably those present realized more vividly than ever before the growth of the denominational spirit, the deepened consciousness of our oneness in faith and service in our beloved Congregational Church . . .[62]

Most of Whitley's Free Church occasions – the opening of Sunday School buildings for Hampstead Garden Suburb Free Church, or of an extension for a Congregationally originated girls' school in Bournemouth, or speaking at Islington's Claremont Central Mission, to give three examples – were less momentous but all testified to the claims of contemporary Nonconformity.[63] Here was a leading layman who could be carefully pigeon-holed by co-religionists and political opponents alike. To the latter he was bound to remain a mystery. The lengths to which he went to ensure that he should not be offered a peerage and his manifest ignorance of London society contrasted with his knowledge of parliamentary tradition and his concern for Parliament's fabric. As Speaker he worshipped at St Margaret's, Westminster, but he was at determined and successful odds with its rector, his chaplain, Canon Carnegie, over the adaptation of the Palace of Westminster's Crypt Chapel for parliamentary weddings and baptisms, free of the Prayer Book if so required.[64]

The secret lies in the accent of Whitley's Congregationalism. Independency can be awkward, obstinate, and fissiparous. Its twin, Congregationalism, can be collegial and constructive, Christian logic pointing to a third way. The outworking of Congregational polity, its disciplines of church meeting, deacons' meeting, teachers' meetings, countless committees in fact, when translated to town councils and works councils, can prove to be remarkably useful – and wholly unexpected by those who see themselves as habitually in command. Such qualities might make for a good Whip. It is not surprising that when the Chief Whip, Percy Illingworth, a Baptist, died early in 1915, the Prime Minister, Asquith (whose own background, it should again be recalled, was closer to theirs than might be thought), turned pressingly to Whitley.[65] Whitley, however, declined, indicating to Asquith that his health might not stand up to the pressures of the role involved. His Chairmanship of Ways and Means, his Deputy Speakership, was more useful and more rewarding. The chief product of those years lay in the Whitley Councils, more notable for their potential than their achievement, but what remains striking about those Councils – local, district, national – is their similarity to contemporary Congregational polity. That thread remained constant in Whitley's industrial and public life. Thus, when the distinctive contribution of the London Missionary Society to Christianity in India is recalled, and its role in influencing British Congregational attitudes to India is taken into account, Whitley's careful Chairmanship of the Royal Commission on Labour in India assumes fresh interest.[66] The same thread might be seen in his overlapping chairmanship, that of the Governors of the BBC. Harry Whitley represented a secularised Congregationalism and took some pleasure in setting it within a broad tradition.

An unlikely yet wholly characteristic incident provides a closing, perhaps clinching, illustration.

Whitley, it is generally agreed, was a good, or at least half-decent, Speaker. Some, finding understated strengths in what others felt to be weaknesses, have argued that he was a great Speaker. All, however, agree as to his diligence in upholding tradition. Sir Ralph Verney illuminated this in a reminiscent postscript.

Lt. Col. Verney was Speaker Whitley's secretary.[67] He expressed all that the establishment felt itself to be: Harrow and Christ Church, a fine military record with the Rifle Brigade, Aide-de-Camp or Secretary to the Governors of Queensland, New South Wales, and a Viceroy of India. His family shared

Buckinghamshire with the Rothschilds, his ancestor had been King Charles's standard bearer at Edge Hill. Needless to say, the establishment springs its surprises. The Verneys tended to be Liberals. Ralph Verney's father had been a Liberal MP; Florence Nightingale was his great-aunt. Let Oliver Whitley set more of the scene:

> When the Whitley family first met Colonel . . . Verney, we were all rather scared. He seemed, and indeed could have been, the ADC to end all ADCs; and we had never imagined father as a General or Governor-General or anyone who needed such a Secretary . . . Verney was every inch a military man. Guards officer moustache. Immaculately dressed, he wore a frock coat as if born in one. Slight patrician stoop. Voice to match.[68]

Verney and Whitley were the perfect team. Their mutual respect was unbroken. One of Whitley's more visible memorials lay in the large paintings which enmythed English parliamentary history in St Stephen's Hall. Opinions must differ as to their artistic merit but as a celebration of myth and as period pieces they remain beyond compare. Colonel Verney takes up the story:

> Their Majesties had expressed their willingness to see these pictures, and graciously accepted Whitley's request that they should honour him by coming to tea in the Speaker's House on a Sunday afternoon. After tea, Whitley took Their Majesties to St Stephen's Hall, where the team of artists, each in front of the picture he had painted, was assembled, who explained in turn the details and historical events depicted. When this was over, on the way back to the Speaker's House, Whitley arranged a very private visit by Their Majesties to the House of Commons' Chamber itself.
>
> H.M. King George fully appreciated the significance of this private visit and Whitley took not a little pleasure in reminding H.M. of the last occasion when a Reigning Monarch visited the House of Commons.[69]

Had the Civil War and its pre-history been laid to rest at last by the lineal descendants of King Charles, his standard bearer, and Speaker Lenthall, each one in his office and his person the guardian of a tradition? The painstaking nature of the scene will be clear to all – pictures meticulous in every detail save genius, artists explanatory to the last degree, Majesty determined to ask the right question. Yet perhaps the prime focus should be on that Sunday afternoon tea in the Speaker's House, en route to the Speaker's work-place. For the Speaker's sort afternoon tea was at the heart of friendly celebration. Harry Whitley's boys at Filey, or their gym classes at the Albion Street British Schools, or in Park Church's Sunday School, and his fellow Free Church people at chapel stone-layings and jubilees, would have been in their element. Here, with such diplomatic choreography, was the ultimate outworking of the Congregational mindset and perhaps a demonstration that family characteristics do not just happen.

Notes

1. I am particularly indebted to John P. Whitley for his encouragement. He was indefatigable in furnishing family lore and in alerting me to likely sources. Material in his possession is hereafter JWC (John Whitley Collection). I must also express my debt to Robin Morley-Fletcher, genealogist without equal, for material, meticulously gleaned, provided many years ago.
2. O. Whitley. 'Percival Whitley and his Forbears: and their Concern for Education', typescript, 1988, pp. 1–2, (JWC).
3. Ibid., p. 13.
4. For Oliver John Whitley (1912–2005) see *Who's Who 2003*, London, A & C Black, 2003, p. 2315.
5. *The Times*, 24 March 2005.
6. The Church of the Peace of God, Oxted. See also J. Whitley, 'A Family of Brantwoods', typescript, c. 2015, pp. 8–11 (JWC); R. Bretton, 'The Whitleys of Halifax', *Halifax Antiquarian Society*, April 1963, 70–1.
7. Park Congregational Church, Halifax. For Percival Nathan Whitley (1893–1957) see Whitley, 'Percival Whitley'; Whitley, 'Brantwoods', pp. 5–6; Bretton, 'The Whitleys', 68–70. For John Percival (1834–1918) see *Oxford Dictionary of National Biography* (hereafter *ODNB*), Oxford, Oxford University Press, 2004–17.
8. M. Snape (ed.), *The Back Parts of War: The YMCA Memoirs and Letters of Barclay Baron, 1915 to 1919*, Woodbridge, The Boydell Press, Church of England Record Society, 16, 2009, p. 109.
9. 'Mr. Whitley's War Service. / Rev. J.F. Shepherd's Personal Experience', *Halifax Courier and Guardian*, undated cutting (JWC). For James Francis Shepherd (1871–1963), minister at Park Congregational Church 1919–24, see *Congregational Year Book* [hereafter *CYB*], 1964–65, 448; *Yorkshire Congregational Year Book* [hereafter *YCYB*], 1934, 11–13.
10. For John Henry Whitley (1866–1925) see *ODNB*.
11. For Edward Algernon Fitzroy (1869–1943) see *ODNB*.
12. For James William Lowther (1855–1949) see *ODNB*.
13. For an encapsulation of the office see JAC, HB, 'Speaker', in J. Cannon (ed.), *The Oxford Companion to British History*, Oxford, Oxford University Press, 1997, pp. 881–2.
14. Lord Hemingford, *Back Bencher and Chairman*, London, John Murray, 1946, pp. 25–9.
15. This was Lord Hemingford (Dennis Henry Herbert, 1869–1947, MP Watford 1918–43), for whom see *Who's Who 1948*, London, A & C Black, pp. 1263–4.
16. Bretton, 'The Whitleys', 54–9, 62–3.
17. Whitley, 'Percival Whitley', p. 8; the houses are fully described in Whitley, 'Brantwoods'.
18. John Crossley (1812–79) was MP Halifax 1874–77; Sir Francis Crossley Bt (1817–72) was MP Halifax 1852–59, West Riding 1859–72.
19. Joseph Crook (1809–84) was MP Bolton 1852–61; William Rawson Shaw (1860–1932) was MP Halifax 1893–97; Thomas Shaw (1823–93) was MP Halifax 1882–93.
20. Thomas Wayman (1832–1901) was MP Elland 1885–99; Sir Albert Spicer Bt (1847–1934) was MP Monmouth 1892–1900, Central Hackney 1906–18.
21. Sir Frederick Whitley (1851–1925; Whitley-Thomson from 1914) was MP Skipton 1900–06; Joseph Montague Kenworthy (1886–1953; 10th Baron Strabolgi, 1934) was MP Central Hull 1919–31.
22. Sir Savile Crossley Bt (1857–1935; 1st Baron Somerleyton 1916) was MP Lowestoft 1885–92, Halifax 1900–06. For the Crossleys, Congregationalism, and Halifax, see C. Binfield, 'Industry, Philanthropy and Christian Citizenship: the Great Paternalists', *Journal of the United Reformed Church History Society* [hereafter *JURCHS*], 9/5 (October 2014), 282–96.
23. The election is described in W.A. Davies, 'The Rt. Hon. J.H. Whitley', typescript, 1953, pp. 11–12 (JWC). Alfred Billson (1839–1907) was MP Barnstaple 1892–95, Halifax 1897–1900, N.W. Staffordshire 1906–07.

24 James Parker (1863–1948) was MP Halifax 1906–18, Cannock 1918–22; he was appointed Companion of Honour in 1918.
25 John Crossley was Mayor of Halifax 1851–52, 1862–63; Sir Francis Crossley was Mayor 1849–50; their nephew, Edward Crossley (1841–1905; MP Sowerby 1885–92) was Mayor 1883–85. For Nathan Whitley (1830–89) see Bretton, 'The Whitleys', 63–4; Davies, 'J.H. Whitley', pp. 2–3.
26 Davies, 'J.H. Whitley', p. 9.
27 Bretton, 'The Whitleys', 63–4; Davies, 'J.H. Whitley', pp. 2–3.
28 For John Whitley (1827–1912) see Bretton, 'The Whitleys', 61–2.
29 For Alfred William Whitley (1868–1945) see Bretton, 'The Whitleys', 71–2.
30 *Halifax Evening Courier*, 25 March 1905, quoted in D. Pye, 'The Guild of Help Movement 1904–1914', University of Huddersfield MA Thesis, 1993, p. 16.
31 For Samuel Rinder Whitley (1869–1933) see Bretton, 'The Whitleys', 74–5; the Lingfield Colony was founded by a Congregational minister, John Brown Paton (1830–1911), in 1895.
32 KCB – Knight of the Bath; CMG – Companion of the Order of St. Michael and St. George; DSO – Distinguished Service Order; DL – Deputy Lieutenant (this is a Crown Appointment to a county); JP – Justice of the Peace.
33 For Sir Edward Nathan Whitley (1873–1966) see Bretton, 'The Whitleys', 75–6.
34 Lucy Delf (1827–1917) came from a Norfolk Dissenting family; her school at Buckhurst Hill, Essex, attracted girls from similar families.
35 Bretton, 'The Whitleys', 64–5.
36 Elizabeth Lucas Sutcliffe (1888–1962); see Bretton, 'The Whitleys', 73–4.
37 This section is drawn chiefly from Davies, 'J.H. Whitley'.
38 For Stanley Davenport Adshead (1868–1946), Professor of Civic Design at the University of Liverpool from 1912, and a pioneer in the field, see *ODNB*.
39 Adshead's chair was founded by Lever; for Lever (1851–1925) see Binfield, 'Industry, Philanthropy and Christian Citizenship', 296–325.
40 O. Whitley, 'Percival Whitley', p. 9.
41 Alfred and Edward were at Trinity; Thomas Ashley Crook (b. 1862) was at Balliol.
42 Harry's elder sister, Ada Rinder Whitley (1865–1902), was at North London Collegiate followed by Girton (1883–86); Alfred's daughter Helen was at Newnham (1938–40), as was Samuel's daughter Ada Joan (1925–28); her younger sister, Margaret, was at Somerville (1926–29). Ada Joan was at Abbey School and Margaret was at Abbey School (1913–20) and Wycombe Abbey (1920–26).
43 William Willans Asquith (1851–1918) was the elder brother of H.H. Asquith. For their background see C. Binfield, 'Asquith: the Formation of a Prime Minister', *JURCHS*, 2/7 (April 1981), pp. 204–42.
44 For Percival see *ODNB*; J. Potter, *Headmaster. The Life of John Percival, Radical Autocrat*, London, Constable, 1998. For James Maurice Wilson (1836–1931) see *ODNB*; [A.T. Wilson and J.S. Wilson (eds)], *James M. Wilson: an Autobiography 1836–1931*, London, Sidgwick & Jackson, 1932.
45 O.F. Christie, *Clifton School Days (1879–1885)*, London, Shaylor, 1930, p. 66.
46 Christie, *Clifton*, p. 66.
47 Christie, *Clifton*, p. 93.
48 Christie, *Clifton*, pp. 48–9; the future Presbyterian missionary was John Sinclair Stevenson (d. 1930), at Clifton 1882–86.
49 Bretton, 'The Whitleys', 52–3.
50 Congregationalism in Halifax and Warley is outlined in J.G. Miall, *Congregationalism in Yorkshire*, London, John Snow and Co., 1868, pp. 267–9, 377–8.
51 John Whitley's contribution can be assessed in *YCYB*, 1913, 39, 43, 100–1, 109, 154; 1914, 140. The Misses Whitleys' subscriptions are listed in successive *YCYBs* to 1939.
52 *YCYB*, 1919, 35.
53 *YCYB*, 1923, 34.

54 *YCYB*, 1913, 9. Alfred Whitley's close involvement in Germany is referred to in the Emily Hobhouse papers being worked on by Rebecca Gill, http://emilyhobhouselettersprject.wordprecess.com. He was also co-leader of the 1906 LMS Delegation to India.
55 Lilian Mary Whitley (1861–1941), daughter of John Whitley (1827–1912), married Ernest William Place (1862–1933), minister at The Quinta, Oswestry, 1887–89, an Anglican from 1891; John P. Whitley, son of Oliver Whitley, became a Quaker.
56 He was President 1928–35; for Douglas, 1st Earl Haig (1861–1928, Clifton 1877–79) and William, 1st Baron Birdwood (1865–1951, Clifton 1877–82) see *ODNB*.
57 *YCYB*, 1914, 63; for Charles Silvester Horne (1865–1914) see below.
58 *YCYB*, 1913, 50–1, 58–9; *YCYB*, 1919, p. 23; Sir H. Norman Rae (1860–1928), MP Shipley 1918–23, was a wool merchant.
59 *YCYB*, 1915, 72; for Sir George Henry Fisher-Smith (1846–1931) see *Who Was Who 1929–1940*, London, Bloomsbury, 2014, p. 451; his sister Bertha (1861–1943) married Sir Frederick Whitley-Thomson (1851–1925).
60 *YCYB*, 1917, 63. The Shaws, too, were family connections, and at that time Edward N. Whitley lived at Holywell Hall.
61 *YCYB*, 1930, 32.
62 *CYB*, 1914, 6–7; *CYB*, 1915, 8.
63 *CYB*, 1926, p. 151; J.D. Jones, *Three Score Years and Ten*, London, Hodder and Stoughton, 1940, p. 270; F.W. Newland, *Newland of Claremont and Canning Town*, London, Epworth Press, 1932, pp. 64, 158.
64 Hemingford, *Back Bencher*, pp. 32–3; Sir John Verney Bt to Oliver Whitley, 9 January 1981 (JWC); for William Hartley Carnegie (1860–1936), Speaker's Chaplain 1916–36, see *Who Was Who 1929–1940*, pp. 222–3.
65 Asquith touched on this in his letters to Venetia Stanley; see M. and E. Brock (eds), *H.H. Asquith. Letters to Venetia Stanley*, Oxford, Oxford University Press, 1982, pp. 366, 368, 378. Percy Illingworth (1869–1915), whose family were Bradford industrialists, was MP Shipley 1906–15, Chief Whip 1912–15. Also look at Chapter 8 of this volume by Graham E. Seel.
66 Alfred Whitley went as part of a London Missionary Society deputation to India, September 1906 to January 1907: J. Sibree (ed.), *London Missionary Society. A Register of Missionaries, Deputations, etc. from 1796 to 1923*, 4th ed., London, London Missionary Society, 1923, p. 211.
67 For Sir Ralph Verney Bt (1879–1959), Speaker's Secretary 1921–55, see *Who's Who 1948*, p. 2840.
68 Oliver noted, in parenthesis: 'Father's Secretary as Liberal Member for Halifax was a cross between Eddie Waring and Michael Parkinson [two popular BBC commentators], so the contrast was breathtaking'. O. Whitley, ms note, 13 January 1981 (JWC).
69 Sir Ralph Verney Bt to Lord Hemingford, 5 January 1945 (JWC). Also see Chapter 8 of this volume by Graham E. Seel.

5 J.H. Whitley and Halifax politics between 1890 and 1906

The politics of social reform

Keith Laybourn

John Henry Whitley, famously a Speaker of the House of Commons in the 1920s, was a politician deeply influenced by his Halifax roots. Better known as Harry in his early years in Halifax, he was one of those political figures who transcended the usual characteristics of Old and New Liberalism, terms so readily used by modern historians researching Liberal politicians of the pre-First World War era.[1] Indeed, he was more than just a local businessman, amateur politician or party hack, who emerged to represent his constituency in the style of an Old Liberalism, and yet he was clearly not the locally unconnected professional politician imposed upon a community, so often associated with the New Liberalism. He was, instead, a mill owner, from Halifax family business partnerships of cotton spinners, and a Nonconformist, who considered himself to be a radical reformer, advanced and progressive in his views on issues of social reform for the betterment of his fellow citizens, and thus a promoter of social harmony and citizenship. Thereby he might be considered something of a hybrid of Old Liberalism and New Liberalism, which possibly accounts for his political success in Halifax. He was certainly influenced in his social reformism by his commitment to Congregationalism, which helped to take him beyond a mere concern about drink as a cause of poverty to tackling the wider problems of poverty, challenging privilege, demanding the reform, indeed removal, of the House of Lords, and fostering a commitment to both full male and female suffrage. Convinced of the need for charitable involvement as a sign of good citizenship, a view which was projected forward by Clem Attlee the later Labour Prime Minister, Harry Whitley was driven by a belief in the need for citizen service to the community. In the final analysis he was truly an 'advanced', community-based, rather than individual, Liberal with local roots, who hesitantly, indeed reluctantly by his own admission, assumed a role in national politics. Yet what is even more significant is that he achieved his political success in Halifax, a community which, related to its size, was one of the most powerful centres for the growth of embryonic socialism in Britain between 1891 and 1914. Harry Whitley never managed to establish a truly close relationship with the Halifax Independent Labour Party (ILP) or Labour Party, except for a brief honeymoon period of the local political pact between 1903 and 1906. Neither was he able to establish a close relationship with its local figureheads, which included the local landowner John Lister of Shibden Hall, Edward Marsden, Arthur Taylor and James Parker, though he willingly shared one of the two Halifax parliamentary seats alongside James Parker in 1906, and for some years afterwards until Halifax became a single-seat constituency in 1918. Nevertheless, his background and advanced views allowed his political career to prosper in Halifax, and indeed flourish in parliamentary politics.

In many senses, therefore, Harry Whitley is a fascinating transitional political figure in turn of the century British history, a period of fundamental change in British politics, who gained local respect for his policies and ideas raising themes of citizenship in a community which was moving significantly to the left of the normal Liberal politics of the day. His career, in such circumstances, rather endorses the view that the reputation of respected individual politicians can often transcend mere party politics. Yet precisely how did he gain and maintain such local respect in a growing heartland for Labour in the years before the First World War, and more particularly in the 'socialist decade' of the 1890s? Certainly his concern to alleviate poverty and to extend the franchise endeared him to the working classes of Halifax and this probably captured him support in the unusual situation of two-seat constituency politics, although these concerns fell far short of the socialist and labour demands for a fundamental change in how society was organised. He was also seen as a politician capable of bringing about 'fusion', with the rare ability and credentials to unite Old Liberalism and the New Liberalism in a time of political turmoil and disunity.

Early life and Harry's social and political activism

John Henry Whitley was born in Halifax, the son of Nathan Whitley (1830–92) from Huddersfield, a Congregationalist who was a director and later the Senior Director of Samuel Whitley & Son, cotton spinners of Hanson-lane mills, Halifax. After being educated at Clifton College, Bristol, he immediately entered work at the family business to assist his father, following the death of his uncle Samuel. (It was during this period that he completed his external degree London University degree in his spare time.) The firm was considered to be generous to its employees, distributing the profits to its workforce from time to time.[2] With strong Halifax credentials Whitley built himself a reputation for social, educational, charitable and municipal work in Halifax. Indeed, in 1900 Whitley was a reluctant and late convert to parliamentary politics and even then much preferred to be involved in local charitable work and municipal politics. He was reported as stating in November 1901, a year after his return as MP for Halifax:

> To go to London and spend more than half a year there, to give up work in which he had become very much attached – municipal and education work – was for him rather a big wrench. He had so rooted into the local life of Halifax that for his part he had no desire to exchange that for any other sphere.[3]

This statement almost defines the man who remained a Halifax councillor until 1902, two years after having secured his seat in the House of Commons, and who, in the 1920s, was to reject the offer of a peerage, the usual reward for being a Speaker of the House of Commons.

Influenced by his religious upbringing as a Congregationalist, of which John Hargreaves and Clyde Binfield have written in Chapters 2 and 4 of this volume, Harry took an early interest in social reform and charitable work. He was particularly concerned with the problem of the high levels of poverty in Halifax, and other industrial towns, which social surveys by Seebohm Rowntree, and Charles Booth were suggesting was probably in the region of about 30 per cent of the urban working-class population at any one time in the 1880s and 1890s and something which most working-class families were subject to in their lifetime.[4] He was not moved to demand a change in the economic system, as socialists wished, but felt that something could be done to alleviate the problems of the poor. And so in 1889 he helped set up the Boys Camp, sometimes referred to as the Poor Boys Camp, at Filey where for many years two groups of about 100 or 110 boys, one for each of consecutive weeks, camped at Long Whinn Farm to enjoy outdoor life by the sea and away from their urban poverty in Halifax.[5] He also campaigned to improve the educational standards of children who worked half-time in both in the schools and the mills, there being several thousand such children in Halifax.[6] He was also involved in developing a gymnasium for working-class boys in Halifax and in offering evening education classes for them as well. This interest in social and educational activities continued throughout his life and, even as an MP, he became a strong supporter of the Halifax Citizens' Guild of Help. The Guild was formed in Halifax in 1905 as part of a wider national philanthropic movement which had begun in Bradford in 1904, with the purpose of undertaking social casework amongst the poor and providing them with health provision and opportunities to raise them out of poverty and avoid them falling into destitution and ending dependent on the poor law.[7] Inevitably, as an MP and embroiled in national politics, he could only play a supportive role to his brother Alfred Whitley, who became the leading local figure and one of the leading national figures in the National Association of the Guild of Help.[8] Nonetheless, it was Harry who presided over a private meeting on 4 January 1905, held at his residence of Brantwood, to consider how to deal with poverty in Halifax and out of which the Halifax Citizens' Guild emerged.[9]

As a young but prominent member of the Halifax millocracy and showing concern about social distress in the community, Harry quickly assumed community and civic duties. He was raised to the magisterial bench in the early 1890s. Then, inspired by his father Nathan Whitley (1830–99), who was Mayor of Halifax on three occasions in the 1870s and 1880s, Harry became a Liberal councillor for West Ward in Halifax in November 1893 – though four times previously he had been 'asked to give his service by different committees',[10] but stressed that he would make his own judgement on matters that came before the Council.[11] Though he often expressed his doubts about his abilities he stated that he 'now owed it to the town in which he was born and brought up that he should not shirk the share of responsibility that came to him'.[12] Significantly, he won his seat by 991 votes to 279, trouncing Henry Backhouse of the fledgling Labour Party (Labour Union soon to be ILP), which had expected defeat but not a rout. This suggests that Harry was already appealing strongly to the working-class municipal voter who might have otherwise been tempted to vote Labour.

From that moment onwards he made clear his laudable, if impossible, lifetime political ideal of raising himself above party politics to fulfil his duties, stating that:

> above all things party shall not be brought into municipal affairs. It would be one of his aims, in which he trusted he would never allow himself to falter, to try not to divide men into parties, but to try to unite them to promote the best interests of the commonweal (applause) . . . He would take no notice whether the proposal was brought forward by the Liberal, Tory or Labour parties, but simply and solely whether they would be for the interest of the town.[13]

This claim defined Harry's community-bound focus as someone essentially focused upon the needs of the community.[14] However, he was just as much a political figure as any socialist demanding the reorganisation of society and control of the means of production in order to tackle poverty, for he selected from a restricted and confined canon of Liberal and progressive ideas designed to alleviate, or patch up, rather than solve, the social consequences of capitalism.

Indeed, in many respects Harry was a deeply traditional Liberal entrenched in the beliefs about the impoverishing results of drink and that the problems of urban society could be solved by land taxation. He was strongly supportive of attempts to control the liquor trade, although he was not a teetotaller, stating that 'Some years ago my doctor advised me to take a beer to dinner, and I have never regretted following his advice.'[15] Nevertheless, he often cited drink as the greatest evil to be tackled,[16] and he was happy to support temperance and took pride in the fact that the average expenditure on beer was 3d (1.2p) in the Halifax Liberal clubs as compared with 7.5d (3p) in Leeds and 5d in the Heavy Woollen District.[17]

The overcrowding of towns was to him the second great evil and again he drew from the canon of traditional Liberal policies. Like many traditional Liberals he felt that overcrowding was caused by the rising cost of land in the centres of cities and that the 'taxation of land values was the cure'.[18] Indeed, following a conference on land taxation in Bradford in 1899, Harry suggested that land values had increased by £2,500 million in the nineteenth century and emphasised that 'Wealth comes from brain and labour – and should not come from land.'[19] In 1902 he attended a meeting at the Hotel Metropole in Leeds where he moved a resolution in favour of municipal authorities levying a tax on land, suggesting that it should be levied at a rate of 3 or 4 per cent on annual values.[20]

Digging deeper into Gladstonian Liberal values, Harry was also wedded to Home Rule for Ireland, that other defining issue for Liberalism at this time (referred too also in Chapter 12 of this volume), for 'He was a Home Ruler – Empire depends upon it'[21] and it was said by Mr. T. Flanagan, of the United Irish League Halifax Branch, that 93 per cent of the Nationalist electors had voted for Mr. Billson and Mr. Whitley in the 1900 General Election.[22] However, Home Rule was rather a given for him than something advocated on the occasion of every political meeting.

Whilst entrenched in the above Old Liberal values, Harry was very much aware of the differences between Old Liberalism and the new forms of Liberalism, some of which he espoused.[23] P.F. Clarke has argued that Edwardian Liberalism in Lancashire was not merely surviving on the strength of local Nonconformity and a free-trade tradition but was rapidly extending its support, especially in the Edwardian age, from community to class politics. He maintains that this growth of class politics was of benefit to the Liberal Party since its organisation became increasingly national in focus, with career politicians replacing local Liberal 'big-wigs' and Liberal intellectuals encouraging Lloyd George, and others, to introduce a synthesis of Liberal and Socialist policies which would attract working-class support. This 'New' Liberalism, a reforming ideology which placed its emphasis upon state intervention extending, in a positive way, liberty by equalising opportunities, replaced the 'Old' Liberalism with its emphasis upon removing the impediments to individual freedom.[24]

There have been serious challenges to this notion, but Martin Pugh has argued that Yorkshire presents a mixed picture of 'New' Liberals being returned with 'Old' Liberal support, the main reason being that 'there was less sense of change than in Lancashire because there was less need for change'.[25] In Halifax, however, there was much need for change but little evidence of it within the majority of the Liberal Party. Harry Whitley, imbued with a Radical and progressive approach to politics, emphatically community based but aware of the problem posed by class politics at the national level, was ideally suited to arrest the growth of the ILP/Labour Party. Sensitive to the needs of the community and the demands of the working classes, he was, for the Halifax Liberal Party, the right man at the right time.

The 'New' Liberalism was much to do with establishing social harmony in British society and was to be associated with David Lloyd George's attempt to provide social insurance, pensions and to reduce the powers of the House of Lords in favour of the national community and greater democratic rights. Within this framework of social harmony, however, Harry saw trade unionism as just as irrelevant to free trade and *laissez faire* as many other Liberal millowners would have felt, since they did not feel that their actions could permanently force up wages against the market, but he was determined that the economic benefits of production should be more equitably divided and that conflict could be avoided, in the manner that the Whitley Councils, named after Whitley, sought to do in the First World War.

Harry Whitley agreed with many of these progressive policies of New Liberalism and tried to apply their principles to the local community, fully aware of the national perspective New Liberalism entailed. At the local level, Harry felt that the community and democracy were more important than the rights of a privileged, often landed, few. By 1895 he was declaring his support for the 'Registration of every man on the [municipal] register . . . and he hoped every woman as well.'[26] He wished to attack privilege *per se*, and particularly the House of Lords, the bastion of landed privilege, which he felt should be relieved 'of their duties altogether'.[27] He went further at about the time of the General Election of 1895 when he felt the need for a clean sweep of the House of Lords: 'Let them come down from their gilded chamber and meet them like men on the floor of the House of Commons.'[28] On another occasion, in speaking to the Elland Liberal Association, he was even more direct on the House of Lords: 'For his part he could see no satisfactory solution to the difficulty except by removing the institution altogether.'[29] These were, indeed, progressive ideas.

Some of Harry's ideas were clearly undeveloped, indeed almost automatic Liberal policies, but there is no denying the advanced nature of some of them. His commitment to the municipality and local political democracy defined him, for he frequently stated his support for the extension of the role of municipal politics and felt that 'We ought to have men at the head of our local affairs with the courage and fight to take in hand large schemes for municipal progress, as well as legislative ability to carry them out.'[30] Indeed, he felt of Halifax that it had an 'abundance of honest, honourable, well employed citizens; who wanted to tackle the serious problem of poverty and unemployment'.[31] Yet Harry Whitley was wise enough to realise that municipal resources could not tackle these problems alone and that there needed to be a change in the national policies of Britain to remove, for instance, the enormous problem of unemployment. This may be why he eventually stood for Parliament in 1900, in a period of significant political change in Halifax.

The Labour challenge at the municipal and parliamentary level

In the 1890s, at the time of Harry's rise in Halifax local politics, there were two main challenges to the Liberal Party in Halifax. One was a Conservative Party galvanised by Liberal Unionists who had split from the Liberal Party over Home Rule for Ireland in 1886. The development of this party is partly discussed in an essay by Pat Dawson and involves the move of the Crossleys, the Halifax carpet manufactures, to Unionism in 1886, and the formation of up to eight Conservative clubs by 1903.[32] The result was that Alfred Arnold, a wire manufacturer, won one of the Halifax seats for the Conservative and Unionists in the 1895 General Election and that Sir Savile Brinton Crossley won one of the two parliamentary seats in the 1900 General Election, following the formation of the Central Association of the Conservative and Unionist Party in 1899. However, much of this Conservative success was placed, probably correctly, at the door of the ILP, which was seen as dividing the progressive vote in Halifax and allowing in the Conservative and Unionists parliamentary success, even though they remained only a significant minority in municipal politics up to the First World War.

The second challenge was that from the Labour movement. In the late 1880s and early 1890s the working classes of Halifax developed two organisations to represent their interests. These were the Halifax Trades and Labour Council, formed in 1889, and the Halifax Labour Union, formed out of it in August 1892 to separate its economic and political actions. The two organisations formally re-established their connection in September 1894[33] and formed the Municipal Election Committee in 1900 which, with Halifax Trades and Labour Council, became the Workers' Election Committee in 1900.[34] There was clearly a closeness between trade union and political action for the trade unions had first looked towards the Liberal Party for political representation only to be rebuffed in the early 1890s and to have some of its leading political figures, such as James Beever, one-time Secretary of the Boothtown Liberal Club, and James Tattersall, victimised and dismissed by the Clayton, Murgatroyd Silk Spinners in April and July 1892.[35]

There was significant industrial and strike action in Halifax in the 1890s. There was a wiredrawers strike in 1889, gas strikes and, most important of all, a national engineering strike called by the Amalgamated Society of Engineers in 1897. The details of these strikes, which certainly called into question the attitude of the Liberal Party in Halifax to industrial disputes are partly dealt with in the essay by Pat Dawson. However, the important point here is that Whitley was concerned to avoid industrial conflict by improving workers' conditions and rights or by seeking to settle conflict. In 1893 and 1894 Whitley pressed Halifax Council to continue to engage only those firms who paid 'fair contracts' – trade union wage rates. He was later to claim credit for improving the conditions of work and indeed wages amongst the gas workers working for Halifax Council, although this was disputed by some who felt that that course had been established before he joined the Gas Committee.[36] He was also involved in Council attempts to resolve the engineering strike in the Halifax region in 1897.

The political expansion of Labour, the Halifax Labour Union/ILP, had emerged out of a mixture of socialist agitation, religious concern and trade union frustration in the early 1890s. In 1891 John Lister, of Shibden Hall, had read Karl Marx's *Das Kapital* and with others attended a lecture on 29 May 1892 given by W.S. De Mattos, a Fabian lecturer, and immediately formed a Fabian branch with the Reverend Bryan Dale, a Congregational Minister and sometime chair of the annual Congregational Union, as its President.[37] Just after this the Halifax Trades and Labour Council resolved 'to form a "Labour Union" on democratic lines to take the political part of the Trades & Labour Council work, so as to allow the Council to devote its time to trade matters.'[38] The Halifax Trades Council and the local trade union movement raised money for Beaver and Tattersall to set up their own businesses but it was clear that there was much disquiet within the Halifax Trades Council from many Liberal members who were by no means fully committed to the new socialist groups that were emerging. As a result, in the first week of August 1892 a meeting was held at the Central Hall, Halifax, where it was resolved that a Labour Union would be formed distinct from the Halifax Trades Council. John Lister, landowner and socialist of Shibden Hall, Halifax, records that 'This resolution was proposed by J.H. Beever & seconded by myself & a Committee to draw up the Constitution was appointed.'[39] From these beginnings the Halifax Labour Union, which changed its name to the Halifax ILP after the formation of the National ILP at Bradford in January 1893, emerged quickly. It had eight clubs with 500 fee-paying members by the end of 1893, 600 members in 1894 and 591 members in 1899.[40] It had its own paper, *The Record*, there was a Labour Church movement, socialist Sunday schools, and Montague Blatchford, the brother of Robert Blatchford of *The Clarion*, organised the Clarion movement in Halifax with its bands, glee clubs and fellowship societies.[41] As an organisation, the ILP won seats on Halifax Council and the Halifax School Board – though the number of municipal seats was never large – there being three successes each in 1892 and 1893, one in 1894, one each in 1897 and 1898, and two each in 1899 and 1900.[42] With the comings and goings of ILP councillors, and aldermen, this meant that Labour had no councillors in 1896, one in 1898 and two in both 1899 and 1900, before gradually increasing in the early twentieth century before the First World War.

The parliamentary situation was more promising. John Lister was selected as the ILP candidate for both the January 1893 by-election and the 1895 General Election in Halifax. In 1893, when the ILP was at the height of its powers and voters had only one vote, since only one of the two Halifax seats were up for election, Lister received 3,028 votes, 23.4 per cent of the votes. In 1895, when each voter had two votes or could plump for one candidate (using one vote but not the other), Lister received 3,818 votes, 20.3 per cent of those caste, having 1,751 Plumpers, sharing 1,351 votes with Arnold, the Conservative candidate who was returned, and sharing 638 votes with Shaw (returned as a Liberal) and 98 with Booth (Liberal). The intriguing situation here is that the ILP vote had increased since 1893 and that almost twice as many Conservative voters as compared to Liberal voters were using their second vote for the ILP candidate. This was almost certainly a tactical ploy by both Conservative and Labour voters but it worried the Liberal Party, who feared that a joint Labour and Conservative squeeze could help undermine its political hold on Halifax – a concern amplified by the fact that the Liberals had lost one of their two seats to the Conservatives in 1895. This was the first time since the reform of the parliamentary system in 1832 that Halifax had not been represented by two Liberal MPs and was clearly a shock to Halifax Liberalism. The ILP further developed and built up alliances with the Halifax Workers' Election Committee, which it helped to form in 1900, had 22 trade unions and the ILP affiliated to it, representing between 4,000 and 5,000 workers in 1905, and was becoming a major force in Halifax parliamentary politics.

Halifax Liberalism was now faced with a serious parliamentary challenge to keep the progressive vote, though this was a two-way relationship. However, Harry's local reputation as a progressive Liberal rose to such an extent that Edward Marsden, a leading figures in the ILP, clearly felt that he could approach him during the 1895 General Election with the hope that he would endorse John Lister. However, Harry was a firm believer that the cause of Liberalism would serve the people of Halifax better, explaining his position in a letter to Marsden.

> Private Letter from Brantwood 10 July 1895
> Dear Sir,
> I have spent a night in anxious consideration of the present political situation in Halifax, and I have come to the conclusion that I cannot give my support to Mr. Lister. My reasons are mainly these: (1) the best information I can get does not confirm your view that to support Lister is the only chance of keeping Arnold [the Conservative candidate] out, or even the best chance (2) I feel bound to look at the matter from a national, rather than from a local and personal point of view & much as I deplore the backwardness of some Liberalism in Halifax, I still look to the Liberal party nationally as the most hopeful instrument of progress in our times at any rate. I believe I have the same earnestness for social reform & financial reform which I gladly recognise in you but I think that I can do more practical good for the objects I have at heart by remaining a Radical outpost than by joining in the 'wrecking' policy which I am sorry to see the leaders of the ILP have avowed.
> You are, of course, at liberty to show this to Mr. Lister who I am sure will credit me with doing right 'according to my lights' though he may think me mistaken.[43]

Harry, however, had competing matters to consider at this time. In the early months of 1895 Sir James Stansfeld, who had held one of the two Halifax seats for the Liberals since 1859, indicated his intention to retire at the end of the current Parliament and before the forthcoming 1895 General Election. As a result, Harry had been approached by the Liberal Four Hundred, which was the organising and representative body for the Liberal clubs in Halifax, to allow his name to be put forward for the nomination as Stansfeld's successor. A deputation was immediately sent to 'Mr. Henry Whitley, JP of Brantwood, cotton spinner' to 'see if he would put his name forward before the General Committee' for it was felt that he 'would be a strong candidate for uniting the various sections of the party'.[44] The ILP's emergence was something that worried Stansfeld, who lamented that there are 'sections within parties/party for special object. One of them is the Independent Labour Party, the danger of the independence of which the Liberal Party the right hon. Gentlemen [Whitley being referred to in an honourable, not parliamentary, term since he was not even an MP] has the political sagacity for fusion, although at the present it is a cloud no bigger than a man's hand.'[45] Stansfeld saw Whitley as a prudent, shrewd and wise successor with the right progressive credentials.

The local Liberal press, the *Halifax Courier*, felt certain that Harry Whitley would take up the task of reuniting the Liberals and confidently predicted that

'Upon Mr. Harry Whitley will probably devolve the Herculean task of reuniting the divergent views represented by the different sections of the party in Halifax.'[46] Yet, in April 1895, after deep consideration he rejected the invite, writing:

> My dear Mitchell
>
> I have given careful consideration to the request so pressingly urged by yourself and other members of the deputation appointed by the Social Selection Committee of the Liberal Four Hundred, and regret to say that I am not able to change the opinions which I have expressed to you.
>
> My position in business is one which makes it impossible for me to accede to your request and many family personal reasons confirm me in this decision.
>
> It has been difficult to say 'No' to an invitation so unanimously given, but in a step of such importance I feel that I must not override my own judgment.
>
> I need hardly say that this testimony of the confidence of my fellow Liberals has touched me very deeply; please assure them of my gratitude and of my earnest hope that they may find another (perhaps of more mature age and experience) to carry their cause to victory.[47]

Nevertheless, Whitley remained active as a local councillor over the subsequent seven years and began to develop his views on the vital issues of British politics and remained active in local politics and in national and parliamentary debates.

Clearly 'advanced' and 'radical' in his views, Whitley began to develop his ideas with increasing confidence. Speaking to the Elland Liberal Association in 1895, on 'The Problem of the Future',[48] his dominant theme was his established commitment to the extension of democracy to all and the removal of privilege, and the removal of the House of Lords. To achieve wider representation he added that 'It seemed to him that payment of members was an absolute necessity in order that people might have a free choice of representatives.' Such a commitment to democracy and the removal of privilege implies substantial social reform. Of his Liberal Party he reflected that 'They wanted every citizen to have an equal opportunity in life, and they looked for the time when ability, character and not wealth, should entitle men to the leading of others . . . (hear, hear).' However, he rejected Joseph Chamberlain's plans for old age pensions, fearing that they would favour only those in a good position rather than the poor, although he became more positive about pensions as time went on. He also wished to control the drink question, and overwhelmingly favoured social betterment.

In mid and late 1890s Halifax, the ILP and the Liberal Radicalism, represented by Whitley, were not far apart, although there were many Liberals who did not support Whitley's more radical and enlightened ideas. Both strands of progressive politics agreed on Home Rule and social reform – although many less progressive Liberals felt that social reform should come only after the introduction of Home Rule for Ireland. Both parties were opposed to, or critical of, of the House of Lords, and both favoured manhood and womanhood suffrage. The only fundamental difference came on the issue of the public ownership of the means of production, although the ILP and socialist groups had not clearly specified how that would operate and felt that it would come only slowly and prosaically as the people gradually moved towards socialism. Even then many trade unionists were still undecided about their commitment to socialism and far more concerned about workers' rights than the distant prospect of public ownership. Notwithstanding the commonality of their progressive policies the Liberal Party now had to accept that the ILP was not just a prodigal son who would one day return to his parents for, by the late 1890s, the local ILP had, as already indicated, a significant political and cultural presence in Halifax. Harry Whitley quickly acknowledged this changed political situation, although other doyens of Halifax Liberalism were reluctant to do so. In many ways, then, Harry Whitley could appeal to traditional Liberal voters, progressive Liberals, and many labourist and socialist members of the Halifax working class.

He was also favoured by circumstances. Nationally, the ILP had done badly in the 1895 General Election – losing some support and credibility, losing the seat of Keir Hardie and losing national membership. The Halifax ILP, which had two, of the nine, members of the National Administrative Council of the ILP – James Beever and John Lister – was also in disarray. In a bitter municipal conflict where Lister, who financed the ILP campaign in the General Election with several other wealthy members of the party, refused to accept the views that the Halifax ILP imposed upon his municipal politics, and in a situation where the Liberals pressed for Beever and the Conservatives for Tattersall in municipal and aldermanic elections and honours – the Halifax ILP found that Lister became distant, Beever re-joined the Liberal Party and Tattersall moved onwards to the Conservative Party.[49] This situation, as indicated in the failure to return even one ILP councillor in 1895 and 1896, had blighted the ILP's municipal presence.

It was at this point, with some hope, that Whitley contacted the ILP leaders in Halifax in the desire that some political arrangement could be made to support Alfred Billson as Liberal candidate in the parliamentary by-election of 1897 resulting from the retirement of the Liberal MP W. Rawson-Shaw. He wrote to Edward Marsden on 15 February 1897, through the local press, stating:

> In view of a possible election, I do hope the two progressive parties may be able to work together. Anyhow, it is worth trying for. Would it be possible that neither party should pledge itself to a candidate until they had met on equal terms, to see if they could find one agreeable to both, as at Walthamstow?
>
> Let us try again, before we agree to differ. If you think any good can be done this way I will do all I can to ensure a satisfactory result.[50]

Edward Marsden replied, through the *Halifax Courier*, the next day, 16 February 1897, stating:

> Whilst as anxious as yourself to see the forces of progress for a common purpose still, as one only of the ILP in Halifax, I am unable to promise anything on my own responsibility. The Executive of the party meet tonight and with your consent I will place your letter before them. Of course I shall not do so without I hear from you per the evening post. Speaking strictly on my own responsibility, and without compromising the party in any sense, it will be important to come to some understanding. Had we to deal only with someone as advanced as yourself, it might be possible to come to some arrangement. But so long as a large number of the Liberal party are determined to oppose the ideas we hold, it will be (in my opinion) impossible to fuse our forces. Had we a second ballot the position might be different and until we get it I can see no possible chance of understanding between us.[51]

It is clear that the ILP would consider a political pact if the Liberals were prepared to accept one Labour candidate in general elections at the side of a Liberal candidate but not in a situation where only one candidate was to be returned and the approach was quickly dismissed by James Parker, the Secretary of the Halifax ILP, who wrote to Whitley.

> To Brantwood, Halifax, Tuesday
>
> Dear Sir, After hearing your letter read I was instructed to forward you the following: That we thank you for your endeavour to bring about an understanding between us and the Liberal Party, but regret that the knowledge we possess of those who manage the affairs of the Liberal party renders any understanding altogether out of the question. We fought on independent lines and we feel since that the righteousness of our ideals will ultimately bring success. There is no denying that the official element of the Liberal party is thoroughly individualistic in its character and will fight us to the last, and we suggest that this element must be broken down, and men with different ideals put in their place before we could consider the question . . .
>
> James Parker, Secretary to the ILP[52]

In the end Alfred Billson stood as the Liberal candidate for Halifax in the parliamentary by-election, supported by J.H. Beever, who had drifted back to Liberalism and by James Tattersall who was slowly moving towards the Conservatives after having advised Labour supporters to use their second vote for the Tory candidate in 1895, against the decision of the National ILP that Labour voters should plump for Mann.[53] In the end Billson was returned with 5,664 votes, despite the contest being challenged by Tom Mann, the national and international socialist and trade unionist, who did considerably worse than Lister in 1985 in winning only 2,000 votes, and Sir Savile Crossley with 5,252 votes.

Uplifted by what appeared to be a nadir in the fortunes of the Halifax ILP, and given that Halifax was represented by a Conservative MP as well as a Liberal MP, Whitley now clearly felt that he could act as a unifying force for the progressive vote and win back the seat lost to Arnold, the Conservative MP, in 1895. The Liberal Party in Halifax was keen to win his candidature and he wrote a letter from Brantwood on 1 March 1898:

> Dear Mr. Booth,
> I have, as requested by yourself & Mr. Mitchell, carefully considered my position with regard to the next Parliamentary election & have come to the conclusion that if and when the time comes, the Liberals of Halifax again wish me to serve them in Parliament it will be my duty to put aside personal inclinations & accept the nomination. If they call on me I shall leave no stone unturned to regain the seat for the cause of Progress & if elected I shall do my best to be a representative worthy of the traditions of Halifax.[54]

Eventually, in anticipation of a general election, Harry Whitley was adopted, alongside Alfred Billson, on 30 January 1900 at a meeting of the Liberal Four Hundred.[55]

The General Election of 1900

The General Election took place in Halifax on Monday 3 October 1900. The Boer War was at the centre of the contest. Sir Savile Brinton Crossley, the Liberal Unionist/Conservative candidate, was absent from the campaign on Voluntary Active Service as Captain in the 71st Company Imperial Yeomanry of Shropshire, being later raised to Lt. Colonel. The *Halifax Guardian* contained numerous reports of his patriotism and sense of duty urging voters to 'Let them on the day vote for England, vote for Empire, so that they could say that they had carried a step forward the Banner of England for the honour of England . . .'[56] Whitley (pictured in 1900 in Figure 5.1) disagreed with this view, criticising the absence of the Conservative candidate, and expressing the concern that Britain should not have been involved in the war, and highlighting the 'Government's blunder and bluster in the war'.[57]

Sir Savile Crossley was returned at top of the poll, in his absence, with J.H. Whitley. Billson, defending his seat, was defeated along with James Parker (ILP), who received fewer than the 3,276 votes – fewer than Lister had won in the 1895 General Election but more than the 2,000 won by Tom Mann in 1897 when electors had one vote. Crossley's victory was thus much less emphatic than the result in the country, where the General Election was clearly a Khaki election in which the Conservatives won over 400 seats and 52.5 per cent of the vote – a

80 *Keith Laybourn*

Figure 5.1 Portrait photograph of J.H. Whitley c. 1900 by Greaves & Co., Halifax.

landslide victory in anyone's language. Richard Price has suggested that in this election the working-class voter was involved in imperial jingoism but did not fully succumb to patriotic and imperialist sentiments. Indeed, it is evident that the national vote was down from the 80 per cent plus of previous elections to 74.6 per cent of the electorate, suggesting that there was an element of abstention by the Liberal and Labour working-class voter, though this may have been less in Halifax than elsewhere.[58] The breakdown of the vote, indicated in Table 5.1, is difficult for one can never fully explain why electors split their votes. It is a fair supposition that some Labour voters were either voting for Crossley because the Liberal Party were failing to work with Labour, or that Conservative voters were wishing to reduce the Liberal chances of challenging their own candidate. Whatever the reasons it did not fully work because Whitley commanded sufficient support from both Liberal and Labour voters to place him in second place, behind Crossley but ahead of Billson, an Old Liberal.

Table 5.1 General Election result, Halifax Constituency 1900

Sir Savile Brinton Crossley (Liberal Unionist)	5,941		
		Plumpers	4,212
		Crossley and Parker	1,290
		Crossley and Whitley	271
		Crossley and Billson	158
J.H. Whitley (Liberal)	5,543		
		Plumpers	42
		Whitley and Billson	4,869
		Whitley and Parker	361
		Whitley and Crossley	271
Alfred Billson (Liberal)	5,325		
		Plumpers	77
		Billson and Whitley	4,869
		Billson and Parker	221
		Billson and Crossley	158
James Parker (ILP)	3,276		
		Plumpers	1,404
		Parker and Crossley	1,290
		Parker and Whitley	361
		Parker and Billson	221

Aftermath

In the wake of Whitley's election success both parliamentary and local politics was to change fundamentally in both Britain and Halifax. The formation of the Labour Representation Committee in 1900, a body which changed its name to the Labour Party in 1906 – an alliance of trade unions and socialist groups, including the ILP – gained enormous support from the Taff Vale Judgement of 1901, which decided that trade unions could be held legally liable for costs of the strikes to employers. It gained rapid gradual parliamentary success, eventually returning 29 MPs to the House of Commons in 1906. One of these was James Parker, who by this time had risen to be President of the Halifax Trades and Labour Council and was promoted by what became the Halifax Workers' Council, to sit alongside Whitley as one of the two MPs for Halifax.[59] This understanding, rather than arrangement, was facilitated by the fact that both the ILP and the Liberal Party opposed the Education Act of 1902, which allowed private schools to gain rate assistance, opposed the protective Tariff Reform policies of Joseph Chamberlain, and deeply opposed a Conservative and Unionist government that had taken Britain into the Boer War. In what seems to have been an unwritten agreement and understanding, both parties, fighting on the policy of free trade and Home Rule for Ireland, put forward one candidate each and implied to their voters to divide their votes between the two progressive parties to dupe the Conservatives. This is exactly what they did and on 13 January 1906 J.H. Whitley and James Parker were returned as Liberal and Labour MPs for Halifax with thumping majorities over the Conservatives, and with most progressive voters dividing their votes between the Whitley and Parker.

John Henry Whitley (Lib)	9,354
James Parker (Lab)	8,937
Rt. Hon. Savile Crossley (Con)	5,041
Split votes Whitley/Parker	8,572[60]

Much of this arrangement and the prominence of Whitley was a product of the work he had done in the 1890s.

Final word

It seems likely that Whitley's success in the General Election of 1900, and indeed later in 1906, is the result of a combination of three main factors. The first is that he had strong local connections and was deeply involved in the community politics of Halifax, something which Billson, his running partner, did not have. This means that he held a status which outside candidates could never enjoy. Secondly, he was in the unusual, possibly unique, position of transcending the full range of local Halifax Liberal politics, espousing both Old Liberal and New Liberal values, which allowed him to represent the wide spectrum of Liberal opinion in Halifax. That made him an important figure of fusion politics in Halifax at a time when Liberalism was divided and under attack. Thirdly, Harry Whitley's concern for social and political reform, and his community work in Halifax, allowed him to slow down the exodus of working-class support to the emerging local political Labour movement and to engage with the ILP leaders about possible political arrangements. These advantages were not to last long, as Labour strengthened its political position in Halifax to such an extent that, successfully, Whitley effectively stood on a joint progressive ticket with James Parker in the 1906 General Election. Whitley's success in the October 1900 General Election was effectively summed up by the *Halifax Courier* ten days before the General Election when it summarised the credentials he had gathered in more than a decade in community action.

> Mr. Whitley, worthy man of a noble father, stands well with the young people of Halifax for the part he has taken in their Recreation Evening Classes, and in the boy camps at the seaside, which provided a delightful change for a class who have far too little brightness in their young life. Mr. Whitley's work in technical education in the Town Council, and in other spheres, has been most valuable and a fine preliminary training for that other place to which, we trust, the electorate will shortly call him.[61]

To this might have been added his commitment to social reform and political equality, vital factors in making him politically attractive to the working-class voter.

Notes

1. P.F. Clarke, *Lancashire and the New Liberalism*, Cambridge, Cambridge University Press, 1971.
2. *Halifax Courier*, 22 September 1900.
3. Whitley Collection in the University of Huddersfield Heritage Quay, JHW 2/3/44, 8 November 1901, extract from the *Halifax Courier*, 8 November 1901.
4. B. Seebohm Rowntree, *Poverty: A Study of Town Life*, London, Macmillan, 1901.
5. Harry Whitley helped to form the Boys Camp at Filey in 1889 and often acted as Captain working alongside E. Whitley, G.B. Crossley, E.H. Hill, and other members of well-established Halifax business families. See in the press cuttings books of the Whitley Collection the following references: JHW 2/1/1, 2/1/66, 2/1/22, 2/1/25, 2/1/28, 2/1/31, 2/1/37, 2/1/66, 2/1/73, and 2/1/81, which cover the period 1889 until 1899. See also the essay by John Hargreaves, Chapter 2 of this volume.
6. JHW 2/1/6/7, a cutting from the *Halifax Guardian*, 5 October 1889.
7. Keith Laybourn, 'The New Philanthropy of the Edwardian Age: The Guild of Help and the Halifax Citizens' Guild 1905–1918', *Transactions of the Halifax Antiquarian Society*, 23, n.s. (2015), 73–94.
8. Ibid.
9. Ibid., p. 78 and *The Helper* (journal of the Halifax Citizen's Guild of Help), 2 (2, September 1910), 4.
10. *Halifax Guardian*, 14 October 1893.
11. *Halifax Courier*. 20 June 1912.
12. Ibid.
13. JHW 2/1/13, in an interview with the press.
14. This was much like the attitude of Clem Attlee, one of his younger contemporaries, portrayed in John Bew, *Citizen Clem: A Biography of Attlee*, London, Riverrun, 2016.
15. JHW 2/1/32.
16. *Halifax Courier*, 3 February 1900.
17. *Halifax Courier*, 13 February 1897, contains an editorial noting that of 119 clubs with 16,375 members, 15 were within the Halifax Federation. There were 64 which enabled liquor to be sold and the average expenditure, other than indicated in the text, was 3.5d in Huddersfield, 3.5d in Shipley and 5.5d in Sheffield.
18. *Halifax Courier*, 13 February 1897.
19. JHW 2/1/64, quoting from a cutting which was clearly, from the context, written in 1899.
20. JHW 2/4/36, newspaper report, 25 October 1902.
21. *Halifax Courier*, 3 February 1900.
22. *Halifax Courier*, 6 October 1900.
23. JHW 2/2/6 in a newspaper article on 'Old and New Liberalism', 11 February 1900, which Whitley gave in Preston on behalf of the Eighty Club and the Preston Reform Club.
24. Clarke, *Lancashire and the New Liberalism*, p. 7.
25. Martin D. Pugh, 'Yorkshire and the New Liberalism', *Journal of Modern History*, 50/3 (September, 1978), D1139–D1155.
26. JHW 2/1/68 to the Elland Liberal Association, circa 1895.
27. JHW 2/1/59.
28. JHW 2/1/44.

29 JHW 2/1/68, in a lecture on 'The Problem of the Future' given in either 1895 or 1896.
30 JHW 2/1/32 in an interview with the press.
31 JHW 2/1/59.
32 Patricia A. Dawson, 'The Halifax Independent Labour Movement: Labour and Liberalism 1890–1914', in Keith Laybourn and David James (eds), *The Rising Sun of Socialism: The Independent Labour Party in the Textile District of the West Riding of Yorkshire between 1890 and 1914*, (Bradford, West Yorkshire Archives, 1991), pp. 52–53; P.A. Dawson, 'Halifax Politics, 1890–1914', Huddersfield Polytechnic, unpublished PhD Thesis, 1987; Jonjo Ward, 'The Rise of a Local Liberal: An Examination of the Success of John Henry Whitley, 1890–1906', University of Huddersfield, unpublished MA by Research Dissertation, 2014.
33 Keith Laybourn and Jack Reynolds, *Liberalism and the Rise of Labour*, London, Croom Helm, 1984, pp. 43, 52.
34 Workers' Municipal Electoral Committee, Minute Book, 1906, HILP, TU:114/1, Calderdale Branch of the West Yorkshire Archives.
35 Dawson, 'The Halifax Independent Labour Movement'.
36 *Halifax Courier*, 6 October 1900.
37 John Lister, 'The ILP in Halifax' (handwritten MSS of 89 pages), p, 8, West Yorkshire Archives, Calderdale SH& JH7 JH/B/45.
38 John Lister, 'The ILP in Halifax' (hand written MSS of 89 pages), p. 47, West Yorkshire Archives, Calderdale, SH7 JH/B/45.
39 Ibid., p. 47. James Beever was a worker who had been a Liberal, indeed Secretary of Boothtown Liberal Club, who had been driven from his job with Clayton, Murgatroyd & Co, Silk Spinners, along with James Tattersall, who later became the President of the Halifax Labour Union/ILP. Beever later returned to the Liberal Party. Tattersall, also a Liberal who joined the ILP eventually left and became a Conservative candidate in a general election for the Preston seat in the early twentieth century.
40 *The ILP Directory 1895*, London, ILP, 1895. Also Keith Laybourn and Jack Reynolds, *Liberalism and the Rise of Labour 1890–1918*, Beckenham, Croom Helm, 1984, p. 62. In 1895 there were twenty-nine branches of the ILP in Bradford, eleven in Colne Valley, nine in Spen Valley, eight in Leeds, eight in Halifax and five in Dewsbury. Keighley and other areas had branches and it is clear that the West Riding textile movement was the epicentre of the ILP.
41 Dawson, 'The Independent Labour Movement: Labour and Liberalism 1890–1914'.
42 Laybourn and Reynolds, *Liberalism and the Rise of Labour 1890–1918*, Table 3.4, p. 65.
43 JHW 2/1/37, a private letter from H. Whitley to Edward Marsden?
44 JHW 2/1/33, a cutting for March/ April 1895.
45 JHW 2/1/33.
46 JHW 2/1/33.
47 JHW 2/1/35.
48 JHW 2/1/68.
49 Fuller details of this conflict are to be found in Laybourn and Reynolds, *Liberalism and the Rise of Labour 1890–1918*, pp. 90–94; also JHW 2/2/61 which contains a newspaper cutting connected with this matter from the *Halifax Courier*, 13 March 1897.
50 JHW 2/1/61.
51 JHW 2/1/62, likely to be the *Halifax Courier*, 16 February 1897.
52 JHW 2/1/62.
53 *Halifax Courier*, 13 March 1897.
54 JHW 2/1/43. The date was 1 March 1898 and not 1 March 1890 as indicated in the catalogue.
55 JHW 2/1/86 and likely to be the *Halifax Courier*, 3 February 1900.
56 JHW 2/2/27, possibly *Halifax Guardian*, 29 September 1900.
57 JHW 2/2/22.

58 Richard Price, *An Imperial War and the British Working Class: Working Class Attitudes and Reaction to the Boer War 1899–1902*, London, Routledge & Kegan Paul, 1971, reprinted by Routledge in 2006 and 2014.
59 Keith Laybourn and Jack Reynolds, *Liberalism and the Rise of Labour*, London, Croom Helm, 1984, pp. 14–20; West Yorkshire Archive Service, CD, Halifax Trades and Labour Council and Workers' Committee, circular dates 17 March 1906, TU 106/3, HXM 14–20.
60 *Halifax Courier*, 14 January 1906.
61 JHW 2/2/ 24, possibly the *Halifax Courier*, 22 September 1900.

6 Industrial relations and joint industrial councils

The UK and beyond 1916–39

Greg Patmore[1]

John Henry Whitley[2] had two important impacts on labour relations. They were the Whitley Reports in 1917 and 1918 in Great Britain and the Royal Commission on Labour in India, which he chaired and reported on in 1931. The recommendations of the Royal Commission, like the Whitley Reports, included the collaboration of employers and trade unions through works committees.[3] This chapter focuses on the Whitley Reports and their influence not only in the UK but beyond, particularly in the USA, Canada and Australia during the interwar period.

Whitley had direct experience with labour relations. He managed the family firm of cotton spinners, S. Whitley & Co., in Halifax, England, where he had begun at 'the bottom of the ladder' as an 'operative', and was a fervent Congregationalist, who was widely respected for his impartiality and high principles. While he was not a social reformer, he was an advocate of co-partnership as a way of sharing responsibility with employees. Whitley also entered politics and by 1916 was a prominent Liberal MP and had served as Chair of the Ways and Means Committee in the House of Commons since 1911 and continued in the role until 1921.[4]

The origins of Whitleyism

The origins of Whitleyism lay in the First World War against a background of industrial unrest. Union officials co-operated with the government in pursuing the war effort, which extended the collective bargaining rights of unions. There was, however, growing tension between union officials and rank-and-file members, particularly in the munitions industries over issues such as dilution or deskilling, which allowed workers to bypass the usual requirements for training to undertake war work and minimise skill shortages. Workplace shop stewards became prominent in leading resistance to dilution and began co-operating across trades and unions in shop committees to represent rank-and-file workers. There were even city-wide committees formed to represent workers' interests, most notably the Clyde Workers' Committee in Glasgow, which led strikes for wage increases and against dilution agreements approved by union officials and the government. The government responded to the Clyde Workers'

Committee resistance to dilution by appointing dilution commissioners to work with moderate local union officials and form joint committees to oversee workshop changes, while repressing left-wing newspapers and arresting and deporting radical leaders from Glasgow. There were employer concerns about radical workers gaining representation on joint committees relating to munitions production. They opposed suggestions to put employee representatives on the boards of the national shell factories and were successful in having joint Local Armaments Committees abolished. Outside munitions production there were Miners' Reform Committees on the Scottish and South Wales coalfields and unofficial vigilance committees on the railways. There was also a growing demand among unions, in particular the National Union of Railwaymen (NUR), for the nationalisation of key industries such as railways and coal mining with workers control.[5]

Against this background, there was developing a general view that the First World War offered a chance for the reconstruction of post-war British society built on wartime co-operation and the 'comradeship of the trenches'. Prime Minister Herbert Asquith established a small Cabinet subcommittee in March 1916 on reconstruction problems. His successor Lloyd George replaced the subcommittee in March 1917 with a Reconstruction Committee of Cabinet Ministers, which he chaired. This in turn became a fully-fledged Ministry of Reconstruction in August 1917. Issues of concern for reconstruction included trade, the demobilisation of the armed forces and the removal of government regulation from industry. Those calling for a reconstruction policy also saw the future of industrial relations as one of its objects.[6]

The Whitley Committee on Relations between Employers and the Employed was a subcommittee of Asquith's subcommittee on Reconstruction and appointed in October 1916. Whitley presided over the Committee and, despite his achievements, later claimed that as Chair he was an 'ignoramus' in 'industrial affairs' compared to other members of the Committee.[7] Despite this, he was concerned with harnessing the 'human factor' in industry by linking 'all the workers in industry in a frank partnership for the common good'.[8] Although neither the Trades Union Congress (TUC) nor the Federation of British Industry (FBI) had direct representation, there was a balance on the Committee between employers or their representatives and union members or their spokespersons. The Committee did not call witnesses and did not keep meeting records.[9]

The Committee issued five reports during 1917 and 1918, notably the first of which is usually thought of as the Whitley Report, and the third, which looked at workplace joint committees. In its first report, which was signed off in March 1917 and published in June 1917, the Committee discussed industries where labour was well organised and proposed Joint Industrial Councils (JICs) composed of employer and employee representatives. Similar committees at a local and workshop level would supplement JIC activities. The JICs could deal with, or allocate to ancillary committees, questions such as methods of fixing and adjusting earnings, technical education and training, and proposed legislation affecting industry. They would also go beyond collective bargaining in that by 'the better utilisation of the practical knowledge and experience of the workpeople' they would bring about the improvement in productivity necessary for Britain to trade in the post-war world. The recommendations were within the voluntarist traditions of British industrial relations, as there was no obligation on employers and unions to do anything if they saw no need for JICs. The government would act in an advisory role in the setting up of JICs if the parties desired and provide relevant information on industrial issues. The only exception to this was the railways. Where there was no adequate organisation of employers and employees, Trade Boards would continue or be established to provide statutory regulation and develop industrial organisation to the point where the JICs would be able to replace the boards.[10]

The report on works committees was a supplementary report signed off by the Committee in October 1917. It emphasised that the works committees were an essential element of Whitleyism and that better relations between employers and employees could only be obtained if workers had a greater say in the matters with which they were concerned. While the works committees could not alter matters in the collective agreement, they could bring grievances before local management and also make suggestions concerning improvements in working conditions and production methods that would improve workplace efficiency. The Committee did not set out any form of constitution for these works committees, beyond recommending that they meet on a regular basis, not less frequently than once a fortnight, and emphasising 'constructive co-operation'. Given the potential benefits of the works committee for 'commercial and scientific efficiency', it was recommended that a management representative in the workplace should devote a 'substantial' amount of 'time and thought' to the working and success of the committee. There was concern that the success of works committees would be undermined if there were any perception employers might use them as a substitute for trade unions. Trade unions and employers' associations had to co-operate in the setting up of works committees. The report recommended against setting up works committees in industries where workers were not organised or only partially organised into trade unions, as there was a danger that employers might use works committees as an anti-union strategy.[11] As the report noted, 'these committees should not, in constitution or methods of working, discourage Trade organisations'.[12] While the works committees were not designed to undermine trade unions, they were a challenge to the shop committee movement and a 'strategy to bypass shop steward authority'.[13] Whitley was to later argue that the works committees were not a 'glorified form of welfare work' but a 'means whereby there can be spread throughout the ranks of workers a real understanding of the problems of industry as a whole'.[14]

The War Cabinet gave, in principle, support on 9 October 1917 to the Whitley Report after obtaining responses from 103 trade unions and employers' organisations, which indicated that none opposed the report's principles. There were some employers, however, that had doubts about the advisability of the works committees on the grounds of interference with managerial prerogative and belief that this would hamper efforts to improve workplace efficiency.

Employers in staple industries such as cotton argued that Whitleyism was not applicable to them as they had developed their own industrial relations processes, but did not oppose the creation of JICs elsewhere.[15] The recognition of trade unionism was not an issue, as 'the war had already made this a foregone conclusion in most British industries'.[16]

While the TUC did not provide a response to the Cabinet request for a viewpoint, the TUC Parliamentary Committee gave qualified approval in April 1918 to the Whitley Report, recognising the need to avoid 'serious industrial strife' in the post-war reconstruction period. There were divisions within the TUC that muted total endorsement by the union movement. While unions covering skilled trades with a strong shop steward organisation and collective bargaining processes, such as the Amalgamated Society of Engineers (ASE), saw little need for Whitleyism, less organised workers in unskilled or semi-skilled occupations such as shop assistants believed that Whitleyism could enhance their bargaining position. While the NUR executive initially supported the Whitley principles in July 1917 as they were broadly in line with union policy, it concluded at its AGM in June 1918 following the release of the Final Report that the Whitley Scheme did not 'sufficiently safeguard the interests of Labour'. This union was calling for a broader agenda of workers' control that included equal representation in the management of the railway companies and their nationalisation.[17]

The impact of the Joint Industrial Council

The JICs did not develop at the industry level despite Whitley's continued hopes for their adoption and his belief that Whitleyism 'would get the maximum from each individual for the benefit of the commonwealth'.[18] Initially there was some degree of enthusiasm for JICs with seventy-four being created between 1918 and 1921. Collective bargaining and trade unionism was so well established that Whitleyism was redundant for much of private manufacturing such as the iron and steel industry. JICs tended to flourish in industries where unions were weak, but in the case of the wrought hollow-ware trade, which produced metal tableware and already had a statutory Trade Board to cover this poorly organised industry, the JIC lapsed after increased powers conferred on the Trade Boards in 1918 led parties to believe the JIC was superfluous. In the wake of the First World War the JICs that were established generally fell into abeyance, with the Civil Service being a notable exception. Many JICs only met a few times or very infrequently. Only 42 JICs still functioned in 1930 and by 1939 only 20 JICs survived. Employers feared that union militants would use the scheme for 'class war' rather than 'constructive collaboration', while unionists feared that employers would use the scheme to eliminate the union presence in the workplace.[19]

There are a number of reasons why the JICs failed to develop during the interwar period. The post-war economic boom broke in 1920 and there was a severe economic recession during 1921–22. The UK economy remained sluggish during the 1920s and was hit severely by the Great Depression. Trade union membership declined and employers became more belligerent and determined to reassert managerial prerogative in the workplace and do what was necessary to challenge overseas competition. The threat posed by militant shop stewards and shop committees also dissipated. Where shopfloor organisation survived the economic downturn, it was integrated into and subordinated to official union structures.[20]

There was also decline in political support. During the General Election of December 1918 Prime Minister Lloyd George weakened any push towards JICs by hardly referring to them in the campaign. The Wartime Coalition Government did organise a National Industrial Conference of employers and unions in February 1919 against a background of an upsurge of industrial discontent during the winter of 1918/19. While there was discussion of forming an elected National Industrial Council of employers and unions to advise governments on major industrial issues, there were virtually no positive results in terms of industrial reform. The Ministry for Reconstruction was disbanded quickly in 1919, with most of its duties being transferred to the Ministries of Labour and Health. While the Ministry of Labour did continue to promote JICs, the funding for allocated staff was cut by Treasury insistence in 1919 and there was a further funding cut in a government financial crisis of 1922, which saw the Industrial Relations Division of the Ministry, the heart of the bureaucratic support for Whitleyism, reduced from 115 to twenty staff.[21] Stitt has noted that after then the Ministry of Labour 'provided advisors and monitors for the JICs that existed but moved away from any active attention to the creation of new JICs'.[22] The Ministry became more focussed on Trade Boards, which provided the Minister of Labour with a more direct method of addressing industrial conditions than the JICs, which operated independently from the Ministry.[23]

JICs remained a feature of the Civil Service. While the Civil Service was not considered in the original report, some Civil Service unions recognised the benefits of Whitleyism for enhancing their role in determination of wages and conditions. The Second Report of the Whitley Committee in October 1917, which recognised that its recommendations covered state and municipal authorities, weakened initial opposition by the government to union support for the extension of Whitleyism into the Civil Service.[24] Civil Service Whitley Councils were essentially joint conciliation boards with broad terms of reference including wages and conditions, but without an independent Chair. There was a National Whitley Council, which held its first meeting on 23 July 1919, departmental councils, district committees and office committees. The functions of the office committees were not spelt out and were subject to the discretion of the departmental councils. By March 1928 there were 68 departmental councils and ten Whitley Industrial Councils, which covered blue-collar workers such as engineers in government workshops, in the UK Civil Service.[25]

While the JICs did not achieve their promise, there were attempts to extend them further by giving them legal powers to prevent unorganised employers undercutting the wages paid by employers loyal to the JIC agreements. The Association of Joint Industrial Councils and Interim Reconstruction Committees (AJICIRC), which was founded in March 1921, lobbied for legislation to allow the JICs statutory enforcement of agreements if they wanted to exercise them. The main support for the AJICIRC came from the Pottery JIC, with Fred Hand being secretary of both organisations. While the TUC did give support to the idea at its 1925 Conference, there were later reservations about the application of penalties to unions and workers who broke agreements, and the movement was weakened by a lack of support among JICs for the idea, with the Tinplate Industry JIC arguing that it had a long and successful history without the need for legal powers. Between 1924 and 1935 there were five unsuccessful attempts to have a Bill passed in Parliament to give the JICs the necessary powers.[26]

The impact of the Whitley works committees

The development of works committees under the Whitley Scheme was also disappointing. While it is difficult to estimate the number of works committees, the Ministry of Labour estimated in 1923 that there were over 1,000 had been formed in the UK, but this figure included works committees in industries where there were no JICs. From 1925 the number of works committees remained stable and were particularly found in large firms, where managers had a desire to maintain a means for the 'more intimate and frequent contact' with employees found in smaller firms.[27]

In the UK Railways works committees or Local Departmental Committees persisted until the outbreak of the Second World War. After 1921 the British railway networks were dominated by four giant private companies with extensive welfare programmes and developed labour administration. Unlike other industries, there was a statutory basis for Whitley works committees through the 1921 Railways Act for occupations covered by the NUR, the Associated Society of Locomotive Engineers and Firemen (ASLEF) and the Railway Clerks Association.[28]

While there is no data available on the number of office committees in the UK Civil Service, office committees were active in several notable Civil Service Departments. In the Admiralty office, the committees operated in most of its headquarters. But as Leonard White noted, many of them were 'without real vitality' and operated 'under very real handicaps' as they did not deal with many major issues, with a lack of business leading to the frequent suspension of meetings.[29] There were also active office committees in the Post Office with committees in Birmingham in 1927 for a time preventing the employment of women in branch offices.[30]

There are a number of reasons why works committees generally failed to take off. Only some JICs showed enthusiasm at the outset and very few persisted with them. The Pottery JIC did try to organise works committees through special campaigns and keep up ongoing interest by organising quarterly conferences of existing workplace committee representatives. While there were 100 pottery work committees organised by August 1929, only approximately half of them survived and it was estimated that not more than six were 'really functioning'.

Works committees did not take root where the collective bargaining machinery was weak, as in the Silk and Hosiery Industry and Quarrying, for example. Some employers, such as the Cliffe Hill Granite Company quarry in Leicester, believed that works committees were inappropriate for their workplaces because of the small numbers of employees. Where employers were suspicious of trade unions, such as in the Soap and Candle Trades, they did not encourage works committees.[31] The Secretary of the London Brewers Council noted in June 1920 that he was not in favour of Whitley works committees because they encouraged 'employees to join trade unions'.[32] In the engineering trades both labour and management preferred the existing system of union shop stewards and shop committees. Colliery owner opposition to works or colliery committees in the coal mining industry by legislation led the government to abandon the proposal.[33] As the International Labour Organisation (ILO) generally observed for Great Britain 'few employers are willing to surrender any part of their control not only over the works but over the workshop.'[34]

There were union concerns about the works committees and a decline in government support for the extension of works committees. Unions objected to non-unionists voting for works committee representatives and running for positions on works committees. The understanding developed that while non-unionists could vote for the committees, they were ineligible for election to office. Some unions saw works committees as 'inadvisable' if they did not have a significant presence in a workplace. Similarly, the Ministry of Labour, when it was directly encouraging the formation of works committees in 1920, refused to help employers where there was insufficient union organisation. The financial cuts to the Ministry of Labour also weakened the push towards work committees, with staff who focussed on the encouragement of works committees either being dismissed or transferred to other government departments where vacancies existed in December 1920. While the Committee of Industry and Trade or the Balfour Committee, which was appointed by the Labour Prime Minister Ramsay MacDonald in July 1924 to investigate the decline in the UK's economy since the First World War, did present a report favouring works committees in March 1929 on a voluntary basis, there was no revival of the earlier interest shown by the Ministry of Labour.[35]

Beyond the UK

What was the impact of Whitleyism beyond the UK? There was an interest in examining the ideas underlying Whitleyism in a number of countries. The German Ministry of Labour, for example, looked at Whitleyism, with a representative visiting the UK in May 1930 to explore the role of JICs in industrial relations. The *Allgemeiner Deutscher Gewerkschaftsbund*, the socialist union movement, published an overview of Whitleyism, including works committees, in its journal in October 1931.[36]

In the USA reprints were published of the Whitley Reports. An Industrial Commission of Employers, nominated by the US Secretary of Labor, visited

Great Britain in February and March 1919 to study industrial conditions and post-war reconstruction, with a particular interest shown in the Whitley system.[37] R.J. Caldwell, an owner of cotton mills and member of the Industrial Commission, later argued in a *New York Times* article that Whitleyism as a form of 'industrial democratization' was 'proving most successful' in Great Britain and 'we must adopt that or something like it . . .'[38]

Employers and commentators in the USA, however, generally dismissed it as inappropriate for US conditions. Waddill Catchings, an influential US economist,[39] argued that Whitleyism was an extension of the British labour movement and inappropriate for the US industry where large numbers of workers were unorganised and where there was a desire in firms such as Standard Oil New Jersey to 'develop a common enterprise'.[40] Cyrus McCormick from International Harvester went even further and argued that Whitleyism had 'organised British industry into two opposing camps, whereas the American system of employee representation is based solely on mutual co-operation' and proclaimed that 'class prejudice has no place in this country'.[41] John D. Rockefeller Jr. congratulated Whitleyism for uniting organisations of 'Labor and Capital by a bond of common interest in a common venture' and then drew favourable comparisons with the non-union Employee Representation Plans (ERPs) or Rockefeller Plans at the Rockefeller-owned Standard Oil of New Jersey and Colorado Fuel and Iron, which were generally joint committees of management appointees and elected worker representatives.[42] US employers had increasingly adopted ERPs as a means of stopping union expansion during the labour shortages that accompanied the First World War.[43]

Where Whitleyism did have an influence, it was in regard to the idea of union–management co-operation. The American Federation of Labor (AFL) faced declining union membership and aggressive anti-union campaigns by employers, which included the establishment of ERPs, following the First World War. Following major strikes in 1919 and 1920 and the whipping up of a 'Red Scare', the AFL wanted to challenge perceptions that it was irresponsible and emphasised that it wanted to increase production through scientific means and co-operation with management. The AFL found an ally in the Taylor Society, which championed scientific management but shifted towards a view that some form of co-operation between organised labour and management was needed to increase industry efficiency. There were precedents for union–management co-operation such as in the building trades and clothing trades.[44]

Union–management co-operation was promoted by civil servants such as Otto Beyer during and immediately after the First World War. Beyer, a mechanical engineer, worked in the iron and steel industry, railways and the Arsenal Orders Branch of the Ordnance Department, remaining in that post until 1919. By the mid-1920s Beyer worked as an industrial relations consultant and technical advisor for AFL's Railway Employees Department. Beyer was a member of the Taylor Society and strongly influenced by Whitleyism.[45]

While the AFL saw Whitleyism as an endorsement of unionism as a cornerstone of industrial relations, there were concerns. Samuel Gompers, AFL

President, believed that committees at the workplace level would act independently of the union, undermine union authority and exacerbate strife with employers, which would lead to 'demoralization'. Any workplace scheme involving union-management co-operation therefore had to be an extension of existing union organisation and not be independently elected by employees at the workplace.[46] Beyer supported Gompers' view by arguing that if the committees were independent of unions then the scheme would lose its 'vital essence' and take on the 'anemic complexion' of an ERP.[47]

The Beyer Plan of union-management co-operation promoted unionism and collective bargaining. On the basis of a collective agreement, union representatives and managers met together on committees to discuss a range of issues that could eliminate waste, improve productivity and enhance safety. Wages and working conditions were left to the regular negotiations between the company and the unions. Under this scheme, management were to accept trade unions as necessary and constructive in the running of their enterprise, while unions agreed to go beyond their traditional concerns with collective bargaining and assist the companies in the marketing of their services and the winning of government contracts. There were also other objectives, including the stabilisation of employment and sharing the gains of co-operation. Employees did not generally directly elect their representatives on these union-management committees. Given the AFL's concerns about unofficial rank-and-file action and the ERP, current union workplace representatives were the employee representatives on the co-operative committees. The work of the committees was done in company time, with no impact on the wages of employee members, and management provided the venue for the meetings. Beyond the workshops there was provision under the Beyer Plan for union representatives and management to regularly meet on a regional and/or company-wide basis to review the progress of the works committees and discuss issues of importance for the whole railway not covered by collective bargaining.[48] The AFL was reluctant to allow management to pay the expenses, including time lost, for union representatives at these regional and company-wide meetings, as this would compromise, as in the ERP, the independence of the representatives, who would lose 'full control' of the scheme.[49] The impact of union-management was limited, with notable examples being the Baltimore and Ohio Railroad in the USA and the Canadian National Railroad in Canada.[50]

As in other countries, wartime labour shortages enhanced the power of Canadian unions, with union membership growing from 160,000 in 1916 to 378,000 in 1919 and growing interest in alternative forms of labour management. There was a surge of industrial unrest in 1917 with 1,123,916 striker days lost. The reason for the discontent included inflation and demands for shorter hours. The popularity of the appeals for labour solidarity and mutual support encouraged employers to seek forms of workplace organisation that would insulate workers in each establishment from those in others such as ERPs.[51]

The Canadian Federal Government responded to the growth of labour power by appointing the Mathers Royal Commission, whose inquiries from April 26 to 13 June 1919 coincided with the greatest period of industrial unrest in Canadian history, with 3,401,843 striker days lost in 1919 including the Winnipeg General Strike. As in the UK, the Canadian Federal Cabinet led by Prime Minister Robert Borden was concerned with the impact of the end of the First World War on the economy and society. It established a Reconstruction and Development Committee and in December 1917 announced the formation of a tripartite 'Sub-committee on Labour Problems'.[52]

The Cabinet accepted a recommendation from the Sub-committee to set up a Royal Commission led by Chief Justice T.C. Mathers of Manitoba. Representatives from labour, capital and the 'public' assisted Chief Justice Mathers. One of the Commissioner's tasks was to investigate progress made by 'joint industrial councils' in Canada, the UK and the USA. When the report of the Commission was completed in late June 1919 reference was also made to Whitleyism in Great Britain and to ERPs in the USA. The Commission praised both the Rockefeller ERP and Whitley schemes as a means of reducing unrest and recognising the 'human factor' in industry with recommendations to establish a 'bureau for promoting Industrial Councils' and that steps be taken to establish joint plant and industrial councils. It saw workplace plant councils as the first step towards district and national industry councils given the sparse population and large geographical area of Canada. The report emphasised that these councils were not intended to be anti-union devices or interfere with workers' freedom of associations or current industrial relations arrangements. Where unions existed then unions should choose the representatives, but in non-unionised plants employees should choose their representatives in whatever manner they saw fit. While it was not clear at what level these issues would be dealt with, the Councils covered a wide range of questions including wages, workplace conditions, welfarism and production improvements. Two Commissioners, Frank Pauzé, a representative of capital from Montreal, and Smeaton White, a representative of the 'public' and managing editor of the *Montreal Gazette*, in their minority report favoured the Rockefeller scheme because of the lack of organisation of employers and workers in Canada relative to Great Britain, the ethnic diversity of the Canadian workforce and the wider geographical dispersion of industry in Canada.[53] As Naylor argues, however, the 'Canadian government, unlike the British, lacked either the will or the power (or both) to initiate such schemes on a large scale'.[54]

The Federal Government did call together a National Industrial Conference of employer and labour delegates in Ottawa in December 1919 to discuss the Mathers Report. Employers were not convinced there was any need for change, particularly if organised labour was involved and the Canadian Manufacturers' Association (CMA) drew advice from the anti-union National Association of Manufacturers in the USA. While there was a favourable presentation by Colonel D. Carnegie from England on Whitleyism, including the works committees, Canadian employers, with the exception of the building employers, dismissed the idea because it recognised unions and would stop the roll back of union gains during an anticipated post-war depression. The CMA refused to recognise labour interests beyond the individual firm. Despite these differences, there was support for the establishment of JICs, because of the 'urgent necessity' for greater co-operation between employer and employee. There was also a call for the Department of Labour to establish a bureau to gather data and furnish information on JICs.[55] However, there was an unwillingness to endorse either Whitleyism or the Rockefeller Plan, with a view that it was 'not wise or expedient to recommend any set plan for such councils'.[56]

There were some examples of JICs based on the Whitley Scheme. Gideon Robertson, the Minister for Labour from 1918 to 1921 and a former telegraphist with a conservative trade union background, preferred the Whitley Scheme with its focus on sector, rather than enterprise, bargaining. Robertson, however, had limited political influence and his approach was fickle when he urged striking militant Toronto metal workers to bargain on an enterprise rather than a sector basis. The Canadian Federal Government also refused a Whitley Council for civil servants unlike their UK counterparts. The Canadian Building and Construction Industries also had a National Joint Council Board with equal representation from the employer association and the international building trade unions with a Chair appointed by the Department of Labour. This Council was short lived with the employers' association voting to discontinue the Board in January 1922 until union representatives recognised a number of principles including the open shop, the prohibition of sympathy strikes and the right of employers to directly deal with employees rather than union business agents. While these Boards operated at national level, there were more localised examples of Whitley type councils such as the Toronto building industry, where there was a union presence and the Whitley Council reinforced a move by building unions towards industrial unionism. Toronto builders found the Whitley Council a useful instrument for cutting wages during the post-war economic recession and the Council was disbanded in early 1923 as it had served its purpose for employers and offered little protection for unions. By contrast to the Federal Government, the Saskatchewan Liberal provincial government did establish the Civil Service Joint Council in 1920, which consisted of three deputy ministers and three members of the Saskatchewan Civil Service Association.[57]

As with the Canada and the USA, so in Australia there was also an interest in the labour question during and immediately after the First World War. The British Government directly communicated with the Australian Government highlighting the benefits of Whitleyism. In 1919–20 the Commonwealth Advisory Council of Science and Industry published reports on industrial co-operation and welfarism, which included a discussion of Whitleyism. In 1918, George Beeby, a barrister, former Labor Party parliamentarian and by then Minister for Labour and Industry in the New South Wales (NSW) Nationalist Government, following an overseas trip to the USA and the UK, issued a report that recommended the introduction of Whitleyism rather than ERPs to defeat worker militancy and increase productivity. J.B. Holme, the Deputy President of the NSW Board of Trade, also published reports in 1919 and 1920 on Whitleyism, which included a detailed discussion of Whitley works committees. Holme emphasised the need to recognise the 'paramount' importance of the 'human factor' in industry and close co-operation between employers and employees.[58]

Beeby actively promoted Whitleyism through his roles as Minister for Labour and later as a judge of the NSW Court of Industrial Arbitration. Beeby amended the NSW Industrial Arbitration Act in 1918 to empower a Board of Trade to establish 'mutual welfare committees', 'industrial councils' and 'shop committees'. Drawing directly from the British experience it was hoped that the legislation 'would find a solution for some of the graver of the industrial problems which militate against the internal peace and the prosperity of the nation'.[59] As in Great Britain there was a clear statement that these committees were not to be used by employers to undermine trade unions. The proposed shop committees would meet fortnightly to discuss grievances. If there were no grievances then meetings would still occur to discuss suggestions 'tending to the improvement of industrial conditions or the better utilisation of the practical knowledge or experience of employees . . .'.[60] Beeby wanted to shift industrial regulation away from state tribunals and judges towards industry and the workplace with the state tribunals only dealing with wages and hours. These provisions attracted little interest from employers and unions and, while the provisions persisted in the NSW arbitration system, they were practically moribund. In 1923 Beeby varied the Boot and Shoe (State) Award in his capacity as a judge, tying the implementation of a 'satisfactory system of piecework' in the industry with the establishment of joint committees of employers and employees to discuss any scheme.[61]

There continued to be Australian interest in ideas of employee representation during the 1920s. The Nationalist Federal Government, led by Prime Minister Stanley Bruce, had already tried to reform Australian industrial relations by unsuccessfully initiating a referendum in September 1926 that would have led to the Federal Government taking over state industrial jurisdictions thereby removing concerns relating to conflicting jurisdictions and potential industrial conflict. Bruce also hoped that the changes would have allowed for a more flexible approach to industrial relations, including the establishment of Whitley JICs.[62]

There was some interest in Whitleyism in state enterprises. Beeby argued that state enterprises, such as the railways, should be the initial starting point for the introduction of Whitleyism. With Beeby's encouragement, the NSW Government Railways tried to establish Whitley committees in 1919. They were supposed to deal with all matters relating to 'staff well-being and comfort', but exclude award matters dealt with by industrial tribunals. However, the bitterness between management and the railway unions following the 1917 General Strike prevented co-operation. Eveleigh workshop employees in Sydney rejected the scheme at a time when management was trying to introduce an unpopular Halsey bonus scheme. Workers saw the proposed committees and the bonus scheme as part of a 'speed-up'. The Labor Council of NSW, the peak council of unions in NSW, condemned the committees for being an objectionable form of 'labour exploitation'. The Australian Socialist Party published a pamphlet entitled *The Danger of the Whitley Scheme*, which claimed that the scheme was against workers' interests. It widely circulated the pamphlet among railway workers. The Railway Commissioners were more successful at the Randwick tramway workshops in Sydney, where a committee was still operating in 1924.[63]

The Federal Department of Defence did not share the enthusiasm of Beeby for Whitleyism. Senator George Pearce, the Nationalist Minister for Defence, requested in November 1920 that a report be made to investigate the application of the Whitley Scheme in Defence Factories. In November 1921, an internal memo concluded that Whitley committees were not needed in the defence factories due to the existence of industrial tribunals and the greater 'power' of Australian workers through their strong trade union movement. In the factories managers already recognised the union representatives of workers and therefore there was no need for works committees. The report also questioned the value of worker suggestions, claiming that workers lack knowledge of prior patents and the costs involved in implementing new ideas.[64]

There was private sector employer interest in Whitleyism. The NSW Master Builders' Association (MBA) examined the Whitley Scheme of Industrial Councils, while the NSW Chamber of Manufactures published a detailed analysis of the Whitley Report in its journal. Both the MBA and the NSW Employers' Federation, however, were concerned that Whitleyism was incompatible with the Australian industrial arbitration system and would have to be redrafted to meet Australian needs. In the NSW boot making industry, employers and unions did agree to introduce Whitleyism in 1919. This scheme was little more than an attempt to formalise collective bargaining and it broke down in 1920 over the issues of the forty-four-hour week and unemployment.[65]

Conclusion

Whitleyism arose against a background of wartime industrial unrest and the growth of workplace rank-and-file movements in Great Britain that challenged unions and the state. While Whitley downplayed his role on the Committee that bore his name, he was concerned with harnessing the 'human factor' of British workers in co-operation with management to meet the challenges of the post-war world. Despite initial support for the recommendations of the Whitley Committee, government and employer interest in Whitleyism diminished as the post-war economic boom broke in 1920, labour militancy declined and the economy remained sluggish in the 1920s.

There were, however, some employers and unions who persisted with Whitleyism. There were still twenty JICs in existence by 1939. Innovative firms of medium to large size maintained Whitley workplace committees in confectionery, chemicals, steel products and the railways, with the latter being underpinned by legislation. The Civil Service found the Whitley system valuable for regulating the labour relations of its employees and its Whitley Council lasted for more than fifty years.

There was an awareness of Whitleyism outside the UK, where there were similar concerns with labour militancy and post-war reconstruction, with the idea having some influence in the USA, particularly in regard to the development of union-management co-operation. Whitleyism also had some influence in Australia, with an attempt by Beeby, the Minister for Labour and Industry in NSW, to provide a favourable legal environment for Whitleyism in that state through amendments to industrial arbitration legislation, and in Canada, as in seen in the findings of the Mathers Royal Commission. While there was awareness of Whitleyism in these three countries, there was a limited impact, ironically because of the weakness of organised labour in Canada and the USA, and the strength of trade unionism and industrial regulation in Australia.

Notes

1 This chapter is drawn from a broader study of employee representation in the inter–war period, see G. Patmore, *Worker Voice: Employee Representation in the Workplace in Australia, Canada, Germany, the UK and the US 1914–1939*, Liverpool, Liverpool University Press, 2016.
2 Known as Harry to his friends, family and to his constituents in his early years. Email from John Whitley, grandson, 12 September 2016.
3 *The Times* (London), 2 July 1931, 4 February 1935.
4 R. Charles, *The Development of Industrial Relations in Britain 1911–1939*, London, Hutchinson, 1973, p. 96; J. Stitt, *Joint Industrial Councils in British History: Inception, Adoption, and Utilization, 1917–1939*, Westport (CT), Praeger, 2006, pp. 66–7; *The Times* (London), 4 February 1935.
5 Charles, *The Development of Industrial Relations*, pp. 83, 92–3; H.A. Clegg, *A History of British Trade Unions since 1889. Volume II 1911–1933*, London, Clarendon Press, 1985, pp. 134–8; R. Darlington, 'Strike waves, union growth and the rank-and-file/bureaucracy interplay: Britain 1889–1890, 1910–1913 and 1919–1920', *Labor History*, 55/1 (February 2014), 13–14; J. Haydu, *Making American Industry Safe for Democracy. Comparative Perspectives on the State and Employee Representation in the Era of World War I*, Urbana and Chicago, University of Illinois Press, 1997, pp. 36–41; Stitt, *Joint Industrial Councils*, chapter 2.
6 Charles, *The Development of Industrial Relations*, p. 82; Stitt, *Joint Industrial Councils*, pp. 47–8.
7 A. Fox, *History and Heritage. The Social Origins of the British Industrial Relations System*, London, Allen & Unwin, 1985, p. 293; J. Whitley, *Works Committees and Industrial Councils. Their Beginnings and Possibilities*, London, Longmans, Green & Co., 1920, p. 1.
8 J. Whitley, 'Introduction', in S. Chapman (ed.), *Labour and Capital After the War*, London, John Murray, 1918, p. ix.
9 Charles, *The Development of Industrial Relations*, pp. 96–8; Fox, *History and Heritage*, pp. 293–5; Stitt, *Joint Industrial Councils*, pp. 67–8.
10 Charles, *The Development of Industrial Relations*, pp. 94–110; Clegg, *A History of British Trade Unions since 1889*, pp. 204–5; Fox, *History and Heritage*, pp. 294–5; Great Britain. Reconstruction Committee. Subcommittee of Relations between Employers and Employed, *Interim Report on Joint Standing Industrial Councils*, London, His Majesty's Stationery Office (hereafter HMSO), 1917, p. 6.
11 Great Britain. Ministry of Reconstruction. Committee on Relations between Employers and Employed, *Supplementary Report on Works Committees*, London, HMSO, 1918.
12 Great Britain, *Supplementary Report on Works Committees*, p. 3.
13 Richard Hyman, 'Rank and File Movement and Workplace Organisation', in Chris Wrigley (ed.), *A History of Industrial Relations 1914–1939*, Brighton, Harvester, 1987, p. 136.
14 Whitley, *Works Committees and Industrial Councils*, p. 14.
15 Patmore, *Worker Voice*, p. 72.
16 H. Gospel, 'Employers and Managers: Organisation and Strategy, 1914–1939', in C. Wrigley (ed.), *A History of British Industrial Relations Volume II: 1914–1939*, Brighton, The Harvester Press, 1987, p. 162.

17 Philip Bagwell, *The Railwaymen. The History of the National Union of Railwaymen*, London, George Allen and Unwin, 1963, pp. 304, 372–3; Patmore, *Worker Voice*, p. 73; Stitt, *Joint Industrial Councils*, pp. 120–1.
18 Whitley, *Works Committees and Industrial Councils*, p. 14.
19 Charles, *The Development of Industrial Relations*, pp. 124–5; Letter, R. Wilson to Sir W. Ashley, 19 January 1918, Letter, H. Eyles to Sir W. Ashley, 29 October 1924. William Ashley Papers, British Library; G. Patmore, 'Unionism and non–union employee representation: The interwar experience in Canada, Germany, the US and the UK', *Journal of Industrial Relations*, 55/4 (September 2013), 536; Stitt, *Joint Industrial Councils*, p. 147.
20 Clegg, *A History of British Trade Unions since 1889*, pp. 270–1; Gospel, 'Employers and Managers', p. 163; R. Hyman, 'Foreword to the 1975 edition', in C. Goodrich, *The Frontier of Control*, London, Pluto Press, 1975, p. xv; A. Pugh, *Men of Steel. By One of Them*, London, Iron and Steel Trades Confederation, 1951, p. 292.
21 Charles, *The Development of Industrial Relations*, p. 204; Stitt, *Joint Industrial Councils*, pp. 137–41.
22 Stitt, *Joint Industrial Councils*, p. 141.
23 Ibid.
24 A JICIRC, Memo, 27 July 1934. UK Treasury, T 162/604/E1067/1, The National Archives, Kew, UK (hereafter NA); Charles, *The Development of Industrial Relations*, pp. 205–10; Letter, General Secretary to J. Gilmour, 2 December 1936. MSS.292/221/1, TUC Collection, Modern Records Centre, University of Warwick, UK (hereafter MRC); Stitt, *Joint Industrial Councils*, pp. 145–53; *The Times* (London), 18 May 1927, p. 11.
25 A. Clinton, *Post Office Workers. A Trade Union and Social History*, London, George Allen & Unwin, 1984, pp. 90–3; Patmore, *Worker Voice*, p. 133; L. White, *Whitley Councils in the British Civil Service*, Chicago, University of Chicago Press, 1933, pp. 3–15.
26 A JICIRC, Memo, 27 July 1934. UK Treasury, T 162/604/E1067/1, National Archives, Kew, UK (hereafter NA); Charles, *The Development of Industrial Relations*, pp. 205–10; Letter, General Secretary to J. Gilmour, 2 December 1936. MSS.292/221/1, TUC Collection, MRC; Stitt, *Joint Industrial Councils*, pp. 145–53; *The Times* (London), 18 May 1927.
27 J. Richardson, *Industrial Relations in Great Britain*, 2nd ed., Studies and Reports Series A (Industrial Relations) No. 36, Geneva, ILO, 1938, pp. 158–9; UK Ministry of Labour, *Report on the Establishment and Progress of Joint Industrial Councils 1917–1922*, London, HMSO, 1923, p. 8.
28 R. Fitzgerald, *British Labour Management & Industrial Welfare*, London, Croom Helm, pp. 25–43; Patmore, 'Unionism and non–union employee representation', 537.
29 White, *Whitley Councils in the British Civil Service*, p. 89.
30 Clinton, *Post Office Workers*, pp. 452–3.
31 Charles, *The Development of Industrial Relations*, p. 204; Great Britain Ministry of Labour, Industrial Councils Division, Works Committee Section, 'Report for week ending 12th June, 1920', p. 1, 'Report for week ending 11th September, 1920', p. 1. JIC186/1920/PSTSII, NA; Patmore, 'Unionism and non–union employee representation', 536; J. Seymour, *The Whitley Council's Scheme*, London, P.S. King & Son, 1932, p. 85; *The Ministry of Labour Gazette*, August 1929.
32 Great Britain Ministry of Labour, Industrial Councils Division, Works Committee Section, 'Report for week ending 12th June, 1920', p. 1. JIC186/1920/PSTSII, PRO.
33 Patmore, *Worker Voice*, pp. 131–2.
34 Weekly Report, London, 30 October 1920, p. 11. C25/*25/2/1/1, International Labour Organisation Archives, Geneva.
35 Great Britain Ministry of Labour, Memo, Establishments Officer, 31 December 1920. JIC 186/15 1920 A465/12, NA; Patmore, 'Unionism and non–union employee representation', 536–7; *The Ministry of Labour Gazette*, March 1929; *The Times*, 12 March 1929.
36 *Gewerkschafts–Zeitung*, October 1931; Letter, Secretary, Research and Economic Department, TUC to Fred Hand, 16 May 1930. MSS.292/221/2, TUC Collection, MRC.

37 Bureau of Industrial Research, *The Industrial Council Plan in Great Britain*, Washington, DC, Bureau of Industrial Research, 1919; UK Ministry of Labour, *Report on the Establishment and Progress of Joint Industrial Councils*, p. 173.
38 *New York Times*, 22 June 1919.
39 M. Hendrickson, *American Labor and Economic Citizenship. New Capitalism from World War 1 to the Great Depression*, Cambridge, Cambridge University Press, 2013, p. 130.
40 W. Catchings, *Our Common Enterprise. A Way Out for Labor and Capital*, Newton, MA, Pollack Foundation for Economic Research, 1922, p. 20.
41 Cyrus McCormick, 'Employees' Representation. Co–operation and Industrial Progress', in *National Safety Council, Advance Copy of papers to be presented before the Employees' Representation Section of the National Safety Council Eighth Annual Safety Congress. Cleveland. October 1–4, 1919*, Chicago, National Safety Council, 1919, p. 11.
42 J. Rockefeller, Jr., *Representation in Industry*, no publisher indicated, 1918, pp. 18, 20.
43 Patmore, *Worker Voice*, pp. 90–1.
44 Hendrickson, *American Labor and Economic Citizenship*, p. 142; S. Jacoby, 'Union–Management Cooperation in the United States: Lessons from the 1920s', *Industrial and Labor Relations Review*, 37/1 (October 1983), 18–24; G. Patmore, 'Industrial Democracy', in M. Dubofsky (ed.), *The Oxford Encyclopedia of American Business, Labor & Economic History*, vol. 1, New York, Oxford University Press, 2013, p. 365; David Vrooman, *Daniel Willard and Progressive Management on the Baltimore & Ohio Railroad*, Columbus, Ohio State University Press, 1991, pp. 38–9.
45 Patmore, *Worker Voice*, pp. 81–2.
46 *American Federationist*, October 1917; Letter, S. Gompers to B. Berg, 23 January 1920 in P. Albert and G. Palladino (eds), *The Samuel Gompers Papers, Volume 11: The Postwar Years, 1918–21*, Urbana and Chicago, University of Illinois Press, 2008, p. 244.
47 O. Beyer, 'B&O Engine 1003', *Survey Graphic*, 4/4 (January 1924), 313.
48 O. Beyer, 'Union–Management Cooperation in the Railroad Industry', *Proceedings of the Academy of Political Science*, 13/1 (June 1928), 124–7; L. Wood, *Union–Management Cooperation on the Railroads*, New Haven, Yale University Press, 1931, pp. 106–9, 113–15.
49 Letter, B. Jewell to J. Corbett, 27 September 1927. File – 'Correspondence, 1927', Container 70, Otto S. Beyer Papers, MS12633, Library of Congress, Washington, DC.
50 Patmore, *Worker Voice*, pp. 109–14, 185–9.
51 G. Kealey, *Workers and Canadian History*, Montreal, McGill–Queens University Press, 1995, p. 295; G. Patmore, 'Employee Representation Plans in the United States, Canada, and Australia: An Employer Response to Workplace Democracy', *Labor*, 3/2 (Summer 2006), 51.
52 Kealey, *Workers and Canadian History*, p. 289; J. Naylor, *The New Democracy. Challenging The Social Order in Industrial Ontario*, Toronto, University of Toronto Press, 1991, pp. 160–2.
53 Canada, Department of Labour, *Report of the Royal Commission*, Supplement to *Labour Gazette* (Canada), December 1919; Kealey, *Workers and Canadian History*, p. 289; Naylor, *The New Democracy*, pp. 162–4, 188.
54 Naylor, *The New Democracy*, p. 164.
55 Canada. Department of Labour, *Report of a Conference on Industrial Relations held at Ottawa. February 21st and 22nd, 1921*, Bulletin No. 2, Industrial Relations Series, Ottawa, pp. 18–23, 164–5; Margaret McCallum, 'Corporate Welfarism in Canada, 1919–1939', *Canadian Historical Review*, 71/1 (March 1990), 59; Naylor, *The New Democracy*, pp. 192–6.
56 Canada. Department of Labour, *Industrial Relations Conference*, p. vii.
57 Canada. Department of Labour, *Joint Councils in Industry*, Bulletin No. 1, Industrial Relations Series, Ottawa, 1921, p. 8; McCallum, 'Corporate Welfarism in Canada, 1919–1939', 60; Naylor, *The New Democracy*, pp. 164–5, 185–7, 201–5.
58 Patmore, *Worker Voice*, p. 192.
59 J. Holme, *The British Scheme for Self-Government of Industry; and its Counterpart in New South Wales*, Sydney, Government Printer, 1918, p. 15.
60 Ibid., p. 17.

61 G. Patmore, 'A Voice for Whom? Employee Representation and Labour Legislation in Australia', *The University of New South Wales Law Journal*, 29/1 (2006), 14; L. Taksa, 'George Stephenson Beeby 1920–1926', in G. Patmore (ed.), *Laying the Foundations of Industrial Justice. The Presidents of the Industrial Relations Commission of NSW 1902–1998*, Sydney, Federation Press, 2003, pp. 141–3.
62 Patmore, *Worker Voice*, p. 194.
63 M. Baritz, *The Danger of the Whitley Scheme*, Sydney, Australian Socialist Party, 1919; G. Patmore, 'A History of Industrial Relations in the NSW Government Railways, 1855–1929', University of Sydney, PhD Thesis, 1985, pp. 355–8.
64 Memo, B. Chomley to the Controller-General, Munitions Supply, 8 November 1921. Minute, G. Pierce to the Factories Management Committee, 11 November 1920, National Archives of Australia, A1952, E404/17/21.
65 Patmore, *Worker Voice*, pp. 197, 199.

7 J.H. Whitley as Speaker of the House of Commons, 1921–28

Richard Toye

This chapter describes and assesses J.H. Whitley's period as Speaker of the House of Commons. Whitley presided over a House that – following the General Election of 1922 – for the first time included a large number of Labour MPs. It was his view that, inexperienced in customs and procedure as they were, it was necessary 'to drive them with a loose rein'. This brought him criticisms from some Conservatives for excessive laxity, but others defended him, on the grounds that stricter treatment would play into the hands of the disrupters. On balance, he was probably quite effective in his efforts to guide Labour into the approved channels of behaviour. Drawing on the Whitley Papers, as well as on contemporary press and diary accounts, this chapter will place Whitley's Speakership within the context of the parliamentary and wider political developments of the time.

There were some striking features to J.H. Whitley's Speakership. He had a background in the cotton industry, whereas previous Speakers tended to be lawyers or squires. He was also – although of course no-one knew it at the time – the last Liberal Speaker. (The Conservatives then monopolised the position until the election of Horace King, the first Labour Speaker, in 1965.) He served during five premierships: Lloyd George (to 1922); Bonar Law (1922–23); Baldwin (1923–24); MacDonald (1924); and Baldwin again (to 1928). Whitley's Speakership witnessed the dramatic fall of the Lloyd George Coalition, the first (minority) Labour Government under Ramsay MacDonald and the 1926 General Strike. As his entry in the *Dictionary of National Biography* notes, during the strike 'he arranged for parliamentary votes and proceedings to be produced by emergency means. In reply to a threat to withdraw workmen from the houses of parliament he declared that he would not allow the work of the House of Commons to be interfered with, and would, if necessary, conduct the business of the house without printing and by candlelight.'[1] As all this suggests, it was a rather tumultuous time.

The turbulence of the period should not be overstated, however. Although much was still up in the air in political terms at the point of his retirement from the Speaker's Chair, Stanley Baldwin's Conservative Government did appear to have restored a measure of stability to the country. More than arguably, the tenure of Whitley's predecessor, James Lowther, had seen greater upheavals, including the constitutional crisis of 1909–11 and the admission of women to the House of Commons from 1918. On the other hand, Whitley's time in office was much more eventful than that of his successor, Edward FitzRoy. It might best be said, then, that Whitley's Speakership represented an important transitional phase, one of the most important outcomes of which, along with the decline of the Liberals, was the full integration of the Labour Party into the conventions of Westminster politics.

As David M. Craig has shown, there is no necessary methodological conflict between a 'high politics' approach, focussed on the manoeuvrings of a select number of the elite, and the techniques of the 'new political history', which investigates the culture of popular, extra-parliamentary politics. In fact, the two schools have more in common than is usually believed, and can be brought into fruitful relationship with one another.[2] This chapter therefore seeks to put Whitley's Speakership in its broader political context. (Whitley's role in the commissioning of the Palace of Westminster 'Building of Britain' mural is dealt with elsewhere in this volume.) It considers how developments outside the House of Commons shaped challenges that Whitley had to cope with within its walls. It examines how the Speakership was understood by contemporaries, and the extent to which it was politically contested. Finally, it suggests that Whitley's conception of Liberalism, based fundamentally on the notion of rational conciliation, provides a key to understanding his approach to the Speakership.

Whitley's career as a whole needs, of course, to be viewed in the perspective of the rise of Labour and the decline of the Liberals. As was seen in Chapter 5, Whitley was first chosen as Liberal member for Halifax in 1900 in what was then a two-member constituency. In 1906 he was in tandem with a Labour candidate, James Parker, who was duly elected. This was a sign of Whitley's commitment to the 'Progressive Alliance'.[3] The relationship between the Liberal Party and Labour was soon to come under severe strain, though. In 1911, Whitley became Chairman of Ways and Means and Deputy Speaker. This was a particularly toxic moment in the battle between the Liberals and the Conservatives/Unionists, not least because the conflict over Irish Home Rule was just starting to heat up. As we shall see, Whitley was perceived on one occasion – fairly or otherwise – to have abused his position in the Chair. However, the Deputy Speakership provided valuable preparation for his further elevation, although it did not make it inevitable.

By the time of the 1918 General Election, the Liberal Party had split into a Coalition wing led by Prime Minister David Lloyd George and an Independent one led by his rival and former Prime Minister H.H. Asquith. Lloyd George and Conservative leader Andrew Bonar Law sent a message – the so-called 'coupon' – to candidates they backed. However, who was sent a coupon and who was not was a very haphazard affair.[4] There is, therefore, nothing especially strange about the fact that Whitley was returned as a Coalitionist candidate without receiving the coupon; indeed, he may have actively disdained to receive it. As his only opponent was a fringe socialist candidate, there is no doubt that Lloyd George and Bonar Law would have wanted to see him returned. The Coalition swept the board at the election, but Lloyd George's popularity started to decline quite soon thereafter. From 1920 onwards, following the puncturing of the brief post-war boom, rising unemployment fuelled industrial unrest and calls for extra-parliamentary 'Direct Action', which in turn stoked fears of a Bolshevik-style revolution. In Ireland, the War of Independence raged from 1919 to 1921, to be followed by the Anglo-Irish Treaty, one consequence of which was to remove Southern Irish MPs from the House of Commons.[5] Meanwhile, the partial female enfranchisement of 1918 had been followed in 1919 by Lady Astor becoming the first woman MP to take her seat. Labour secured only fifty-seven seats at the General Election, but added to this tally at subsequent by-elections.[6]

By 1921, the Coalition was certainly in difficulties, but it was not quite on its last legs. In March that year, the Halifax Unionist Association chose a prospective candidate to challenge him were he to decide to stop supporting the Coalition. This was not, we may be sure, because the Association had any great love of Lloyd George; rather, to them he was a lesser evil than the Asquithians, and it seems clear that they feared that Whitley might switch sides. He, for his part, reiterated that his position had not changed since the General Election: 'although he was no coupon candidate, he considered that a Coalition Party was still necessary for the country, and if [re-]elected he would give a general support to the Coalition Government in any steps it might take to secure a sound peace'.[7] Thus he gave out a slight air of detachment which might well have given the Unionists cause for concern about the true extent of his loyalty to the government.

By custom (occasionally breached, but not in Whitley's case) the Speaker is not opposed at General Elections.[8] We cannot know, had he remained an ordinary MP, and had thus had to fight in the General Elections of 1922, 1923 and 1924, whether or not he would have won. It is striking, though, that after he retired the ensuing by-election was won by Labour (Halifax having become a single-member constituency in 1918). There is no evidence that Whitley was influenced in his decision to accept the Speakership by the prospect of avoiding contested elections and thereby prolonging his career. Yet it cannot have failed to occur to him that he would no longer have to undertake the labour of campaigning, which was likely not especially congenial to him. When his name was mooted for the Speakership, an article in the *Observer* approvingly noted that, although he was an MP of longstanding, he was 'not a politician'. True, it argued, he had 'worn throughout his political career the Liberal label; but he is no violent partisan revelling in the clash of controversy'. And yes, he had progressive views on education and social reform, but although he felt about these things strongly, 'he is not a man who would carry the fiery cross throughout the land.'[9]

But although Whitley's patience and judicial-mindedness seemed to make him well qualified to inhabit the Speaker's Chair, his selection, which occurred in April 1921 upon Lowther's retirement, did not take place without incident. According to Ralph Verney, who acted as Whitley's secretary when he was Speaker, Whitley 'was not enthusiastically keen to occupy the position'. He made two conditions, which were agreed to by Austen Chamberlain as Leader of the House of Commons. First, regarding himself as something as a stop-gap, he wanted to be free to relinquish the reins after a period of two years had elapsed. Second, he did not wish to accept a peerage at the end of his Speakership.[10] However, after the government nominated Whitley, Unionist backbenchers, led by Sir William Bull and Ronald McNeill, resolved to put up their own candidate.

The objectors had two reasons for opposing Whitley. The first was constitutional, it being claimed that appointment to the Speakership should not be allowed to become the preserve of the government. This was a weak argument because although private members certainly did have the right to make their own nominations, and the House as a whole had the right to make the final choice, it was quite normal for the government to nominate one of its own supporters. Underlying this aspect of the anti-Whitley case was the broader sense, prevalent at the time, that Lloyd George was operating a high-handed and 'dictatorial' style of government that ran roughshod over the rights of Parliament. The second objection was a personal one. 'It is suggested that an incident in 1913, when the Liberal Government was in danger of defeat, is a disqualification of Mr. Whitley, who was then in the Chair.' (This was according to the *Times* parliamentary correspondent, who found the notion far-fetched.) 'The imputation is that Mr. Whitley on that occasion showed less impartiality than is associated with the Chair, and that the overlooking of irrelevancies in a particular speech gave the Government time to rally its supporters.'[11] An alternative (though reluctant) candidate was found: Sir Frederick Banbury, member for the City of London, who said that he would allow his name to go forward if at least 100 MPs would pledge their support to him. However, sufficient support was not forthcoming, and Banbury withdrew.[12] Therefore, when it came to the day of the election, Whitley's opponents had to content themselves with expressions of regret at the way the issue had been handled. McNeill objected in particular to the announcement in the press that 'The Prime Minister has offered the Speakership to Mr. Whitley.'[13] Austen Chamberlain replied for the government, but Whitley's opponents were 'not much impressed' by his defence against the complaints.[14]

The scene was described by the Liberal MP Cecil Harmsworth in his diary:

> Mr. Whitley elected Speaker nem. con., the proposed Opposition candidature of Sir Frederick Banbury having been withdrawn.
>
> What an unnerving place the H. of Commons is. Here is Whitley, who has been Chairman of Ways & Means for 10 years, going white as a sheet when he is conducted to the Chair which he has so often occupied in a deputy capacity, by [Francis Bingham] Mildmay and Arthur Henderson. In its moments of ceremony the House is very grand indeed.[15]

The dispute over Whitley's selection was a kerfuffle rather than a crisis. Nevertheless, it illustrated the developing tensions within the Coalition, which intersected with virtually antique Tory resentments dating back to the Edwardian years. In other words, in spite of the general agreement as to Whitley's capacity, the supposedly apolitical question of the Speakership was a site of controversy – or a lightning rod for the expression of other grievances. It would be wrong to make too much of this. Nevertheless, as Whitley's time in office progressed, some Conservatives came to feel disgruntled with his approach, and this may have been connected to a lingering sense that (given that they were the majority party) one of their own should have been chosen instead.

The initial phase of Whitley's Speakership proved unproblematic. He was humorous and self-deprecating. In a speech to the annual Parliamentary Press Gallery dinner, he spoke of his fear of going down in history as being absent-minded, telling of how on one occasion, having called a division, he forgot to put the question and name the tellers before calling out: 'Lock the door!' In consequence, 'The Minister of Transport exceeded the speed limit trying to squeeze through one of the side doors. (Laughter).' He also told the story of a new MP who, having had his speech ripped to shreds by another member, plaintively asked if it was in order for another member to contradict him. 'I felt it was my duty to tell him that was what we came here for', Whitley quipped. On a more serious note, he stated his belief that 'the quality of Parliament lay quite as much in the quality of its listening as in the quality of its speaking, and it was in that perhaps that our British Parliament stood supreme amongst the legislative bodies of the world'.[16] The statement of British constitutional superiority was entirely conventional, but Whitley's emphasis on listening was characteristic of his faith in political reason. New developments, however, were soon to raise doubts about the capacity of Parliament to function as a rational public sphere.

In 1922, the Unionist backbench discontent that had manifested itself in the abortive opposition to Whitley's election at last welled up and brought down the Lloyd George Coalition. In the ensuing General Election, Bonar Law's Conservatives won a substantial majority. At the same time, the Labour Party secured an unprecedented 142 seats and – with the Liberals divided and reduced in overall number – became the official Opposition for the first time. As I have described elsewhere, a significant number of the new Labour MPs, notably the radical Clydeside group, adopted a challenging rhetorical style within the Chamber. The party's opponents portrayed these frequently disruptive tactics as a form of rowdyism that was designed to undermine parliamentary government. To Labour's leader, Ramsay MacDonald, this type of behaviour was problematic, not least because he was accused of not being able to control his own followers. But as far as the more militant socialist MPs were concerned, this kind of conduct was an urgent moral necessity, a virile form of rhetorical conduct that was an essential means of drawing the nation's attention to the plight of the poor and the unemployed.[17]

According to a story relayed in the press when Whitley retired, 'when a friend asked Mr. Whitley how he managed to "hold himself in" with such a lot of lively members, he replied, "If you want to know the real truth, I learnt it when I was teaching in the night schools in Halifax."'[18] Labour 'rowdyism' was at its greatest intensity in 1922–23. One of the most notorious parliamentary 'scenes' of the era arose over the issue of the government's treatment of ex-servicemen, and involved the singing of 'The Red Flag'. At last, Whitley suspended the sitting.[19] Nor were the problems restricted to the Chamber itself. Much of the work of the House was done in Committee, and one Conservative MP complained to Whitley of frivolous Labour amendments and of lengthy and repetitive speeches that held up progress.[20]

Whitley's attempts to manage these problems were subject to criticism by some Tories – although not by all of them. A letter from Bonar Law to the King in December 1922 gives an insight into how Whitley's handling of Labour was viewed:

> Yesterday's proceedings were marked by an unfortunate exhibition on the part of Labour Members who indulged in a demonstration such as has not been witnessed in the House for a very long time. . . .
>
> There were some Members of the Conservative Party who thought that the Speaker showed excessive patience which erred on the side of weakness, but the Prime Minister cannot share that view. Probably the true explanation of the demonstration was that Labour Members wished to advertise their cause by being suspended themselves or by bringing about the suspension of the sitting. It was the Speaker's patience which alone prevented them from attaining their object.[21]

The allegation of weakness was reiterated in the autobiography of the Conservative MP Dennis Herbert (Lord Hemingford). Herbert was one of those who had objected to Whitley's candidature 'on constitutional and not personal grounds'. The two men in fact got along well and, bearing no grudges, Whitley soon appointed Herbert to the panel of temporary Chairmen. In his memoirs, Hemingford judged that although Whitley 'may not have been a bad Speaker, he will not rank as a great Speaker'. He referred to Whitley's opinion that it was necessary 'to drive them [Labour MPs] with a loose rein'. He argued: 'Though there was no doubt much to be said for this view, he carried it rather far, with the result that during his Speakership the House tended to get rather out of hand.' Furthermore, 'experienced members of the House belonging to other Parties felt that he sometimes gave far more licence and liberty to members of the Labour Party than to other members'.[22]

Ralph Verney reviewed Hemingford's manuscript and, in a lengthy private letter to him, indicated that he had been aware of the Conservative criticisms of Whitley at the time:

> I faithfully, but I hope tactfully, made Whitley fully aware of what I had gathered; he never resented or took amiss, anything I told him; his treatment of the Labour Party was deliberate, and he was not diverted by any hostile criticism: he was out to help them to take their position as His Majesty's Opposition, though never allowing them to transgress the Rules of Order

or to act contrary to recognized Procedure, which, when necessary, he used to take great trouble in explaining personally to individual Members in the privacy of his Library.

Verney also emphasized that Whitley, 'unattracted as he was personally to social activities and completely and frankly ignorant of London society', had taken pains to restart the tradition of Speaker's dinners and levees which had 'lapsed completely during the last 6 years off Lowther's Speakership'.[23] This is not to say that these events were a complete success. According to the minutes of a 1927 meeting of the Parliamentary Labour Party, 'The Chairman [Ramsay MacDonald] reported that the Speaker had made representations to him regarding the failure of many Members of the Party to attend his levees at the beginning of the session, and in addition, those who were absent did not take the trouble to send a letter of apology.'[24]

In June 1928, upon Whitley's retirement, MacDonald paid eloquent tribute to him in the House of Commons: 'You have shown us in a most remarkable way how to be patient and courteous without being lax; how to be strict and severe without being mechanical and formal; and you have also demonstrated to us, in a way that few of your predecessors have done, how gentleness can rule and how persuasiveness can subdue.'[25] An affectionate cartoon in *Punch* portrayed him as boxing referee, surrounded by leading politicians of the day (Figure 7.1). There is no reason to doubt that the warmth was genuine. It should not, however, be allowed to obscure the tensions and difficulties that had surrounded Whitley's Speakership.

Although it should not be suggested that Whitley always handled things perfectly, he deserves considerable credit for successfully surmounting the challenges he faced. Hemingford may have been right to judge that he was not one of history's 'great' Speakers, but he was certainly an effective one. He arguably achieved more than many of his successors, albeit his opportunity to do so derived largely from the interesting parliamentary times in which he was condemned to live. If he was to some extent responsible for integrating the new Labour MPs into the conventions of Parliament, this was possible only because of the uniqueness of the moment of their sudden influx in 1922. Moreover, although he brought important personal qualities to the job of Speaker, his success was in part attributable to broader factors. In particular, he benefitted from MacDonald's determination to mould his crew to become 'House of Commons men'.[26] In turn, the success of this project was facilitated by the fundamental faith in Parliament that was manifested by even the most radical of the Clydesiders. No matter what the allegations of the critics, the 'scenes' he created were never intended to weaken parliamentary government. Rather, they were symbolic – a sign of a conviction that the House of Commons could be used as a venue for morally forceful rhetorical displays, albeit they were designed to arrest the attention of the nation more than to persuade the immediate audience in the Chamber.[27] In this sense both Whitley and MacDonald were pushing at an open door – if admittedly one with slightly stiff hinges.

It remains to us to ask what Whitley's Speakership owed to his ideological background. A 1927 news-cutting retained in his papers said of him: 'May a Liberal dare to say that he owes a great deal to his Liberalism? He is eminently reasonable without expecting in other people an equal grasp of the principles of reason, yet with a profound faith in the essential reasonableness of the human species.'[28] We need not assume that Whitley on all occasions fully lived up to such noble principles – and certainly many other Liberals spectacularly failed to do so – but the comment does offer an insight into his political approach. Many Liberals of the period saw Liberalism less as a specific set of policies than as an approach to political problem-solving or as a mindset; that is to say a way *doing politics*.[29] Whitley's powerful sense of duty, which was connected to his roots in Halifax civic life, was thus connected to a Liberal creed based on the notion of rational conciliation. This made him a cooperative, consensual figure who believed in progress without being a 'hot gospeller' for it.[30] There was therefore a link between his belief in the Edwardian-era Progressive Alliance, the development of the Whitley Councils, his cautious support for Coalition Liberalism, and his emollient Speakership. Indeed, his career and his Speakership can be taken to represent the persistence of Liberal ideology and influence beyond the

Figure 7.1 Punch Cartoon: Raven-Hill, Leonard. *The Referee's Farewell*. (Reproduced with permission of Punch Ltd, www.punch.co.uk.)

point where the Liberal Party itself entered near-terminal decline. Whitley can therefore be seen as an early embodiment of what has been termed 'the strange survival of Liberal England.'[31]

Notes

1. H.J. Wilson, 'Whitley, John Henry (1866–1935)', rev. Mark Pottle, *Oxford Dictionary of National Biography*, Oxford, Oxford University Press, 2004 [http://www.oxforddnb.com/view/article/36875, accessed 25 October 2016].
2. David M. Craig, '"High Politics" and the "New Political History"', *Historical Journal*, 53/2 (June 2010), 453–75.
3. Patricia A Dawson, 'Liberalism and the challenge of Labour: the 1906 progressive election in Halifax', *Transactions of the Halifax Antiquarian Society* (1994), 107–24.
4. Trevor Wilson, *The Downfall of the Liberal Party 1914–1935*, London, Collins, 1966, pp. 157–9.
5. Given that the Sinn Féin MPs elected in 1918 had declined to take their seats, the immediate impact on the atmosphere of the House of Commons was not great.
6. Kenneth O. Morgan, *Consensus and Disunity: The Lloyd George Coalition Government 1918–1922*, Oxford, Clarendon Press, 1979, p. 43.
7. 'Mr. Whitley's Seat', *The Times*, 19 March 1921.
8. However, according to one authority, 'it appears that opposition in Speaker Whitley's constituency' was 'seriously contemplated' in 1924. Philip Laundy, 'The Speaker and His Office in the Twentieth Century', in S.A. Walkland (ed.), *The House of Commons in the Twentieth Century*, Oxford, Clarendon Press, 1979, pp. 124–203, particularly 135.
9. 'The Next Speaker', *The Observer*, 24 April 1921.
10. Ralph Verney to Lord Hemingford, 5 January 1945, J.H. Whitley Papers, University of Huddersfield.
11. 'The Next Speaker', *The Times*, 7 April 1921.
12. 'The Speaker's Farewell', *The Times*, 27 April 1921.
13. 'House Of Commons', *The Times*, 28 April 1921.
14. Lord Hemingford, *Back-Bencher and Chairman: Some Parliamentary Reminiscences of Lord Hemingford, KBE, PC*, London, John Murray, 1946, p. 29.
15. Andrew Thorpe and Richard Toye (eds), *Parliament and Politics in the Age of Asquith and Lloyd George: The Diaries of Cecil Harmsworth, MP, 1909–1922*, London, Cambridge University Press for the Royal Historical Society, 2016, p. 321 (entry for 27 April 1921).
16. 'The Speaker's Slip', *Manchester Guardian*, 30 July 1921.
17. Richard Toye, 'The Rhetorical Culture of the House of Commons after 1918', *History*, 99 (2014), 270–98.
18. 'Mr. Speaker', *Daily News*, 4 June 1928, cutting in Whitley Papers.
19. 'Uproar in the Commons', *The Times*, 12 April. 1923. For a similar view, expressed a few years later by a pseudonymous Conservative MP, see 'The Man in the House', 'Inside the House', *The Man in the Street*, August 1926.
20. C.W.C. Oman to Whitley, 8 June 1923, Whitley Papers.
21. Andrew Bonar Law to George V, 14 December 1922, Stanley Baldwin Papers, 60, Cambridge University Library. It should be noted that Bonar Law's letters to the King were probably drafted for him, but there is no reason to think that they did not represent his views.
22. Hemingford, *Back-Bencher*, p. 31.
23. Verney to Hemingford, 5 January 1945, Whitley Papers.
24. Minutes of the Parliamentary Labour Party, 29 November 1927. Consulted on microfilm: *The Archives of the Parliamentary Labour Party*, Brighton, Harvester, 1985.
25. Parliamentary Debates, House of Commons, 5th Series, Vol. 218, 19 June 1928, col. 1597.
26. J. Ramsay MacDonald, 'The Ball Opens', *Forward*, 2 December 1922.

27 Richard Toye, '"Perfectly Parliamentary"? The Labour Party and the House of Commons in the Inter-war Years', *Twentieth Century British History*, 25/1 (2014), 1–29.
28 Hugh Martin, 'Mr. Speaker', 1927 but otherwise undated, Whitley Papers. The publication is not identified, but earlier in the 1920s a journalist called Hugh Martin had worked for the Liberal *Daily News*.
29 Richard Toye, 'Keynes, Liberalism, and "The Emancipation of the Mind"', *English Historical Review*, 130/546 (2015), 1162–91.
30 'The Next Speaker', *The Observer*, 24 April 1921.
31 Duncan Tanner and E.H.H. Green (eds), *The Strange Survival of Liberal England: Political leaders, moral values and the reception of economic debate*, Cambridge, Cambridge University Press, 2007.

Plate 1 Interior of St Stephen's Hall, c. 1910 (Looking East). Note the empty panels are dressed with red flock paper.[1]

Plate 2 Interior of St Stephen's Hall as it appears today, showing the adornment sponsored by J. H. Whitley. (© The Palace of Westminster, Curator's Office.)

8 J.H. Whitley and St Stephen's Hall in the Palace of Westminster

Graham E. Seel

J.H. Whitley, Speaker of the House of Commons, described St Stephen's Hall in the New Palace of Westminster as 'one of the most famous shrines of British history'.[2] On this site stood the medieval royal chapel of St Stephen, the crypt of which still survives. The original chapel was occupied by the House of Commons from 1547 until its destruction by fire in 1834. Charles Barry and Augustus Pugin designed the replacement building. Completed by the mid-nineteenth century, St Stephen's Hall was built on the footprint of the chapel and thus sits on the site that over the course of some 300 years witnessed all the most important parliamentary events in English history and, following the Acts of Union with Scotland (1707) and Ireland (1801), British history too. This was 'the exact spot where many of the great struggles of our Parliamentary history took place – where words were spoken and decisions taken which have ever since affected the course of our national life', according to the poet and naval historian Sir Henry Newbolt.[3] It was the place where, for instance, Charles I attempted to arrest the Five Members; Cromwell dissolved the Rump Parliament; Wilberforce called for the abolition of slavery; and the Great Reform Act was forged.

Notwithstanding the importance of St Stephen's Hall and its resonance with the nation's history, as Whitley's Speakership began in 1921 the Hall stood as the only part of the New Palace in which the internal adornment remained significantly incomplete.[4] Indeed, Whitley believed that the empty panels stood as 'eyesores and reproaches to those who remembered the vision of the Prince Consort in 1851' and he therefore determined upon a programme of adornment.[5] Over a period of roughly six years he presided over a decorative scheme so extensive that the St Stephen's Hall of today is significantly a manifestation of his vision – elements of the glazing, the mosaics above the east and west entrances and, above all, the eight paintings in the lateral panels (collectively known as the *Building of Britain*) stand as monuments to his ambition, vigour and political wherewithal. Yet the lack of adornment in 1921 partly reflected the enormous challenges to any such scheme of decoration – how to identify and agree a theme that animated all eight paintings, and, separately, the two mosaics; how to ensure that the content of any one image did not foment politically motivated complaint sufficient to demand its removal; how to fund the works; and how to facilitate the project so that it would not suffer the obstacles and delays encountered by so many of the earlier decorative schemes in the Palace. Whitley overcame all.

Whitley's contribution to the decoration of the New Palace of Westminster followed a long line of abortive and partially fulfilled schemes. The first suggestion for how to fill the panels in St Stephen's Hall was made by Charles Barry in 1843, who proposed the theme of 'Great Domestic Events in British History'. This scheme never progressed. The same fate was encountered by the Fine Arts Commissioners' suggestion in 1847 that the panels should be populated with scenes of the greatest epochs of the country's constitutional, social and ecclesiastical history, though by the end of the 1850s the Hall had been lined with twelve marble statues of statesmen and a total of twelve statues of medieval kings and queens had been affixed to the east and west entrance surrounds. Prior to Whitley, the most recent attempt to adorn the empty panels in St Stephen's Hall had occurred in 1909, prompted by an offer of £800 received from the President and Members of the Royal Academy to contribute a fresco for one of the panels, the subject to be of any historical or political event. A committee chaired by the then First Commissioner of Works, Lewis Harcourt, set about considering suitable subjects and, having deliberated for almost twelve months, published their preferred subjects for the eight panels in April 1910.[6] This list was then sent to the Royal Academy who selected Andrew Gow RA to choose and paint one of the eight subjects. Gow selected *Holles and Valentine holding down the Speaker in his Chair*, and the painting was successfully installed in December 1912. Thereafter, however, the scheme lost momentum with Harcourt's translation to the position of Colonial Secretary and the onset of the First World War, by which time the only other painting to have been added was John Seymour Lucas's *Flight of the Five Members*, even though this subject had not been nominated by the committee.[7] In 1920 a bastardised version of the scheme momentarily spluttered into life with the addition of Frank Salisbury's *The Burial of the Unknown Warrior in Westminster Abbey* in 1920, a moving representation of the human cost of the First World War, but which engaged in no dialogue with the two existing paintings in the Hall. Whitley thus inherited a scheme that had been neither substantially implemented nor formally terminated. Moreover, it had drifted from the theme expressed in 1910 and was now composed of three paintings that articulated no common message and whose presence presented a greater challenge to any new scheme of adornment than if all the eight panels had been empty.

Whitley thus devised a particular way forward, displaying a shrewd awareness of how earlier schemes of adornment had foundered on the dual rocks of cacophonous committees and pouting public opinion, the latter frequently empowered by the knowledge that public funds were being expended. Henceforth, Whitley determined that finance was to be obtained wholly from private donors; that progress was to be driven forward by a coterie of individuals rather than a formal committee and the painters were to be overseen by a masterpainter answerable to Whitley, though not in a way that was obvious to interested parties looking in from the outside.[8] Whitley was almost certainly aware of Melbourne's famous lament: 'God help the minister that meddles with Art . . . He will get the whole Academy on his back.'⁹ As he told Sir Lionel Earle, permanent secretary to the Office of Works (1912–33), 'I want to avoid the use of the pernicious word "committee" in matter[s] of art'.¹⁰ Whitley thus advanced his ideas in the first instance only with Lords Crawford and Peel, Chairman of the Royal Fine Arts Commission and First Commissioner of Works respectively.

In avoiding a formal committee, Whitley deprived historians of the benefit of a formal and accessible written record of the project, so instead the story of the decoration of St Stephen's Hall has to be reconstructed through private letters and through the debates and Question and Answer sessions in the Commons. 'I am arranging for a friendly question to be put down by Sir Martin Conway on Monday next', wrote Earle to Stamfordham, private secretary to George V, on 15 December 1925, 'which will enable our representative in the House, Captain Hacking, to answer the question – the answer to which I have drafted, and which both the First Commissioner and Captain Hacking and the Speaker approve'.¹¹ In fact, in this instance Earle had rather elevated his contribution to proceedings as indicated by a later letter in which he thanked the Speaker for his 'suggested alterations [to the first draft of responses to be given by Conway] which I think a great improvement'.¹²

By adopting this *modus operandi*, Whitley was borrowing significantly from an example set by Harcourt's successful decoration of the six lateral panels in the East Corridor in 1908–10. On that occasion Harcourt had argued powerfully that 'my experience is that Advisory Committees seldom do anything, and what they do is almost invariably a compromise and certainly wrong'.¹³ In imitation of the private support for mural painting that had been pioneered by the donor system at the Royal Exchange, Harcourt had obtained finance for each of the panels by personally approaching members of the Lords. This tactic ensured a good degree of independence of action – he employed E.A. Abbey as a master-painter to select and oversee the progress of the other six painters and insisted that the scheme proceed in secrecy because, if not, 'all the Philistines and others would descend upon my devoted head'.¹⁴

Whitley's extraordinary ability to raise private funds vindicated his decision to dispense with a formal committee and expedited progress. As early as October 1923 he had managed to encourage two donations, each of £1,500, to deliver the mosaics above the east and west entrances, prompting Crawford to assure Whitley '[that] private benefactions being responsible, you are at complete liberty to employ [Robert] Anning Bell should the donors approve'.¹⁵ At the unveiling ceremony in 1926 it was remarked that 'to [the Speaker's] efforts is due entirely the collection of funds necessary for carrying out the work.'¹⁶ In January 1925 Whitley informed Peel that 'Lord Devonport whom I have seen today promises 3,000 guineas . . . and makes no condition of any kind . . . This will provide two panels [for the *Building of Britain* scheme] and the fee of the chief painter [i.e. Sir D.Y. Cameron]. I hope I can find six other donors without much trouble.'¹⁷ Later in the same month, breezily espoused in the form of a footnote in a letter to Earle, Whitley informed his correspondent that 'I now have promised £4,400'.¹⁸ Before the end of April Lord Derby had promised

£1,250. At some point the Duke of Bedford had also been persuaded to sponsor a panel, no mean feat if the testimony of his grandson is to be believed: 'my grandfather lived a completely lonely and austere life . . . He had very little time for human beings and rarely spoke.'[19] In January 1926 Whitley reported to Earle that he had seen Lord Fitzalan and that he 'is very much attracted by the suggestion that one panel should come from the Howards'. He asked to reserve Sir Thomas More and Richard the Lionheart 'as the ones that would have special interest for a Catholic family'.[20] As early as February 1925 Earle felt motivated to congratulate the Speaker 'on having had such a substantial success on the question of contributions'.[21] In a display of uncharacteristic awe tinged with bewilderment, Crawford remarked that the Speaker 'has facilities which he alone knows how to exercise of impressing donors with the importance of contributing towards the decoration of the Palace of Westminster'.[22] It is not clear by what date the *Building of Britain* scheme was fully funded but, as Whitley put it in his notes for the Prime Minister on the occasion of the unveiling, 'all the pictures were the gifts of generous donors who have come forward at the appeal of the Speaker'.[23]

Remarkably, at the same time as raising monies for the mosaics and the *Building of Britain* scheme, Whitley was also concerned with funding the re-glazing of windows in St Stephen's Hall, which had been noticed as 'bulging etc,' and about which the artists working on canvases for the eight panels had said that 'they feared that their pictures were going to be detrimentally affected by the vulgarity and badness of the glass'.[24] It betrays something of the confidence that others had in Whitley's ability to raise monies that Earle was able casually to enquire whether the Speaker would be able to get a donor to present replacement windows, to which Whitley immediately promised that he would 'set about trying to get a donor for the new windows . . . and will set the figure at £3000'.[25] This figure was roughly twice the estimated cost of refurbishment, a consequence of the Speaker's personal ambition to re-glaze the windows by installing grisaille – as had been done successfully in the Royal Gallery – and about which Sir Frank Baines had cautioned that 'the expense of this would be very great'.[26] Nonetheless, even before the passing of one month, it was reported that 'the Speaker, with his usual activity, [has] approached Lord Bearsted who was too ill to attend to such matters and he has since approached Lord Cowdray, and succeeded in getting £3,000 to renew this glass'.[27] The proposed installation of new glazing proved problematic, however, each of the artists arguing that they had designed their compositions to match the light thrown by the existing windows. Thus a much simpler scheme involving the redisposition of the existing 150 glazed armorial shields rather than any larger refurbishment involving a new row and rearrangement was agreed, to be effected by Anning Bell working in consultation with Sir D.Y. Cameron.[28] Ultimately, upon installation of their work, 'the painters were one and all of [the] opinion that the light is quite satisfactory and that no alteration in the glass is called for in respect of the quality of the light'.[29] This thwarted the Speaker's desire to install grisaille, though some minor modification took place with the application of a stippling and flattening coat of distemper on the lower tier of glass in an attempt to dampen the crudeness of the reds and yellows. It is not clear what happened to the Cowdray bequest, though it may have helped constitute what from 1928 became known as the Speaker's Fund, devoted primarily, but not exclusively, to the purchase of works of art having a close connection with the House.[30]

Whitley's contribution to determining the appearance and style of the decoration of St Stephen's Hall is on the same scale of importance as his money-raising wherewithal, though since it would have been impolitic for the Speaker to involve himself ostentatiously in defining the character of any such scheme some of the available evidence is necessarily rather opaque. The Speaker's affinity with the historical resonances of the fabric of the Palace of Westminster is nonetheless evident from an early stage. In an abortive attempt in 1924 to fill the west entrance panel facing Westminster Hall, he had instructed Sir Frank Baines, architect and leading architectural preservationist, to 'gather the available material with regard to historic incidents connected with the Great Hall, in consultation with W. Galbraith of the Record Office'.[31] As early as October 1923 the Speaker suggested that mosaics be installed in the two vacant panels above the entrances to the Hall. 'I have nothing but admiration for your idea about having the secular subject over the western door, and St Stephen with his two attendant Kings over the eastern door, and therefore in close proximity to the original altar', wrote Crawford.[32] In terms of determining the detailed composition of the mosaics, Whitley told John Baird, First Commissioner of Works (1922–24), that 'I have come to the conclusion that the best course would be to invite [Robert] Anning Bell to submit designs.'[33] It was a good choice and work on the mosaics proceeded briskly because Anning Bell had 'gathered round him a little atelier of setters, familiar with his style and upon whom he can implicitly rely'.[34] An Office of Works memo notes how 'the completion of the . . . panels owes much to the initiative of Mr Speaker [Whitley] and the enlightened artistic interest he has shown in the work.'[35] The mosaic at the east end was unveiled on 5 May 1925; that at the west end on 21 October 1926.

With the scheme for the mosaics above the entrances in the east and west ends of the Hall underway, Whitley turned his attention to the eight lateral panels below the windows. This task necessitated expanding the coterie. Thus, alongside Peel and Crawford, Whitley nominated Sir Henry Newbolt 'to be chief adviser on the historical side'.[36] Though Newbolt was more of a poet than a historian, Peel approved of the choice, commenting that 'it is known that [Newbolt] is prepared to consult the regular historians and there [will] be less danger of rivalry than if one of these gentlemen was chosen as advisor'.[37] The selection of artists was devolved to Sir D.Y. Cameron, one of the best-known painters in England as well as Scotland and whose work had been critically acclaimed, who was 'to supervise the scheme . . . and . . . to ensure that the painters should cooperate in making the series a logical and homogeneous entity'.[38] This tactic was to deny the individual painter too much independence and so to avoid the likely disastrous effects that would follow: the example of the recently finished twenty-four murals in the panels around the ambulatory of the Royal Exchange was probably uppermost in Whitley's mind, described by one commentator as a 'hideous result . . . which is a standing example of how not to do it'.[39] By the early summer of 1925 an initial list of painters had been drawn up.[40]

Although Whitley had a political motive to create the impression that he was not dictating the nature and character of the decoration of the Hall, there is no doubt that he was both the driving force of the project in general and that he was also responsible for much of the key detail. These characteristics are especially evident in the *Building of Britain* scheme. 'I had lunch with the Speaker today' reported Crawford in a letter of 11 October 1923. '[The Speaker told me] he has an ultimate scheme, much more likely to cause controversy [than the mosaics], namely the preparations of eight great painted cartoons to fill the lateral panels.'[41] From the very start Whitley expressed 'the deepest personal interest in the work and spare[d] no trouble to ensure success'.[42] As early as 1923 he let it be known that he thought the panels should 'illustrate the development of Order and Liberty through the agencies of Parliamentary Government'.[43] In a somewhat animated letter of January 1925 he announced that 'the vision takes form' and presented a draft set of terms of reference for Newbolt and Cameron to work from, asserting that 'actual historical scenes should be adopted and the appropriate medium is undoubtedly painting'.[44] Later in 1925 he again made it clear that he thought the panels should show 'an ordered sequence of [historical] events'.[45] He stipulated that advice as to the historical detail for the panels in St Stephen's Hall should be obtained from the British Museum and South Kensington museums.[46]

Whitley's initial adherence to his ambition that the panels should portray 'actual historical scenes' had apparently diminished by the end of 1925. He told Earle in December that he had 'spent a Sunday hour in jotting down my conception [of how the Hall should appear]'.[47] He now spelled out that:

> what was desired was not to produce a few literal illustrations to the vast volume of our annals, but to symbolize the inner meaning of certain events, to show them as typical and fateful stages in our national growth, our evolution from a tribal state to a worldwide Commonwealth. The theme, then, must be the *Building of Britain*.[48]

The reason for Whitley's change of mind is apparently made clear from a sequence of letters in the Cameron Papers, which reveal a sustained tussle for much of 1925 between Whitley on the one hand and Crawford and Cameron.[49] Described by Crawford as being 'sticky and difficult', the Speaker had for long remained resistant to the suggestion that the subjects for the panels should be based upon a set of broad and comprehensive titles in order to 'humour the painters'.[50] (The titles proposed by Crawford were: 'the Monarch; the Church; the Barons; the Commons; Overseas, Diplomacy, Navy and Army'.[51]) It seems as though the Speaker had been defeated in the debate between the three men. But close reading of the evidence and context better suggests that Whitley's apparent change of heart did not amount to a concession but was more likely dissembling, fashioned to create an impression that he had travelled some way towards the position of Crawford and Cameron in order to maintain the momentum of the project at a crucial point in its gestation. Whitley was using the language of his opponents to appease them, but elsewhere in the same 'jottings' that he sent to Earle he also provided a 'list of the actual historical titles, with the names of the painters to whom they have been entrusted'.[52] Indeed, by December 1925 letters had already been sent to the artists, commissioning each to paint a particular event rather than an historical theme.[53] It seems that Whitley was probably mindful of the fact that he had determined the character of the mosaic panels and, perhaps emboldened by the example set by Harcourt in his successful decoration of the panels in the East Corridor, he may have felt empowered to do the same with the panels in the Hall. In the end Whitley won his corner: the panels expressed recognisable historical subjects.

The subjects chosen – imperial and Whiggish in theme – were undoubtedly a reaction to what must have seemed destabilising change. Indeed, the very notion of 'Britain' in the 1920s must have seemed under threat: in Ireland, Sinn Fein had triumphed over moderate Home Rulers in the election of 1918 and civil war erupted in 1922; in Scotland, tanks and troops were deployed in 'Red' Clydeside in 1919; in India, Gandhi's programme of non-cooperation and his steadily escalating demands were threatening British control of the 'jewel in the crown'; and in 1924 the first Labour government was elected, terrifying many that a party that represented the working class must be revolutionary. Perhaps sensing the end of an era, an astonishing 27 million visitors had attended the British Empire Exhibition at Wembley in 1924–25, and may have felt reassured by the assertion in the Exhibition brochure that the British Empire was 'the greatest organisation of human society that man has ever known'.[54]

According to notes drafted by Earle for the Prime Minister's opening address of the *Building of Britain* in 1927, the precise subject content of the panels 'had been no easy matter and nine months was spent in arriving at a decision . . .; the painters and historians [i.e. Newbolt and those he consulted] decided on the scenes depicted'.[55] Newbolt explains that '[since] it was felt that the later part of [British history] was no very happy subject for the art of today, [it was agreed that the scenes] they were to cover must be the eight centuries which begin with King Alfred and end with Queen Anne'.[56] The available evidence does not however permit the notion expressed by Newbolt that Whitley devolved completely the question of the subject matter of the panels. 'I have no doubt we shall find means to argue . . . with the historical view of the Speaker', wrote Newbolt to Cameron on the question of the subjects of the panels; and on another occasion Crawford warned that 'a good deal depends upon what the Speaker thinks'.[57] Both remarks suggest that Whitley was far from a passive recipient of the ideas of others. Indeed, when it became clear that Whitley did not favour the original proposal for the eighth panel – *Samuel Pepys talking with the London Merchants at Lloyd's Coffee House* – Newbolt reported to Cameron that Peel and Whitley 'will decide' between the two alternatives.[58] In this instance Whitley stated that 'I have not much feeling as between "*William and Mary*" or "*Queen Anne [and the Union with Scotland]*"', but he let it be known that on balance he favoured *Queen Anne and the Union* since he had noted that there was already in the Commons Corridor a small picture of the offer of the crown to William and Mary, evidencing well the typical attention to detail that Whitley expended on his ambition to adorn St Stephen's Hall.[59]

Whitley's close personal involvement in the adornment of the Hall is also evidenced by an occasional impatience and impetuosity, as intimated in a complaining note from Baird to Earle in which the former related that '[The Speaker] knows that he cannot act without Office of Works sanction – but I am glad that Crawford impressed that fact upon him.'[60] There is also a sense of occasional tetchiness between Whitley and Earle, the latter's role as permanent private secretary to the First Commissioner meaning that he found himself increasingly involved as one of the coterie. In one instance Earle felt compelled to tell Peel of his hope that 'before [Whitley] gets his money for [the *Building of Britain*] scheme, I hope the Fine Arts Commission will be in existence', presumably in order to dampen the zeal of the Speaker.[61] Alice Eden interprets this evidence as insinuating that Whitley had a tendency to 'act rashly or without agreement from others', but this is to push the evidence too far and it receives generally little corroborative support beyond an unpopular (and short-lived) suggestion by Whitley to remove the great chandelier in the Central Lobby and substitute eight pendants.[62] For the large part, Whitley ensured that the schemes of adornment moved forward expeditiously and amicably. When necessary he was prepared to make concessions to facilitate progress and to win the bigger prize, as evidenced for example by his giving way on his ambition to re-glaze the Hall in grisaille. Reflecting on progress in January 1926, Earle recorded that 'so far, [there is] no [general] criticism either of the subjects for the pictures, the painters or the removal of the existing pictures – which is all to the good'.[63] But it was not long before the storm broke.

Installation of the *Building of Britain* was dependent on the successful removal of the three existing paintings from St Stephen's Hall, a process anticipated as being 'very odious and difficult'.[64] Indeed, Crawford warned the Speaker in 1923 that this was 'a problem which would make the brain of the First Commissioner of the day reel'.[65] Whitley was thus undoubtedly fortunate that Gow and Lucas had predeceased the removal of their paintings, but Frank Salisbury complained loudly when he learned about Whitley's scheme in the press and the proposal that his painting *The Burial of the Unknown Warrior in Westminster Abbey* was to be 'relegated to the dim inaccessible obscurity of a Committee Room'.[66] For the time being, however, Salisbury's complaint garnered little support, perhaps because it coincided with the controversy swirling around the arrival in the Palace of a painting of Lady Astor and the fact that her portrait had reminded MPs of the rule that no representation of living politicians should be hung in the Palace of Westminster.[67] In addition, Peel's advice to Whitley was clear and helpful: 'I do not think that Mr Salisbury has any ground of complaint . . . [His picture] has no freehold of its present position.'[68] Whitley also overcame the objections of the Duke of Bedford. 'Intensely sensitive of contribution to any scheme where any removals are involved', the Duke now threatened to withdraw his promise of a donation.[69] Using as a go-between Sir Laurence Roper – a colleague of Bedford who had a shared interest in all things Indian – the Duke was reminded that Whitley's ambition was to 'get as many of the great families in the past history of England to associate themselves in the scheme, and was not in any way merely for getting the sum of £1,200'.[70] The Duke duly changed his mind and dropped his protest. Nevertheless, the actual removal of the three existing paintings in 1927 prompted questions and consternation in the House on 27 June of that year, the day before the formal unveiling. It was asserted that the removal of Salisbury's was 'very unpopular'; thorny questions were asked about 'who has the final say in the removal of any gifts by Members of this House to any other section of the Palace at Westminster?'; 'why [were] these removals made without any consultations with Members of the House?'; and 'is there any Committee of Members of the House of all parties to consider the removal of any pictures from one part of the House to another?'[71] These questions, if they had been asked earlier, would have had the potential to delay the scheme, and perhaps even to distort it beyond recognition. But Whitley's *modus operandi* had ensured that the *Building of Britain* had by now achieved an unstoppable momentum. The panels, draped with Union Jacks and Dominion flags, were unveiled by the Prime Minister on Tuesday 28 June 1927 at 11.30 am.

Yet even after the formal unveiling by the Prime Minister the *Building of Britain* was not completely secure. W.T. Monnington's *Parliamentary Union of England and Scotland, 1707* suffered sustained attack because of the subject chosen. Whitley appears to have anticipated some protest at the subject of the Union from those who sought Home Rule for Scotland and had cautioned that the subject should only be chosen 'if the Scots see no objection'.[72] (The Speaker was no doubt keen to avoid a recurrence of the attack on his authority he had suffered during the debate on Scottish Home Rule on 9 May 1924. On that occasion, barely able to make himself heard, he had suspended the debate 'being of opinion that grave disorder has arisen in the House'.[73]) Whitley had nonetheless allowed his concerns to be assuaged when he learned from Earle that Crawford had 'pooh-poohed the idea of any suggestion of trouble from Scottish Home Rulers'.[74] Crawford's reassurance proved hollow.

The attack began only two days after the unveiling. Mr Thomas Johnston, Labour MP for Dundee, asked the First Commissioner of Works 'whether he is aware that the only historical picture in St Stephen's Hall representing an incident in Scottish history deals with an act of national humiliation.'[75] A week later Mr James Brown, Labour MP for South Ayrshire, argued that there existed 'a rare opportunity to get rid of this disgraceful picture and put something in its place which would be more true to history than it is'.[76] These proved only the preliminary skirmishes to a major debate on 19 July. In what amounted to a clearly premeditated assault, Johnston and his allies hijacked a vote on the Salaries and Expenses of the Office of the Commissioner of His Majesty's Works and Public Buildings in order again to attack the painting. Johnston lamented that 'No one can deny that, and if we were to accept without protest a glorification of the incorporated union, engineered as we believe under a cloud of corruption, it would mean that we acquiesce in race suicide.' Brown was also on his feet again and actively sought to mobilise the support of all the Scottish Unionists and the Scottish Liberals so 'that picture would be blotted out. . . . Why should we sit quietly under a picture of that kind? Every time we come up St Stephen's Hall our eyes are drawn to it. They are always drawn to it. One cannot help seeing this Judas thing there. Why should we allow a thing like that to stand there?'[77] That the painting survived was perhaps in part because a latent hostility existed between Brown and Johnston that prevented their effective collaboration, but more especially because Whitley's style of Speakership meant that he administered a surfeit of oxygen so that the quarrel rapidly burned itself out.[78]

Whitley's occupancy of the Chair occurred during a period of unusual political instability and strife. A Speaker who presided over five administrations in seven years, who endured the effects of the General Strike, miners' unrest and significant unemployment and who overcame what one historian calls 'unprecedented scenes of disorder [in the Commons]', knew well how to handle politically inspired debates on the meaning of paintings.[79] In short, Whitley had developed techniques that diminished and defused conflict. Although perhaps amplified by its context, the eulogy given in the House by Ramsay MacDonald on the occasion of Whitley's retirement provides a sense of how the Speaker's style ensured that attacks upon the *Union* painting fizzled out. MacDonald said of Whitley that 'You have shown us in a most remarkable way how to be patient and courteous without being lax; how to be strict and severe without being mechanical and formal; and you have also demonstrated to us, in a way that few of your predecessors have done, how gentleness can rule and how persuasiveness can subdue.'[80] On the same occasion Lloyd-George echoed MacDonald's sentiment when he stated that great difficulties had been overcome due 'not merely to the urbanity, but to the tact, the forbearance, and the good temper which [the Speaker has] exhibited'.[81]

The other painting that endured an assault so fierce that it was for a time questionable whether it would survive in situ was Charles Sims' *King John at Runnymede, 1215*, its protagonists motivated by the way in which the artist had chosen to portray his subject rather than the subject matter *per se* as in the case of the *Union*. Upon unveiling, although *The Manchester Guardian* found 'a hundred touches of brilliant and witty painting', most of the press judged against Sims' canvas.[82] *The Times* complained that 'the colour is imperfectly organised' and that 'the work of Mr Sims falls below the level of the rest'.[83] *The Apollo* described it as 'neither quite cricket nor mural decoration. It is not cricket because the artist has played his own game . . .; nor is it mural decoration because [of the absence] of the static quality which it is the mural decorator's peculiar duty to establish'.[84] By far the most serious and sustained attack was headed by Sir Charles Oman MP, distinguished Oxford historian and very much the voice of the establishment, who asked in the House 'whether measures can be taken to replace [the painting] by a more satisfactory picture?'[85] Seeking to expedite his ambition, Oman stalked the committee rooms and corridors and protested directly to Peel: 'the general colouring of the picture is at variance with all the rest of the series ... dozens of my colleagues ... [have] expressed high disapproval of it'.[86] Four days later he followed this with another letter promising that he could raise a petition signed by 250 MPs to 'clear out the fresco'.[87] The threat to the painting was palpable, and indeed to the whole *Building of Britain* scheme. As Cameron pointed out, 'the removal of this panel would be a very grave matter and lead to serious trouble', not least because those who were antagonistic to Monnington's *Union* would undoubtedly have felt emboldened to try once more to remove that particular painting.[88] The *Building of Britain* appeared as though it was about to crumble. That it did not do so owes much to Whitley.

As the crisis continued to gather pace, Oman had a long meeting with the Speaker, about which he told Peel: 'I had hoped Mr Speaker would agree to some definite move being made at once, to clear out the fresco. But he suggested delay, so as not to hurt the feelings of Mr Sims, Lord Burnham the donor, and Lord Crawford, who had passed the picture as possible.'[89] The buying of time – Whitley had insisted that the painting should remain in situ for twelve months until public opinion was sought in the Spring of 1928 – was a masterly move: it deflated Oman and encouraged sympathetic support for Sims. The painting would thus have probably survived the attacks of its critics, but after the artist took his own life on 28 April 1928 it was henceforth considered too distasteful to contemplate removal of the painting.

Whitley had made clear his ambition that it was important that 'in the Hall, through which tens of thousands of persons pass every year, it is fitting that the appeal [of the decoration] should be direct, so that he who runs may read'.[90] But perhaps the subject matter of the *Building of Britain* panels was an overreaction to the context in which they were produced and their message was not particularly 'direct'. None of the panels dealt with material beyond 1707 and the failure clearly to reference war intimated a lack of confidence, despite the fact that Britain had emerged victorious in the 1914–18 conflict. Most who viewed the panels were not able to discern their meaning, even if standing still rather than running. Upon visiting the murals, Herbert Furst concluded that they showed no 'living, so to speak ... concrete relation to life ... all the subjects seemed remote and hardly in contact with the present at any point'.[91] One MP considered the subject material so removed that he asked in the House whether the artists had known of the miners' strike, a national event which had provided the mood music to their compositions. Upon viewing Philpot's painting *Richard the Lionheart*, the King clearly failed to understand the symbolism and, when he stood before *Magna Carta*, he 'declared that he could not see what Sims' picture meant'.[92] Monnington's *Union* painting was described by Newbolt in his published booklet as an act 'to hold the Empire together', but few viewers seem likely to have perceived such a message and it is equally likely that few fully understood its meaning even with the textual prompt.[93] Thus, it seems that Whitley's aim that 'the story [as told through the panels] should be simple enough to make its impress on the hearts of the visitors who come in tens of thousands through the Hall every year' was probably not achieved.[94] Nevertheless, Whitley insisted in 1929 that 'the real recompense would come when those pictures were, as he hoped they soon would be, on the wall of every school in the Empire, telling the story of the Building of Britain'.[95] Perhaps he was correct. He certainly persuaded the Fine Arts Publishing Company – Bell's – and a number of other publishers to issue reproductions of [the panels] as posters for schools and history textbook illustrations, though quite how extensively these booklets were produced and how penetrative their distribution is difficult to determine. There is no evidence of children's chatter about the *Building of Britain* in the schoolrooms of the Empire, but perhaps that is because such evidence is ephemeral in nature.

By the time of Whitley's retirement from the Speakership in June 1928 the fabric of St Stephen's Hall was substantially different from its form at his accession in 1921. In this transformation Newbolt was undoubtedly correct to describe Whitley as 'the initiator and sympathetic director of the whole scheme [of the Building of Britain]'.[96] It is thus entirely apposite that Whitley's formal portrait, undertaken by Philpot, shows the Speaker at the top of the stairs leading from the earlier exit of St Stephen's Hall with some of the *Building of Britain* panels evident in the background. The scale and extent of the transformation was substantive and significant. Crawford stated that he considered the *Building of Britain*, 'taken as a whole [to be] as important in scale, and in result as creditable to British Art, as anything achieved for generations'.[97] At the end of 1926 Whitley considered the then nearly complete adornment of St Stephen's Hall as 'the greatest scheme of decorative art yet undertaken in Your Majesty's Realm . . . With the two great mosaics recently completed by Anning Bell RA, these paintings will make St Stephen's Hall a real treasure house of Art, in addition to its being the Shrine of British Constitutional History.'[98] Although there is reason to regard these remarks as hyperbole – after all, Crawford was deeply involved in the whole affair and Whitley was describing a scheme that was a manifestation of his own vision and the purpose of his letter was to persuade George V to agree to unveil the paintings – their sentiment was for the large part corroborated by the critics: *The Times* led the way, trumpeting that the project was 'the most important scheme of mural decorations in our time'.[99] *The Spectator*, circumspectly, 'let it be known that this is only one step, though a great one, in the process of beautifying Parliament'.[100]

Whatever the qualities of the schemes of adornment in St Stephen's Hall in the 1920s they are singularly the achievement of Whitley, described at the time 'as the greatest living patron of British pictorial art'.[101] As the Prime Minister, Baldwin, said on the occasion of Whitley's retirement in 1928:

> More than previous Speakers have you exercised your great influence beneficiently and usefully in other directions. Your knowledge of, your interest in, and your love of these historic buildings has made you do more, perhaps, for the beautifying and preservation of them than has been done by any of your predecessors.[102]

It is hard to disagree.

Notes

1. Library of Congress, LC-DIG-ppmsc-08561.
2. TNA Work 11/197 Whitley to Earle 21 December 1925.
3. H. Newbolt, *The Building of Britain*, London, Thomas Nelson, c.1927, p. 1.
4. The statues of statesman (by a number of sculptors) that stand in the Hall were commissioned in 1845 and completed in 1858. The Royal Ancestry statues that decorate the East and West entrances were crafted by John Thomas and the Thames Bank Workshop. Commissioned in 1837, they were completed c. 1854. The empty panels had been dressed with red flock paper.
5. Whitley's address to the R.A. banquet, *The Times*, 6 May 1929.
6. The other members of the committee were Lord Plymouth, Lord Carlisle, Lord Stanmore, The Speaker, Sir William Anson, Mr Birrell and Mr G.M. Trevelyan. The list of proposed subjects was as follows: 1399, Deposition of Richard II; 1523 Wolsey confronts Sir Thomas More in the Commons; 1629 Holles and Valentine holding the Speaker down in his Chair; 1641 the Presentation of the Grand Remonstrance; 1653 Cromwell expelling the Long Parliament; 1780 Franklin at the Bar of the House of Commons; 1830 passage of the First Reform Bill by one vote in the Commons; 1846 repeal of the Corn Laws, Peel in the temporary House of Commons. See TNA Work 11/197.
7. The work was commissioned by Sir Alfred Bird MP and had been intended for the Terrace Staircase. The fact that the painting was repositioned in St Stephen's Hall is indicative of the lack of funding for the Harcourt scheme.
8. In 1883, ex-Commissioner of Works, Austen Henry Layard (1817–94) had sought to revive schemes for the Central Lobby but, as he stated in a letter to *The Times*, 'Unfortunately in England political animosities are allowed to interfere even in matters of art'. A.H Layard, Letter to the Editor, *The Times*, 2 April 1883, p. 8.
9. Lord Melbourne, 25 September 1835, as reported by the artist Benjamin Haydon in *Life of Benjamin Robert Haydon, His Autobiography and Journals*, ed. Tom Taylor, Vol II, London, Longman, Brown, Green and Longman, 1853, p. 398.
10. TNA Work 11/197, Whitley to Earle, 15 December 1925.
11. TNA Work 11/197, Earle to Stamfordham, 15 December 1925. The Question and Answer exchange is recorded in *Hansard*, 'HC Debates', 17 December 1925, Vol. 189 cols 1622–4.
12. TNA Work 11/197, Earle to Whitley, 16 December 1925.
13. British Library, Stanmore Papers, Vol XLIV, Add. MS. 49242, fol. 250, Harcourt to Stanmore, 23 July 1907.
14. Bodleian Libraries, University of Oxford, MS. Harcourt, fol. 256, Harcourt to Stanmore, 23 March 1909.
15. TNA Works 11/277, Speaker to Baird. 'I have £1500 in the bank (on deposit) for this [i.e. mosaics] and given by Sir R. Houston MP (1853–1926); and the Executors of Sir Joseph Walton (1849–1923) have advised that he left £1500 for the other, 15 October 1923.'
16. *Historical Note on the Mosaics at the Palace of Westminster*, Thomas Wilson (private circulation), 1926.
17. TNA Work 11/197, Whitley to Peel, 25 January 1925.
18. TNA Work 11/197, Whitley to Earle, 31 January 1925.
19. John, Duke of Bedford, *A Silver-Plated Spoon*, London, Cassell, 1959, pp. 10–11. William Rothenstein painted the canvas sponsored by Bedford. He was the only one of the painters not to receive written thanks from their donor. He eventually discovered that this was because 'the Duke had never been to St Stephen's Hall to see the painting he had paid for – a truly ducal attitude of beneficence and indifference'. William Rothenstein, *Since Fifty, Men and Memories, 1922–1938*, London, Macmillan, 1940, p. 40.
20. TNA Work 11/197, Whitley to Earle, 30 January 1926.
21. TNA Work 11/197, Earle to Whitley, 3 February 1925.
22. HC/LB/1/106, Cameron Letters, 1925–1927. Letter to Cameron from Crawford, 10 February 1925.

23 TNA Work 11/197. Whitley's notes for the PM, 15 June 1927. Each of the eight artists was paid £1,250 in instalments as the work progressed. Cameron was paid 500 guineas.
24 TNA Work 11/197, Minute Sheet, 17 December 1926; Earle to Crawford, 27 January 1927.
25 TNA Work 11/197, Whitley to Earle, 18 December 1926.
26 TNA Work 11/197, Minute sheet signed by Frank Baines, 14 December 1926.
27 TNA Work 11/197, Earle to Crawford, 27 January 1927.
28 TNA Work 11/197, Notes of inspection made by the artists, 27 March 1927.
29 TNA Work 11/197, Notes of a meeting of the painters, 9 October 1927.
30 *Report of an Advisory Committee on Works of Art in the House of Commons*, Chaired by Viscount Hinchingbrooke, 1955, para. 9.
31 TNA Work 11/197, Speaker to Jowett, 10 July 1924.
32 TNA Work 11/277 15 Oct. Crawford to Whitley. There was some debate about the subject of the western mosaic though it was finally settled as King Edward III commanding the rebuilding of St Stephen's Chapel; the mosaic over the eastern door shows St Stephen, King Stephen and King Edward the Confessor.
33 TNA Work 11/277, Whitley to Baird, 15 October 1923.
34 TNA Work 11/277, Crawford to Whitley, 15 October 1923.
35 Thomas Wilson, *Historical Note on the Mosaics at the Palace of Westminster*. Booklet printed for private circulation on completion of the mosaics in St. Stephen's Hall and handed out at the unveiling of the mosaics, 28 October 1926 by the Earl of Crawford and Balcarres.
36 TNA Work 11/197, Whitley to Peel, 25 January 1925.
37 TNA Work 11/197, Whitley to Peel, 25 January 1925; TNA Work 11/197, Peel to Whitley, 2 February 1925.
38 TNA 11/197, Terms of Reference devised by Whitley, 31 January 1925.
39 E.A. Abbey, quoted in Clare A.P. Willsdon, *Mural Painting in Britain, 1840–1940: Image and Meaning*, Oxford, Oxford University Press, 2001, p. 80; HC/LB/1/106, Cameron Letters, 1925–1927, Letter to Cameron from Crawford, 10 February 1925.
40 At this stage the artist for the yet-to-be confirmed subject of the eighth panel was listed as 'probably Orpen'. Here is the final list of the painters, followed by a short title of their panel and name of donor: Colin Gill – *King Alfred's longships, 877* – Duke of Devonshire; Glyn Philpot RA – *King Richard I, 1189* – Viscount Devonport; Charles Sims RA – *King John at Runnymede, 1215* – Viscount Burnham; George Clausen RA – *The English people read Wycliffe's English Bible* – Duke of Portland; Vivian Forbes – *Sir Thomas More refuses Wolsey's demand for a subsidy, 1523* – Viscount Fitzalan; A.K. Lawrence – *Elizabeth I commissions Sir Walter Raleigh to sail for America, 1584* – Earl of Derby; W. Rothenstein – *Sir Thomas Roe lays the foundation of British influence in India, 1614* – Duke of Bedford; W.T. Monnington – *Parliamentary Union of England and Scotland, 1707* – Viscount Younger of Leckie. The murals, painted on canvas, are each 3.05 m × 4.42 m in size.
41 TNA, Works 11/277, Crawford to Earle, 11 October 1923.
42 HC/LB/1/106, Cameron Letters, 1925–1927. Crawford to Cameron, 10 February 1925.
43 TNA Work 11/277, Crawford memo to the Speaker, 15 October 1923.
44 TNA Work 11/197, Whitley to Peel, 25 January 1925; TNA Work 11/197, Whitley to Earle, 31 January 1925. Interestingly, as late as 22 January 1925 there were discussions about 'decorating St Stephen's Hall with tapestry' and that the estimated cost for eight panels would be approximately £10,000. See TNA Work 11/197, letter from Frank Baines, Director of Office of Works, 22 January 1925.
45 HC/LB/1/106, Cameron Letters, 1925–1927. Crawford to Cameron 29 June 1925.
46 HC/LB/1/106, Cameron Letters, 1925–1927. Newbolt to Cameron, 30 July 1925.
47 TNA Work 11/197, Whitley to Earle, 21 December 1925.
48 TNA Work 11/197, Whitley notes on Scheme for Completion of the Decoration of St Stephen's Hall. Undated but probably 21 December 1925.

49 HC/LB/1/106, Cameron Letters, 1925–1927. Crawford to Cameron 25 June 1925.
50 HC/LB/1/106, Crawford to Cameron 25 June 1925 and 29 June 1925.
51 HC/LB/1/106, Cameron Letters, 1925–1927. Crawford to Cameron, 25 June 1925.
52 TNA Work 11/197, Whitley notes on Scheme for Completion of the Decoration of St Stephen's Hall. Undated but probably 21 December1925.
53 HC/LB/1/106, Cameron Letters, 1925–1 927. See this file for the letters sent by Cameron to each of the artists containing exact historical titles of the subject of their panel.
54 *The British Empire Exhibition*, London, Fleetway Press, 1924 (exhibition brochure).
55 TNA Work 11/197, Notes for PM's opening address. Unsigned but probably composed by Whitley, 15 June 1927.
56 Newbolt, *Building of Britain* pp. 2–3.
57 HC/LB/1/106, Newbolt to Cameron, 18 June 1925; Crawford to Cameron 25 June 1925.
58 HC/LB/1/106, Newbolt to Cameron, 24 July 1925.
59 TNA Work 11/97, Whitley to Peel, 29 July 1925.
60 TNA Work 11/277, Baird to Earle, 16 October 1923.
61 TNA Work 11/197, Earle to Peel, 18 October 1923.
62 See note 55 in Alice Eden, 'Robert Anning Bell (1863–1933) and the mosaics in the Houses of Parliament', *The British Art Journal,* 10/2 (Winter 2009), 22–31; TNA 11/197, Crawford to Earle 11 October 1923.
63 TNA Work 11/197, Earle to Newbolt, 18 Jan 1926.
64 TNA Works 11/197, Letter to Sir Robert Bird from Earle, 18 January 1926. (Bird was the patron of the *Flight of the Five Members* painting.)
65 TNA Word 11/277, Crawford to Whitley memo, 15 October 1923. Whitley's success in removing the three existing paintings contrasts with efforts by some in the House of Lords seeking to replace Gibson's statue of Queen Victoria with a memorial to the relatives of House of Lords killed in the war. Endless committees that met in the 1920s resulted in the statue remaining in situ.
66 TNA Work 11/197, Salisbury to Whitley, 30 August 1925. Interestingly, in his memoirs Salisbury recollects that 'one day [in probably 1920/21], when I was fixing [*The Burial of the Unknown Soldier*] there [i.e. in St Stephen's Hall] the Speaker, Mr Whitley, discussed the question of filling the other panels . . . In requesting me to consider suitable subjects he said that he felt the *The Burial of the Unknown Soldier* would fit in with the idea and should come last, remaining where it then was.' Frank Salisbury, *Sarum Chase*, London, John Murray, 1953, pp. 58–59.
67 This was vigorously debated in the House. See *Hansard*, 'HC Debates', 30 July 1924, Vol 176, cols 2047–9. Salisbury's painting represented George V.
68 TNA Work 11/197, Peel to Whitley, 4 September 1925.
69 TNA Work 11/197, Earle to Whitley, 14 January 1926.
70 TNA Work 11/197, Earle to Whitley, 14 January 1926.
71 *Hansard*, 'HC Debates', 27 June 1927, Vol. 208, cols 18–20.
72 TNA Work 11/197, Whitley to Peel, 29 July 1925.
73 *Hansard*, 'HC Debates', 9 May 1924, Vol. 173, cols 789–874.
74 TNA, Work 11/197, in a note from Earle to Whitley, 29 July 1925.
75 *Hansard*, 'HC Debates', 30 June 1927, Vol. 208, cols 574–5. Tom Johnston was later described by Churchill as 'the king of Scotland'. The notion of 'humiliation' was based on the argument that those who agreed the Union received bribes.
76 *Hansard*, 'HC Debates', 5 July 1927, Vol. 208, cols 1087–9.
77 *Hansard*, 'HC Debates', 19 July 1927, Vol. 209, cols 300–37.
78 '[Brown] bridled what could be a sharp tongue and did not make public his view that a prominent Labour critic, Churchill's future Scottish secretary, Tom Johnston, was "a dirty beggar", or a similar less decorous phrase (Galbraith, 95).' R.D. Kernohan, Brown, James (1862–1939) trade unionist and politician, *Oxford Dictionary of National Biography*, Oxford

79 H.J. Wilson, rev. M. Brown, 'Whitley, John Henry (1866–1935)', *Oxford Dictionary of National Biography*, Oxford, Oxford University Press, 2004 [accessed 9 January 2017: http://www.oxforddnb.com/view/article/36875?docPos=2].
80 *Hansard*, 'HC Debates', 19 June 1928, Vol. 218, cols 1595–604.
81 *Hansard*, 'HC Debates', 19 June 1928, Vol. 218, cols 1595–604.
82 *Manchester Guardian*, 28 June 1927, p. 11.
83 *The Times*, 28 June 1927.
84 Herbert Furst, 'The Building of Britain', *Apollo*, 6/33 (September 1927), 113–19, at p. 115.
85 *Hansard*, 'HC Debates', 21 July 1927, Vol. 209, col. 573.
86 TNA Work 11/197, Oman to Peel, 27 July 1927.
87 TNA Work 11/197, Oman to Peel, 1 August 1927.
88 TNA Work 11/197, Cameron to Peel, 17 September 1927.
89 TNA Work 11/197, Oman to Peel, 1 August 1927.
90 TNA Work 11/197, Whitley to Earle, 31 January 1925.
91 H. Furst, 'The Building of Britain', 114.
92 Newbolt described the King's reaction. 'When he was looking at Coeur de Lion I explained the point about the dates – 11 December 1089, 11 December 1917. He said, "But that was accidental I suppose," and I replied "Yes Sir, accidental – or providential". "Oh!" said the King, "accidental, I think, accidental". (On the latter date occurred the "Battle of Jerusalem", which some newspapers described as the end of the Crusades.)' From a letter by Newbolt to his wife, 27 June 1927 in *The later life and letters of Sir Henry Newbolt*, edited by his wife, M. Newbolt, London, Faber and Faber, 1942, p. 352.
93 Newbolt, *Building of Britain*, p. 22.
94 HC/LB/1/106, Cameron Letters, 1925–1927. Speaker's Draft of the Scheme for Eight Paintings in the panels of St Stephen's Hall.
95 Whitley's address at the R A Banquet. *The Times*, 6 May 1929.
96 Newbolt, *Building of Britain*, p. 2.
97 HC/LB/1/106, Cameron Letters, 1925–1927. Crawford to Peel, 20 September 1927.
98 TNA Work 11/197, Whitley to King George V, 13 December 1926.
99 Although the George V did not unveil the paintings the King and Queen enjoyed a private tour of St Stephen's Hall with the Speaker on 26 June 1927. A reason for the King not accepting the offer to preside at the formal unveiling may have been a realisation that his visit was probably the first occasion that a monarch had entered the Hall since Charles I had attempted to arrest the Five Members on 4 January 1642. *The Times*, 28 June 1927.
100 *The Spectator*, 2 July 1927, p. 13.
101 HC/LB/1/106, Cameron Letters, 1925–1927. Crawford to Cameron 10 February 1925.
102 *Hansard*, 'HC Debates', 19 June 1928, Vol. 218, cols 1595–604.

9 J.H. Whitley and the Royal Commission on Labour in India 1929–31

Amerdeep Panesar, Amy Stoddart, James Turner, Paul Ward and Sarah Wells[1]

In the years after the First World War, the British Empire was at its most extensive and at its most vulnerable. The war necessitated increased British intervention in the Empire and colonies. As well as encouraging nationalism, war also increased industrial development and the growth of trade unionism. The All-India Trade Union Congress was founded in Bombay in 1920, for example. Faced with political upheaval in India, the British government combined repression with an attempt to improve social conditions in industry and in the countryside to counter demands for independence. On the one hand, in the 'Cawnpore Conspiracy case' of 1924 and Meerut case of 1929 radicals were arrested and accused of attempting a Communist revolution and in 1926 the Trade Union Act was passed to regulate and monitor trade unions.[2] On the other, as Michael McNamara argues, 'Continuing labour unrest in India and a British recognition of the importance of addressing its causes, was to precipitate the Royal Commission on Labour appointed in July 1929.'[3] D.A. Low has argued that Britain had a difficulty in maintaining 'two ultimate incompatibles' – the desire to maintain imperial rule while at the same time maintaining liberal ideals of self-government and reform. In this context, J.H. Whitley, recently retired as Speaker of the House of Commons, was appointed to chair the Royal Commission on Labour in India in 1929, which mirrored the work of the Royal Commission on Agriculture (1926–28). Whitley's founding of the joint industrial councils was well known and he had some interest in imperial matters, as was unavoidable for British politicians in the early twentieth century. Whitley was a member of the Empire Parliamentary Association and as Speaker had welcomed parliamentarians from across the dominions and Empire to the Palace of Westminster.[4] In this chapter, we explore Whitley's relationship to India, and what the Royal Commission did in India, including what its recommendations were. Extant papers do not reveal Whitley's detailed thinking on Empire and India and we have relied on the scrapbook compiled and labelled by his second wife, who accompanied him to India, to deduce the milieu of a first-time visitor to India and to speculate on his motives and rationalisation of his role.[5] We have adopted the approach suggested by Antoinette Burton that a sense of 'perpetual insecurity . . . should drive big histories of modern British imperialism rather than serve merely as backdrop to the story of its rise and fall'.[6] We argue that the Royal Commission was initiated in context of the rise of trade unionism, industrial unrest and especially the threat to Empire as Britain struggled to maintain its rule, while it also sought seriously to understand and improve conditions for the labouring poor in India. Burton describes a wave of strikes and other forms of economic disruption during and after the First World War, arguing that:

> Taken together, these labour struggles and the specific cauldrons from which they emerged give a selective yet consistent impression of the extent to which the representatives of British imperialism on the ground were thrown back on their heels in wartime and throughout the interwar period, decades when Britain was struggling to maintain its global positioning under the weight of war debt and the emergence of the United States as an increasingly ambitious imperial power.[7]

In 1928 a memorandum from the Viceroy's Department of Industries and Labour confirmed a twin-pronged strategy in response to the precariousness of Empire:

> Recent labour troubles have . . . convinced us that extremist and communistic elements which have been perverting the course of the labour movement must be checked, but this is not our whole policy, and we are sincerely anxious to devise a measure and method for improving economic condition of Indian workers, which . . . would be the best antidote to communism.

In such circumstances, Whitley's socially concerned Liberalism and approach to industrial relations made him ideal to examine the social causes of imperial precariousness in India. Lord Peel persuaded Whitley to take the chairmanship, telling him that a labour commission in Geneva had recommended reform, through implementation of minimum wages and sickness and unemployment insurances, but, 'Further, there is, as you know, a good deal of subversive action playing upon discontent amongst the industrial communities in India.'[8]

Whitley, the Liberals and Empire

If one listened to the accusations of the Conservative Party in the heyday of the British Empire in the late nineteenth and early twentieth centuries, it would be easy to assume Liberal indifference or even hostility to Empire and imperialism. Yet even W.E. Gladstone, seen as a very reluctant imperialist, could declare in 1878 that 'The sentiment of Empire may be called innate in every Briton . . . It is part of our patrimony . . . a portion of our national stock.'[9] Daniel Gorman explains that 'The Liberal Party . . . turned increasingly to pro-imperial policies after Gladstone's death. Liberal imperialists such as Grey, Asquith, and especially Rosebery, identified themselves with imperial policies in an effort to shed the party's "Little Englander" image.'[10] In a period of imperial expansion and conflict, empire was everywhere. At Clifton College, for example, Whitley was educated in an atmosphere that encouraged adherence to imperial ideals and during the period of his entry into local and national politics, imperialism was widely debated and celebrated, with few opponents of Empire even if many were critical of some of its practices.[11]

Whitley, like most Liberals, thought that the Empire should be held as far as possible by consent and that if Britain relied on the force of arms then it would lose it. In the wake of the Boer War of 1899–1902, he argued for southern Africa's white inhabitants to be governed like Canada and Australia, with considerable autonomy.[12] 'It is better to trust people too soon,' he argued, 'than too late.' His concerns for free association within the Empire, at this stage, appear to extend only to white people. While many Liberal opponents of the South African War were described as pro-Boer, this rarely meant that they were opposed to the Empire. Instead they considered that to strengthen the Empire it was necessary to reform it. In the 1900 general election, Whitley pointed to the collapse of the Roman Empire because of its neglect of the home affairs of the countries it conquered.[13]

On 5 January 1906, when he was standing again as Liberal candidate for the parliamentary constituency of Halifax, Whitley was asked a question that anticipated his later chairmanship of the Royal Commission: 'which is the greatest slavery,' he was asked, 'the Chinese working 10 hours, or the Hindoos 16 hours in the Bombay cotton mills?' The *Halifax Courier* recorded Whitley's response. He said that the difference between the two was that the Chinese in South Africa were compelled to work – 'he could not give up if he wanted' – whereas 'no one could compel the Bombay Hindoo to go out and work'. Nonetheless, he said, 'such hours in those cotton mills ought to be stopped'.[14]

Often, Empire was a national political issue to which local candidates were asked to respond, and most of J.H. Whitley's campaigns focussed on local issues of concern to himself and his constituents, mainly relating to the conditions of poverty in which substantial sections of the population lived. Jose Harris has described a 'surprising indifference among Edwardian Liberal ministers and officials to possible social welfare schemes and economic opportunities within the wider British Empire' and only marginal interest in social reform for indigenous peoples, compared to significant concerns for British imperial settlers.[15] In the Commons, Whitley only occasionally referred to imperial matters and tended to be more concerned with the liberty of labour as well as its conditions in the Empire. In 1903, for example, he looked forward to a time when 'under the British flag no compulsory labour, direct or indirect, would ever be permitted'.[16]

Imperialism in the 1920s

In the 1920s, when Whitley was Speaker, British control of India had come under increased scrutiny both in the United Kingdom and from the Indian people themselves.[17] The First World War exacerbated nationalist grievances and stoked unrest. Anti-imperialist notions within British politics were slow to take hold, however, due to opposition from more traditional thinkers. These differing viewpoints can be seen most clearly in the events surrounding the Simon Commission of 1928. The Simon Commission, or Indian Statutory Commission, was sent to India in 1928 with the aim of studying constitutional reforms and the impact that previous commissions and the 1919 Government of India Act, which expanded the participation of Indians in their own governance, had on the hierarchy of power in India. The Simon Commission alienated many Indian people, because the members of the Commission were exclusively British politicians, and were met in India by organised mass protests and a boycott of its activities.[18] In the aftermath of the Simon Commission, the Nehru Report was produced by an All-Parties Conference to counter the argument that the Indian people were incapable of ruling themselves. It argued for the same status as the white self-governing dominions.[19] In response to this political turmoil, the Viceroy of India, Lord Irwin, initiated dialogue with various nationalist leaders and assured them that dominion status was the goal of the *Raj*, the British government in India. Lord Peel, secretary of state for India, wrote to Stanley Baldwin as prime minister that, 'in view of the troubles that had recently occurred in various branches of Labour in India, it was desirous to undertake, at an early date, a comprehensive enquiry into the conditions of Labour in organised industries in India'.[20] At first an Indian chairman was favoured. Irwin suggested that 'While I do not regard it as absolutely essential that the Chairman should be an Indian . . . I consider it no less important that he should command equal confidence in India . . . If it is possible to secure Whitley for the chairmanship of the Committee, his standing and well-known interest in labour matters would to a large extent outweigh the considerations in favour of [an Indian].'[21]

Membership of the Royal Commission

As well as Whitley, the Royal Commission on Labour in India had eleven other members, drawn from a wide variety of backgrounds. Sir Ellis Victor Sassoon (1881–1961) ran his family's textile business and also served on the Indian Legislative Council. Sir Alexander Robertson Murray (1872–1956) was President of the Bengal Chamber of Commerce, Chairman of the Indian Jute Mills Association and of the Indian Mining Association. Andrew Gourlay Clow (1890–1957) was a member the Indian Civil Service and was governor of Assam between 1942 and 1947. John Cliff was a British trade union leader from the Transport Workers. Beryl Millicent La Poer Power (1891–1974), who was the only female member of the Commission, was a British civil servant and had been a suffragist.[22] There were then six Indian members of the Commission. V.S. Srinivasa Sastri (1869–1946) had been a member of the Indian National Congress and served on the Imperial Legislative Council of India. He had been sent by the government to report on the living conditions of Indians in other parts of the Empire. Sir Ibrahim Rahimtoola (1862–1942) had been mayor of Bombay, president of the All-India Muslim League and president of the Legislative Council. Kabeer-ud-Din Ahmed was a member of the India legislative council. Ghanshyam Das Birla (1894–1983) was a businessman who made his money from moneylending and jute and represented the 'new' Indian entrepreneurs who were 'Indianising' business in the 1920s. He was also a member of the Indian legislative assembly. Narayan Malhar Joshi (1879–1955) was an Indian trade union leader. Diwan Chaman Lall (1892–1973) was a University of Oxford-educated barrister who founded the All-India Trade Union Congress.

This shows a drastic change of approach by the Indian government from that of the all-white British membership of the Simon Commission only a year before. The Commission's members were people who had either been involved in Indian politics or labour conditions in establishments such as textile mills. This might explain why its report recommended significant reforms as opposed to previous commissions headed by British politicians who were keen to maintain the status quo. Whitley, who was considered by his peers to be tactful and restrained, was the ideal chairman of a potentially fractious membership. While Victor Sassoon and Kabeer-Ud-Din Ahmed were to produce separate 'minutes' as comments on the report, both accepted the report and asserted that they 'differed on questions of detail rather than of principle'.[23]

On his arrival in India, Whitley announced his approach:

> India has emerged from the first stage of industrial evolution; and so far as I am able to judge, she seems to have surmounted the difficulties inherent in the transition more easily and smoothly than did some Western countries ... there can be no progress in industry unless that progress is reflected in the conditions of the masses of workers who made industry possible.[24]

The Girni Kamgar Union, recently involved in a series of strikes in Bombay, boycotted the Commission, declaring the 'Commission's motive is "to strengthen the chains of India's slavery", and the Union is attempting to organise a boycott'. However, the Commission's membership and chairmanship by Whitley appeased other unions and it secured sufficient co-operation to compile nineteen volumes of written and oral evidence.[25]

Where they went and what they saw

The Royal Commission undertook two substantial tours of India totalling 16,000 miles. They visited eight provinces of India, followed by a short tour of Ceylon and Burma. The first tour of India took place between 11 October 1929 and 22 March 1930. The Commission assembled in Bombay and they began their work in Karachi four days later. After visiting the North Indian provinces, they travelled to largest Indian cities of Delhi and Bombay. The Commission then investigated central India and the United Provinces. From there, they travelled to the east of India to explore working conditions in Bengal. The final part of the tour was to visit southern India. Before the second tour, the Commission held a series of meetings in London, between 3 June and 31 August 1930. The second tour was shorter and was mainly conducted in the neighbouring countries of the Indian Empire. It began on 15 October 1930 in Ceylon after which they travelled to Burma four days later and they finished their work on 11 November 1930. After completing both tours the Commission met in Delhi to complete the Report.

On their journey, the Commission was exposed to the realities of working conditions in India. Their investigation ranged from the largest employers of factory workers in the textile mills and steel factories, to the smaller industries such as tobacco and paper production. The Report is almost entirely textual, and does not contain any images of the conditions they inspected, but there are sources available which shed light on what the Commission saw when they were in India. Whitley's papers include a scrapbook, compiled and labelled by his second wife, Helen, containing vivid photographs of the conditions they encountered. Similarly the photograph albums of Beryl Power contain numerous photographs, of a sweeper and a water carrier, for example.[26] Whitley seemed saddened and deeply touched about his work in India. Whitley used a photograph of living conditions to illustrate the article he wrote for the BBC's magazine the *Listener* in 1931,[27] which suggests he felt the image was important. In the *Listener*, he describes conditions in one factory as an 'airless box . . . where workers are crowded so thickly on the ground that there is barely room to squeeze'. He continued that:

> Women and children are seated on the earth floor, where they tear or beat with bare hands and iron rods, lumps of dry mud, coagulated blood and other matter from the unsorted wool. No grids or fans to remove the dust, workers covered in powdered dirt and wool fluff. Small children asleep next to their mothers covered in the germ-laden dust.[28]

Whitley and the Commission witnessed the most impoverished conditions in India and their report sought to implement measures that would improve such conditions.

Understanding what the Commission saw is important, but it sheds light on the imperial and 'oriental' gaze on India. Such conceptualisation emerges from Edward Said's formulation of 'orientalism', in which Europeans did not seek to understand the East but to gaze upon it in exoticised fascination which did not honestly encounter difference but consume it as 'the other', regarding it as backward, which justified imperialism (see Figures 9.1 and 9.2).[29]

The Indian members of the Commission, while representative of a variety of business interests and nationalist opinion were not from the labouring classes of the population. The voices of Indian workers were integral to the Commission's findings as nearly 1,000 witnesses were examined in either formal sessions or at their place of work. Despite this, the Report itself has no direct reference to Indian voices heard in the evidence gathering and frequently it was Britons who offered evidence, such as Miss Piggott, reported in the *Sind Observer* as giving evidence on Indian living conditions.[30] In the final report, Indian voices are not included in direct form and judgements were made by the Commission as rapporteurs. This led to some scrutiny, so for example, the *Weekly Mazdoor*, a union

Figure 9.1 Indian Homes in Bengal. (JHW/2/8/71. This image was used by *The Listener* 15 July 1931. University of Huddersfield Archives/Heritage Quay.)

Figure 9.2 Women Workers in Burma. (JHW/2/8/60. University of Huddersfield Archives/Heritage Quay.)

newspaper, suggested that the Commission was interviewing witnesses on behalf of the workers rather than the workers themselves and the *Hitavada* suggested that the Commission in Nagpur examined witnesses who all appear to be in a detached position from the Indian workers and their work.[31]

While the Royal Commission's primary purpose was to investigate working conditions in India, its British members also took advantage of the opportunity for tourism. Whitley, Power and Cliff were visiting India for the first time.[32] The stark differences between the way of life in Britain and in India created an element of sightseeing to the tour, made evident by the Whitley [and Power] scrapbooks. Documenting the interesting things he and his wife saw on his trip for their own personal use, the scrapbook acts almost like a holiday photograph album.

Whitley's scrapbook, comprising photographs, news clippings and various other memorabilia, makes evident the element of an Orientalist tourism for Whitley and the other British members of the Commission. Visiting Indian factories, villages and workers' homes allowed them an opportunity to relish the strange, 'other' way of life of the Indian people. The extent of otherness and how Whitley and others struggled to relate to the experience of the Indian factories can be seen in the way in which they posed at the factories, as if taking holiday snaps in strange and novel places (Figure 9.3).

Whitley and his colleagues had quite a diverse experience in terms of how they enjoyed their leisure time. Helen McCarthy devotes some space to how the Commission enjoyed their free time in *Women of the World: The Rise of the Lady Diplomat*. Focusing particularly on Beryl Power, who was the only female member of the Commission, McCarthy sheds light on how they spent their spare time. Whitley said of Power that she 'pulled her full weight with any man amongst us'.[33] This enables us to deduce that Power's experience was similar to that of her British male counterparts. Power, and most likely the other members of the Commission, enjoyed visiting historical sites, going to the club, playing badminton and travelling to the bazaar to buy local merchandise.[34] This paints a picture of a thriving social life among the members of the Commission who were made to feel at home with their Anglo-Indian friends in their transplanted British way of life. Work and Leisure often functioned in collaboration with each other during the tour, as the many dinner menus and seating plans in Whitley's scrapbook make evident, allowing for socialisation, networking and business to be attended to in a casual and informal atmosphere.[35]

Aside from the seemingly touristic pursuits which Whitley and his colleagues took part in during their free time, India allowed for unique activities for the

Figure 9.3 'Ready for the Mine'. (JHW/2/8/64. University of Huddersfield Archives/ Heritage Quay.)

touring Britons. Included in Whitley's scrapbook are photographs of the team enjoying elephant rides and tiger hunting, showing how the group took advantage of the opportunities India offered them in their spare time (see Figures 9.4 and 9.5). Whitley's involvement in these activities, especially tiger hunting, shows how highly he and his work were regarded by the Anglo-Indians living in India as, by this point, 'tiger shooting for sport was largely left to the VIPs'.[36]

Figure 9.4 Whitley and an elephant. (JHW2/8/49. University of Huddersfield Archives/Heritage Quay.)

Figure 9.5 Assam. (JHW/2/8/56. University of Huddersfield Archives/Heritage Quay.)

Whitley kept a series of scrapbooks across his public career, all of which are very different from the one from his time in India, which has a feeling of exotic adventure about it. The touristic nature of this scrapbook suggests the way in which he and the British members of the Commission viewed their work, relishing the otherness of their Indian surroundings. While some of the members of the Commission were Indian, its findings were largely based on an external view of discovery.

The Royal Commission's recommendations

The Royal Commission's extensive tour and thorough investigation of the industries of India led them to hundreds of recommendations. The *Manchester Guardian* stated, 'From it there emerge 357 recommendations, some for legislative action. But most in the form of advice to employers of labour'.[37] The Commission reported that poverty caused most of India's social and economic problems and that employers contributed significantly to poverty through low wages and working conditions. The Commission felt direct regulation was not always necessary. They perceived that the problem was that the population was not accustomed to factory labour. They considered India to be a country of rural workers, who would only seek factory work if no jobs were available in their villages.[38] While they saw connection to the countryside as an asset to productivity, they wanted to regularise the fluid nature of labour. To begin, they recommended the exclusion of the jobber, who acted as mouthpiece between the employer and potential employees from rural areas and who dealt with employment and dismissals. Jobbers were frequently corrupt and often took bribes. The Commission recommended the creation of Labour Officers 'subordinate to no one except the general manager of the factory'.[39] The Officers would effectively work as a neutral human resource manager and the recommendation affirms that the Commission was seeking the efficiency of labour organisation as a central reform. Other recommendations were that employers should aim to reduce the number of hours worked. The guideline was fifty-four hours per week with a maximum of ten hours per day, with an overtime rate to be paid to workers if these hours were exceeded. They recommended rest days, with at least one day per week or two per fortnight as the norm. Employers were recommended to let their staff have annual holidays with the promise of a job on return. The Commission viewed factory conditions as inadequate. The recommendation was that there should be an annual cleaning of factories and clean facilities such as toilets and canteens. Some India trade unions saw such amelioration as 'stabilising and perpetuating the exploitation of the Indian workers and peasants'.[40]

The Commission were keen to ensure extra provisions were made for women and children. They felt that factories which had a large female workforce should be expected to hire a female labour officer to best suit their needs. The Report recommended that, as with male workers, women should have rest periods in the working day and their hours should be limited. One of the Commission's major aims was to improve the conditions for children, with the working day shortened to seven and half hours. The employer would also be expected to have factory schools and provide a crèche for children under six. They suggested that education in future should also be made available to adult workers. The Commission realised that its recommendations would be difficult to enforce, so they recommended that native inspectors should be hired to make sure standards were maintained. The aim of these recommendations was not only to improve the productivity of Indian factories but attract more Indians to factory work. They show an approach that sought to make sense of the economic complexities of a country with a population of nearly 350 million to improve the conditions of the workers but also improve productivity and capacity.

It is important to emphasise that these recommendations were put forward at an unstable political period of colonial rule. The Great Depression of the late 1920s and early 1930s had a severe impact on the Indian economy. As Bose and Jalal point out, 'The acute economic crisis of the early 1930s provided the context for a revival of the mass nationalist agitations held in suspended animation since 1922.'[41] The Commission was conscious of the combined economic and political situation stating that 'Our work in India has been carried on when political issues have loomed large.'[42] While it detached itself from political considerations, its recommendations were not only made to increase productivity but to contribute to the political stability of India. Whitley was selected because he would uphold the British imperial dominance of India. It is evident he fulfilled the role the British establishment wanted. Whitley received a letter, which he treasured, from Lord Irwin, the Viceroy of India at the time of the Commission, which lauded his contribution. 'I'm sure that India will remember you with gratitude', Irwin wrote, including a photograph of himself in full imperial costume and regalia.[43] Whitley was also awarded the Kaiser-I-Hind Medal for Public Service in India.[44] A.G. Clow of the India Civil Service – and member of the Commission – wrote to Whitley thanking him, as six major pieces of legislation had resulted from the Commission's recommendations.[45] Whitley used this legislation as the basis of his rebuttal of the claim that the work of the Commission 'has been almost forgotten both in India and in England', made by G.T. Garratt in the *Economic Journal* in 1932.[46] Among the imperial elite in India Whitley performed his role well, as they felt the Commission's findings, through the implementation of moderate reform, would strengthen the rule of India. As McNamara has argued the Commission 'led to a number of improvements in the industrial relations area in India and reduced labour unrest in the ensuing years'.[47]

Whitley can be conceptualised as a man of his time, a liberal imperialist. He fulfilled a role needed to maintain the colonial rule of India. Earlier in his career, his views about Empire were of rule by consent and this showed later in the work he did for the Commission. Whitley was an ideal chairman for the Commission. His obituaries praise him for his impartiality and ability to mediate discussions.[48] He lived up to his billing as he settled the conflicting ideas of the members of the Commission such as Sassoon and Ahmed. Perhaps what made Whitley stand out was revealed in his broadcast on the BBC after the publication of the Report. The most striking part is his empathy for the India factory workers: 'I would only ask you remember that all of you have a share in our joint responsibility for India, which was never greater than it is to-day, and that we shall not discharge our responsibility unless we try to understand the lives and circumstances of our fellow citizens across the seas.'[49] Whitley expressed sincere concern and regard for the Indian people and especially its labouring classes, yet his speech suggested that their destiny would remain 'our joint responsibility' rather than being in their own hands.

Notes

1 The research for this chapter and its accompanying exhibition at the Whitley conference in September 2016 (now online at http://blogs.hud.ac.uk/subject-areas/historians-at-work/2017/03/09/jh-whitley-and-the-royal-commission-on-labour-in-india-an-exhibition/) has been an exercise in the co-production of historical research, in which we worked together as a group of university students and staff to undertake the primary and secondary research, with co-interpretation and co-writing drawing together from discussions in a series of workshops. For more on the research process see: http://blogs.hud.ac.uk/subject-areas/historians-at-work/2017/03/09/jh-whitley-and-the-royal-commission-on-labour-in-india-an-exercise-in-the-co-production-of-history/. We are grateful to the Economic History Society for funding Amy Stoddart's research into the Beryl Power papers at Girton College, Cambridge. We are also grateful to Lisa Bates, Katie Langan, Madeleine Longtin and Charlotte Derbyshire for contributions to the research and thinking, and to John Whitley for his support for the project. We would also like to thank the staff of Heritage Quay – particularly Ann Clayton and Lindsay Ince – for their helpfulness and patience. Others in Heritage Quay dealt patiently with a rabble using their reading room and collections.
2 F. Roy and B. Zachariah, 'Meerut and a Hanging: "Young India," Popular Socialism, and the Dynamics of Imperialism', *Comparative Studies of South Asia, Africa and the Middle East*, 33/3 (2013), 360–77.
3 M. McNamara, *A Governor's Raj: British Administration during Lord Irwin's Viceroyalty, 1926–1931*, London, Sage, 2015, p. 138.
4 Royal Commission on Labour in India: Note on summary of Whitley Report; appointment of J.H. Whitley as chairman. India Office Records, British Library, IOR/L/PO/1/38.
5 J.H. Whitley papers, University of Huddersfield Archives/Heritage Quay, especially JHW/2 Scrapbooks.
6 Antoinette Burton, *The Trouble with Empire: Challenges to Modern British Imperialism*, Oxford, Oxford University Press, 2015, p. 4.
7 Ibid., p. 118.
8 Lord Peel to J.H. Whitley, 23 November 1928, British Library, IOR/L/PO/1/38.
9 Quoted in T. Koditschek, *Liberalism, Imperialism, and the Historical Imagination: Nineteenth-Century*, Cambridge, Cambridge University Press, 2011, p. 314.
10 D. Gorman, *Imperial Citizenship: Empire and the Question of Belonging*, Manchester, Manchester University Press, 2006 p. 4.
11 For a sensible account of the impact of Empire see A. Thomson, *The Empire Strikes Back? The Impact of Imperialism on Britain from the Mid-Nineteenth Century*, Abingdon, Routledge, 2014.
12 J.H. Whitley papers, press cutting 29 Nov 1901, JHW/2/3/53.
13 J.H. Whitley papers, unattributed press cutting, JHW/2/2/7.
14 J.H. Whitley papers, unattributed press cutting, probably *Halifax Courier*, 5 January 1906, JHW/2/5/4.

15 Jose Harris, 'The Liberal Empire and British Social Policy: Citizens, Colonials, and Indigenous Peoples, circa 1880–1914', *Histoire@Politique* 2 (2010), 3 [http://www.cairn.info/revue-histoire-politique-2010-2-page-3.htm, accessed 15 November 2016].
16 House of Commons Debates, 19 March 1903, Vol. 119, col. 1265.
17 Judith M. Brown, *Modern India: The Origins of an Asian Democracy*, second edition, Oxford, Oxford University Press, 1994, pp. 231–50.
18 Hester Barron, 'Weaving Tales of Empire: Gandhi's Visit to Lancashire', in B. Frank, C. Horner and D. Stewart (eds), *The British Labour Movement and Imperialism*, Newcastle upon Tyne, Cambridge Scholars Publishing, 2010, p. 73.
19 Brown, *Modern India*, pp. 265–6.
20 Lord Peel to Stanley Baldwin, 17 January 1929. India Office Records, British Library, IOR/L/PO/1/38.
21 Viceroy telegram to Secretary of State for India, 19 November 1928, IOR/L/PO/1/38.
22 Personal Papers of Beryl Power, 1891–1974, Girton College, University of Cambridge.
23 *Report of the Royal Commission on Labour in India*, Calcutta, Government of India, 1931, pp. 476 and 490. Sassoon argued for less regulation and inspection, while Ahmed argued for more.
24 J.H. Whitley papers, unattributed press cutting JHW/2/8/4.
25 Power papers, 'Pandit Jawaharlal Nehru's address at Nagpur Trade Union Congress: Non co-operation with Whitley commission urged', undated press cutting, *Yorkshire Herald*, 14 October 1929. Memorandums sent to the Commission are available in the British Library's India Office Records series.
26 Power papers, photograph album, volume 2.
27 J.H. Whitley, 'Investigating Indian Labour: What the Royal Commission Has Discovered', *The Listener*, 15 July 1931, pp. 83–5.
28 Whitley, 'Investigating Indian Labour', 84.
29 Edward W. Said, *Orientalism*, 25th anniversary edition with 1995 Afterword, Harmondsworth, Penguin, 2003.
30 Power papers, *Sind Observer*, 18 October 1929.
31 Power papers, B 2/2/1 volume 1.
32 'Labour Conditions in India: Report of the Royal Commission', *Manchester Guardian*, 2 July 1931.
33 Helen McCarthy, *Women of the World: The Rise of the Lady Diplomat*, London, Bloomsbury, 2014, p. 27.
34 McCarthy, *Women of the World*, pp. 26, 27.
35 See J.H. Whitley papers, JHW/2/8/48, for an example of a menu saved by the Whitleys as a souvenir.
36 C. Allen, *Plain Tales from the Raj*, London, Andre Deutsch, 1975, p. 99. For tiger-hunting in the nineteenth century, see J. Sramek, '"Face Him Like a Briton": Tiger Hunting, Imperialism, and British Masculinity in Colonial India, 1800–1875', *Victorian Studies*, 48 (2006), 659–80.
37 'Labour Conditions in India', *Manchester Guardian*.
38 For an overview of 'circulatory labour' see I. Kerr, 'On the move: circulatory labour in pre-colonial, colonial and post-colonial India', *International Review of Social History*, 51 (2006), supplement, 85–109.
39 *Report of the Royal Commission*, p. 25.
40 Power papers, *The Servant of India*, 12 December 1929.
41 S. Bose and Ayesha Jalal, *Modern South Asia: History, Culture, Political Economy*, second edition, London, Routledge, 2004, p. 147.
42 *Report of the Royal Commission*, p. 5.
43 J.H. Whitley papers, JHW/2/8/1, JHW/2/81/2. After Whitley's death, Irwin, now Lord Halifax, wrote that 'The Commission was representative of the most widely different views, and apart from the difficulty of guiding its deliberations in an enquiry of great

complexity, the business of hearing evidence constantly called for the exercise of unusual tact and self-restraint.' *The Listener*, 13 February 1935.
44 J.H. Whitley papers, JHW/4/1/95, JHW/6/1/4/3.
45 J.H. Whitley papers, JHW/4/1/96, 5 September 1933.
46 JH Whitley, 'The Royal Commission on Labour in India – A Correction', *Economic Journal*, 43 (March 1933), 168–9.
47 McNamara, *A Governor's Raj*, p. 138.
48 J.H. Whitley papers, JHW/6/1/4/11, JHW/2/7/14.
49 J.H. Whitley, 'The Report of the Royal Commission on Labour in India', BBC Written Archives Centre, Caversham. We are grateful to the late John Barrett for this reference.

10 J.H. Whitley at the BBC 1930–35

David Hendy

And with him light, and understanding, and excellent wisdom.

So wrote John Reith, the BBC's Director-General, in his 1949 memoir *Into the Wind* when remembering the arrival, as Chairman of the Corporation's Board of Governors in June 1930, of J.H. Whitley (Figure 10.1).[1] It is interesting that Reith signally failed in this retrospective account to describe his own initial qualms about the new appointment. Just a fortnight before Whitley turned up at the BBC's Savoy Hill headquarters that summer, the Director-General had filled his private diary with its usual ration of brooding dissatisfaction and suspicion:

> 21 May 1930: 'Heard that Mr J. H. Whitley, late Speaker of the House of Commons, is to be chairman of the BBC. It is very annoying . . . I wrote to the lord chancellor that I was very disappointed. I am feeling very disgusted with the PM.'[2]

His ill-temper was, however, strikingly short-lived. Within a few hours of the formal announcement, Whitley sent Reith a letter. 'May I say with what pleasure I look forward to being associated with you in the great work of which you are the creator', he wrote. 'I hope our association will be mutually helpful in the service to which you have given such unstinted devotion and to which I will bring my very humble contribution in the spirit of an admirer and a learner.'[3]

It was a clever manoeuvre. Reith had a high regard for his own achievements; he was famously thin-skinned. Whitley already knew this, and no doubt sensed the need to tread carefully. When the Postmaster-General, Hastings Lees-Smith, had originally invited him to consider becoming BBC Chairman, he had apparently felt the need to reassure Whitley that Reith's domineering ego would not really present a problem: the Director-General 'was almost certain to be in a lunatic asylum before many months had passed'.[4] According to his own son, Oliver – who would soon have his own distinguished career at the BBC – Whitley almost certainly took Lees-Smith's prognosis 'with a pinch of salt'; he wanted very much to form his own impressions of a man he had only heard about in the pages of the newspapers. '[My] father's way of doing anything ever

144 David Hendy

Figure 10.1 BBC Photo: Whitley, J.H., Chairman of BBC ('August 1931'). (© BBCPhotoLibrary.)

anywhere,' Oliver Whitley explained, 'was to be quiet and bide his time and not to throw his weight around.'[5]

The new Chairman and the Director-General met face to face for the first time on 11 June 1930, Reith worrying – with good reason, it would seem – that Whitley had been 'filled up with all sorts of stories about me'. But, by the time he wrote in his diary that evening, Reith's view was shifting. 'I did not find him as impossible as I had expected . . . he has a quiet dignity and I am not without hope that things will go satisfactorily.'[6] After a second meeting four days later, Reith confided in the diary that this new Chairman 'seems very much to have the right attitude about things'.[7] As the two men sat together in Savoy Hill, they had talked about broadcasting policy in general, and the role of Chairman and of the Board of Governors in particular – 'what he and they should do; about their relationships with me'. Mutual trust was already being established. Indeed, it was the start of an extraordinarily smooth four-year working partnership at the very top of the BBC. 'There was never any unpleasantness throughout the whole of the Whitley rule,' Reith recalled, '– at board meetings, between governors, between myself and any of them'. Was it, the Director-General wondered, all 'a dream'?[8]

Fortunately for Reith, it was not a dream. High politics – and specifically, the relationship between a Director-General and the Governors – has always mattered to the BBC. In 1930, however, it mattered acutely. The Corporation had been in existence for less than eight years, but it was becoming a power in the land. There were already about three-and-a-half million licence-fee paying households, which meant that roughly a third of the entire British population was listening to its programmes. The BBC was establishing a reputation for musical patronage on a decisive scale, not just broadcasting music of various kinds day-in, day-out but appointing a Director of Music to conduct its own newly created – and soon, highly regarded – Symphony Orchestra. It was attracting many leading figures – writers, scientists, historians – to the airwaves. It was forging the art of radio drama through its commitment to regular productions of the classics, as well as more middlebrow fare. It was even starting to build the machinery required for a regular news service of its own. All of this fed into John Reith's grand vision for the BBC – namely that by its commitment to giving people not what they wanted but what they *needed* and would perhaps eventually *come* to want; that by, in his own words, carrying 'into the greatest possible number of homes everything that is best in every department of human knowledge, endeavour and achievement', the universally accessible technology of broadcasting could deliver not just agreeable entertainment but a great cultural transformation, namely the creation of a 'more intelligent and enlightened' citizenry, and more to the point given the recent extension of the franchise, a more intelligent and enlightened *electorate*.[9]

There was something else exercising the Director-General in 1930. Reith reckoned that the BBC might now be capable of setting new standards in how a public corporation should be run. Its own status – a national body licensed by a Royal Charter to act in the public interest, though emphatically not a *state*-run broadcaster – was relatively novel, still precarious. As the government's threatening behaviour during the 1926 General Strike had shown, it needed strong protection and careful nurturing. Handled well, Reith calculated, it could serve the interests of the public *and* of good government: it could be efficiently responsive to the prevailing climate of opinion, while remaining free from political or ministerial or civil service interference.[10] The difficulty facing Reith, however, was that for the past three years or so he had been having to operate with a group of Governors who did not always appear to share his own ambitions for the BBC – and, in particular, did not appear to share his own assessment of the virtues of remaining free from political meddling. Whitley's immediate predecessor as Chairman, the former Conservative Chief Whip in the upper House, Lord Clarendon, had proved especially irksome: 'he is a stupid man and weak', Reith complained. When it came to resisting government pressure, 'I do not see him taking a strong line on anything as required. If he interferes it would most likely be through fear that trouble might come if he did not.'[11] Reith's chief irritant on the Board, however, had been another governor: Ethel, Lady Snowden, a veteran of the suffragette movement now married to the Labour MP, Philip Snowden. Lady Snowden thought Reith's character and ability had been 'overestimated', and had complained to Clarendon about the Director-General's 'overwhelming egoism'. In return, Reith referred to her in his diaries, variously, as the 'Red Woman', the 'Scarlet Woman', and the 'Mother of Harlots and Abominations'. Matters had deteriorated to the point where the Governors took to gathering informally at the Savoy Grill or Clarendon's London home without Reith's knowledge.[12] At its most senior level, the BBC was proving to be dangerously dysfunctional.

Whitley's arrival arrested the downward spiral. The new Chairman simply asked Reith to 'forgive and forget', which the Director-General did. 'Being satisfied that he knew how much he was requiring,' Reith wrote, 'I promised to try; and succeeded . . . The relationship between Mrs Snowden and myself was as if there had never been an angry word or harsh thought.'[13] But if the acute issue of festering relations between the Governors and Reith had been resolved relatively easily and remarkably quickly, Whitley and Reith both recognised there remained a chronic problem: blurred lines of accountability at the top. A strategic fix was required to prevent the same disputatious atmosphere developing again. Whitley, certainly, was keen for some arrangement that would outlast his own tenure. Towards the end of 1931, the pair worked on separate drafts of a statement setting out the Governors' responsibilities, and the necessary limits to their involvement in day-to-day programme-making. Reith's own wording was accepted without demur by Whitley. And, with just one very minor amendment suggested by the Postmaster-General (who was, by now, Kingsley Wood), it became one of the core constitutional records of the BBC – known as the 'Whitley Document', and put in the hands of all new Governors on appointment for the next twenty years.[14] It stated that the Governors' role was to be able to 'judge of the general effect of the service upon the public', and that they had final responsibility for it on behalf of the public. Crucially, however, it also stated that the functions of the Governors were 'not executive':

> Their responsibilities are general and not particular . . . With the director-general they discuss and (then) decide on major matters of policy and finance, but they leave the execution of that policy and the general administration of the service in all its branches to the director-general and his competent officers.[15]

It was the word 'then' – bracketed in the above quotation – that had been inserted by the Postmaster-General. The significance of this insertion was, Reith claimed, 'obvious and unexceptional'.[16] It would be more accurate to say it suited his purposes nicely. Simply put, it suggested that Governors could not initiate policy without *first* discussing matters with Reith – or whoever might one day succeed him. But, in any case the rest of the wording here was clear as could be in establishing the general principle: Governors were not to interfere in day-to-day programme-making issues.

The Whitley Document clearly left the Director-General in a more powerful position. And Reith relished the new sense of freedom this gave him, the freedom to simply get on with the job. He could now press ahead, largely without distraction, on a range of projects: planning the BBC's move out of Savoy Hill, keeping an eye on the technical development of television, dealing with Welsh MPs unhappy about the range of programmes on offer in their homeland. Most dear to his own heart, perhaps, was being able to see to fruition plans for an English-language Empire Service. In this, Reith had little support from politicians – and almost no money to speak of. But he did at least have both the professional backing of his Chairman and a great deal of his personal enthusiasm – for Whitley had a keen interest in colonial affairs through his chairing of the Royal Commission on Labour in India and had seen for himself the ability of radio to banish the isolation experienced by people living in remote areas. When regular transmissions began on 19 December 1932 – with programmes beamed to Australia, South Africa, West Africa, Canada and India – Whitley himself took to the microphone to initiate proceedings. In reality, though, it was Reith's moment: the realisation of his own hard-fought efforts since the very earliest years of the BBC. As one of Reith's biographers, Ian McIntyre, argues persuasively, it was in these early years of the 1930s that 'John Reith was able to give the fullest and most rounded expression to his concept of what broadcasting as a public service should be'. That he could do so owed a great deal to the climate created by Whitley from the outset, and the clarity produced by the document bearing his name.

Yet not everyone working for Reith in the BBC entirely shared their Director-General's concept of what this public service should be – or, indeed, relished the tighter rein on proceedings that Whitley's adept manoeuvring had granted him. The Corporation was not – at least not *yet* – a monolith in terms of outlook and ethos. Ever since its foundation as a Company in 1922, it had contained a heterogeneous collection of people and attitudes. The influential Director of Talks, Hilda Matheson, had joined the BBC in 1926, and when she had first looked around the Savoy Hill headquarters she saw a motley collection of men – for it *was* mostly men – who had served in the First World War and then, as she put it, 'on account of some awkward versatility or some form of fastidiousness, idealism or general restlessness, never settled down to any humdrum profession after war was over'.[17] One of the producers soon working under Matheson, Lionel Fielden, had described himself as 'trained for nothing', 'restless', 'confused', finding the BBC to be a congenial home – a 'port in a storm', as he put it – precisely because the work of broadcasting was still so deliciously ill-defined, so wonderfully improvised.[18] As Reith himself admitted in 1924, 'There were no sealed orders to open . . . Very few knew what broadcasting meant; none knew what it might be.'[19] Moreover, despite his own rapidly cohering sense of what broadcasting *should* be for, the Director-General was often simply too busy getting the BBC onto a firm footing, financially and structurally – in short *politicking* – to keep an eye on everything his underlings transmitted over the airwaves in his name. 'The elemental fact about broadcasting,' Lionel Fielden explained, 'is its tremendous output.' The 'authorities and restrictions and committees and regulations', he said, were 'all defeated' in the last resort by the sheer 'rapidity' of successive programmes.[20] Another pioneering producer from the early years, Cecil Lewis, put it even more succinctly: 'We had the whole thing left to ourselves.'[21]

From the perspective of those working at the coal face, then – ordinary producers and technicians and writers wanting to carry on making programmes with a reasonable amount of editorial freedom – a newly focused, newly empowered Director-General threatened to be something of a mixed blessing. One ominous sign of greater scrutiny from above over day-to-day editorial discussions in the programme-making departments came to a boil during Whitley's first two years at Savoy Hill – though, in truth, it had been simmering for some time. Hilda Matheson, as Head of Talks, was supremely well-connected – with politicians, writers, artists, and, above all, with the Bloomsbury set. Unsurprisingly, therefore, she had always been keen to reflect on the airwaves the widest range of ideas and opinions of the time. At first, one difficulty in her way was that the BBC had long been required by government rules – and very much against its own instincts – to avoid 'topics of political, religious or industrial controversy'.[22] But in March 1928 this debilitating ban was lifted, allowing Matheson to grant more freedom at the microphone to contributors such as John Maynard Keynes, George Bernard Shaw, H.G. Wells and Harold Nicolson. And it was with Nicolson that a particularly tricky problem now arose. In 1931, after he was invited to talk about modern trends in literature, it quickly became obvious that he was determined to recommend books that, from Reith's point of view, 'no decent minded person would wish to read' – specifically, James Joyce's *Ulysses*.[23] Whitley, expressing a horror at this prospect no less strong than Reith's, intervened by asking for the talk to be withdrawn – a step which rather seemed to run against his own principles; Nicolson responded by refusing to continue the series.

A compromise was eventually reached which allowed Nicolson to talk about Joyce but not to mention the book's name. By this point, though, Matheson was at her wits end, tired of arguing with the Director-General, suspicious of his motives and her own future, while Reith himself was increasingly irritated with his Director of Talks, not least because she was trying surreptitiously to enlist support from, among others, the Scarlet Woman herself, Lady Snowden. Four days before Nicolson went on air, Matheson resigned. In a letter to Reith, she attempted to draw out what she saw as the underlying issue at stake. A monopolistic broadcasting service such as the BBC, she suggested, had only two options: to take the middle, traditional, orthodox view on most things, with a minimal degree of latitude either side of that line – a perfectly understandable approach, she admitted, if the BBC's interest was in protecting its listeners from anything too disturbing – or the approach she favoured, which was to make available *all* the most important currents of thought, while preserving a carefully balanced diversity and treating controversial subjects or views with due sensitivity.[24] As she departed, Matheson, and a good number of those colleagues she left behind, suspected that Reith's narrower conception would now prevail.

This unedifying episode was not solely one of a personality clash between Matheson and Reith, then. Their spat reflected genuine differences of opinion about broadcasting and the role of talks which appeared to be coming to a head. As Matheson's biographer, Carney, suggests, there was 'a growing conflict inside the BBC in the period 1929–31', and it was one that 'mirrored the political and economic battles of the time'.[25] The fall of the Labour government, victory in

October 1931 for a National Government dominated by Conservatives, a gathering sense of economic fragility: all this hardly made it a congenial time for liberal attitudes or experimentation. The lifting of the ban on controversy turned out to be less decisive a moment than many BBC insiders had hoped, simply because, like Whitley's arrival, it coincided with this unproductive change of atmosphere.

The BBC was also growing rapidly in size *and* in reputation – and this, too, seemed to be generating an increasingly rigid culture within. As an expanding organisation, the Corporation needed more and more systems and routines, and codes of conduct to ensure that each part of the constantly evolving, increasingly complex machine worked harmoniously with all the other parts. As an organisation increasingly conscious of its status as a national broadcaster – increasingly conscious that it was regarded by many listeners as a guardian of standards in language and taste – it was difficult to avoid becoming obsessed with protecting its own standing by the simple expedient of avoiding all risk of offence in programme-making or policy. The Whitley era was one in which the obverse of smooth-running efficiency could easily shade into something more disturbing, a sclerotic loss of imagination and vigour. Even the BBC's much anticipated move out of the cramped Savoy Hill building and into the purpose-built Broadcasting House in Portland Place, in May 1932, appeared to many insiders to reflect an unwelcome longer-term trend towards greater conformity and professionalism. In his memoir about working at the BBC around this time, the band-leader Jack Payne suggested that the move became associated not only with growth and all the problems that went with it but with a change of mood, even of style. At Savoy Hill, he claimed, the atmosphere had been 'chummy'; now, in Portland Place, there was a regime marked by an air of 'punctiliousness'.[26]

The new, efficient, tightly run, and frankly increasingly conservative BBC had not been created by Whitley's arrival. Nor was it in any way a direct result of his continuing presence. But one unintended consequence of the smoothly functioning senior management system he helped to create was clearly the extra opportunity it granted to those at the Corporation's helm to turn their attention to what was happening below decks – for a hierarchical system of surveillance and accountability, and with it a culture of *cautiousness,* to spread through the organism as a whole. This trend reached a culmination of sorts in 1933, when Reith decided that the BBC should be split organisationally in two, the programme-making division being separated completely from a new 'administrative' division. As Asa Briggs points out in his magisterial history of the BBC, the idea was supposed to be that those engaged in the 'creative' process of programme-making would henceforth be liberated from tasks for which they had little interest or aptitude. But the danger was that administrators who had no direct engagement with programme-making would soon generate rules that had little or no regard for the more intuitive needs of the creative process.[27]

That is certainly how many insiders saw it. Take, for instance, Charles Siepmann, who had already assumed Hilda Matheson's old responsibilities and was at this point in charge of a broader talks division in the BBC. Siepmann was particularly scathing about the new arrangements. His outlook, even more so than Matheson's, had always been distinctly progressive: he wanted the BBC, in his words, to be 'on the cutting edge of contemporary problems and contemporary life'.[28] Now, more than ever before, he reckoned, Reith was surrounding himself with 'yes men'; more than ever before, establishment figures – 'solid, sound and rather conservative' – were being recruited to key posts; more than ever before, 'imaginative' programme ideas were being turned down without good reason.[29] Siepmann professed an admiration for Reith's energy and vision, but he calculated that, whatever outward appearances suggested, the Director-General was no longer entirely his own man: 'strong forces of conservatism' were bearing down on him – from politicians *and* from within the Board of Governors. As an increasingly isolated champion of progressive causes, Siepmann even started to believe that an air of distrust clung to him personally. He suspected, for instance, that a new 'Controller', freshly-appointed to a position above him in the hierarchy – the somewhat mysterious ex-army officer, Colonel Dawnay – had an unhealthy interest in monitoring his activities. As far as Siepmann was concerned, the only problem with Dawnay was that this 'sweet . . . simple soldier' was 'utterly at sea', 'bewildered', 'had no competence in the field', and 'made no contribution of any kind' to the BBC's mission. In other words, he was just one more example of the 'mediocrity' and inertia which Siepmann now detected all around – someone who simply got in the way.[30] As it turned out, incompetence was not the real issue, for the new Controller embodied a degree of surveillance that not even Siepmann appreciated. Half of Dawnay's salary was paid for by the War Office. He also met regularly with senior officials at the security service MI5. The Controller's true role, it would appear, was to conduct an informal though careful and detailed vetting of 'every officer in the BBC' – with a particular interest in detecting any communist infiltration.[31] Siepmann was closer to the truth than he ever realised when he railed against 'sinister forces . . . sinister in their effects on the BBC'.[32] The freedom Whitley had generously created for the Director-General did not appear to be infusing the body politic of the Corporation as a whole.

Yet, in the end, Whitley's decisive support for Reith helped the BBC at a crucial moment in its history by protecting it against the worst excesses of government interference. A supportive Chairman, a largely united Board of Governors, the clarity with which the Whitley Document defined the executive powers of the Director-General and his own senior staff: all this allowed the BBC at the top to present a more united front than ever before whenever politicians poked their unwelcome noses into its day-to-day business – which, in the early-1930s, they appeared to do with increasing frequency. In 1933, for instance, a series of rows erupted over broadcasts about India. Several talks on contemporary political concerns had been planned for the autumn, and on 24 August, Austen Chamberlain, David Lloyd George and Winston Churchill – three distinctly heavyweight politicians, but three politicians who nevertheless no longer served on the front-line of either the Conservative or Liberal parties – wrote a joint letter to the BBC Chairman, criticising their exclusion from the roster of contributors, and complaining bitterly of the BBC's practice, which was to prioritise speakers nominated by the party leaders or whips. In denying the expression of independent views, the trio complained, debates would be reduced to 'regimentations of machine-controlled opinion'.[33] Churchill, of course, had been grumbling about the BBC – and what he saw as its consistent refusal to give him access to the airwaves, especially in relation to India – for years. As for the BBC, there were many inside the Corporation who still remembered Churchill's unseemly desire to take it over and turn it into a government mouthpiece during the 1926 General Strike.

As it happened, Whitley was forthright in his response. He wrote immediately to his complainants, explaining politely that the BBC's decision to select only official Government and Opposition speakers for this particular series did not preclude the expression of independent and unofficial views in future broadcasts. And, indeed, within two months, Churchill had been offered a slot in another series – Whither Britain? – complete with a guarantee that he would be given the maximum latitude in terms of subject matter. An outright breakdown in relations had been avoided, but the portrayal of the whole incident in a celebrated Punch cartoon 'BBSecrecy', showing the three politicians as 'Three Mute Mice' having their 'tales' cut off by the 'Wireless Wife' – a thinly disguised Whitley – captures vividly how disputatious relations between the BBC and politicians had now become, despite the presence of an especially emollient Chairman (Figure 10.2).

Figure 10.2 Punch Cartoon: Partridge, Bernard *BBSecrecy*. (Reproduced with permission of Punch Ltd, www.punch.co.uk).

The role of the Postmaster-General, who might in normal circumstances act as something of an intermediary, was often now a complicating factor. When, in the course of the 1933 row, MPs in the Commons asked the current post-holder Kingsley Wood to use his exceptional power of veto to prohibit some broadcast talks to which they had taken offence, Wood had quite properly refused. But he was, as Reith put it, always 'more party-minded' and 'obviously not so well disposed' as any of his predecessors towards the Corporation.[34]

Indeed, when a broadcast talk with an ex-German submarine commander was planned, Wood put a great deal of pressure on the BBC not to go ahead, on the grounds that it would offend public opinion. He did not use his right of veto, but then he had no need to. The Board of Governors was sufficiently intimidated to insist the talk be stopped – even though Reith himself, no fan of the programme, dissented on principle with the Board's decision. For Charles Siepmann, it was precisely this 'soft power' pressure that mattered because it could be so intangible, yet so pervasive in its effect on programme-makers. He talked later of the 'pressures' and 'warnings' made, of the BBC moving inexorably towards more 'innocuous' output.[35]

In Siepmann's mind, the Governors – even with Whitley in charge – were part of the problem. He would no doubt have been alarmed at Whitley's regular invitation from Reith to meetings of the Control Board, where the heads of department would gather weekly to discuss editorial policy in detail. But Reith had calculated, correctly, that Whitley's attendance would help educate the Chairman – and through him the other Governors – about the Reithian mission, the sheer difficulty of pleasing everyone, the care taken to get things right day-in, day-out – in short, the whole, complex, *messy* business of public service broadcasting. In his diaries, Reith refers to Whitley's presence as providing 'good cover for us': 'one felt certain of his backing in everything'.[36] And a Board of Governors more in tune with Reith and with each other, though hardly conducive to innovation and risk-taking, was surely a more effective shock-absorber between Corporation and Government than a fissiparous one.

The very personal bond of understanding and sympathy forged with Reith was, perhaps, the most striking achievement of Whitley's time as Chairman at the BBC. In 1934, Whitley wrote to his predecessor, Lord Clarendon, who was by then the Governor-General of South Africa. Reith, he told Clarendon, was 'one of those strong men with whom it is a delight to work, and our relationship throughout has been all that one could possibly wish'.[37] The previous year he wrote to Reith himself, reflecting on the alarming forecasts made about the Director-General's sanity on his appointment. 'It did not take me long', he told Reith, 'to discover under the scale a very human heart'. And, Whitley went on:

> Of all the jobs that have come to me in the course of a varied life this last one has given me the most unalloyed pleasure. It is a high privilege to have a small share in the development of a public service so intimately affecting the homes of the people in every phase of their lives, and I am fortunate indeed that this should have brought me into close contact with you.[38]

In return, Reith recorded in his diary that he could 'never be grateful . . . enough' for all that the Chairman had done 'for me'. 'It seemed,' he added, 'that one of his main objects was to make me happy, and if he did not succeed I suppose it was because nothing would make me happy.'[39]

As Whitley's health deteriorated in the closing months of 1934, Reith described these times as being 'shadowed'.[40] He was phoned at 11.45 in the morning on 3 February 1935 by Whitley's son, Oliver, who broke the news of his father's death. 'I am glad that he has gone', Reith recorded in his diary that night, 'because he was so anxious to be off and was so tired of it all. Apart from this, however, I am very sad indeed.'[41]

After cremation, at Whitley's own request his ashes were taken to Broadcasting House. There they rested a moment or two in the entrance hall, just below the gilded Latin dedication:

> *This temple of the arts and muses is dedicated to Almighty God by the first Governors in the year of our Lord 1931 . . . And they pray that good seed sown may bring forth good harvest, and that all things foul or hostile to peace may be banished thence, and that the people inclining their ear to whatsoever things are lovely and honest, whatsoever things are of good report, may tread the path of virtue and wisdom.*

His urn was then left overnight in the religious studio, as flags on BBC buildings throughout the country were lowered to half-mast. In 'Broadcasting House and in the broadcasting service,' Reith said, 'he lives and will live.'[42]

Notes

1. J.C.W. Reith, *Into the Wind*, London, Hodder and Stoughton, 1949, p. 127.
2. C. Stuart (ed.), *The Reith Diaries*, London, Collins, 1975, pp. 151–2.
3. Reith, *Into the Wind*, p. 132.
4. BBC Oral History Interview: Oliver Whitley, 1982, p. 4 of transcript.
5. Ibid.
6. Stuart, *Reith Diaries*, p. 152.
7. Ibid., pp. 152–3.
8. Reith, *Into the Wind*, p. 132.
9. J.C.W. Reith, *Broadcast over Britain*, London, Hodder & Stoughton, 1924, pp. 34, 113.
10. Reith, *Into the Wind*, p. 134.
11. Reith's diary entry for 3 July 1926, quoted in I. McIntyre, *The Expense of Glory: A Life of John Reith*, London, Harper Collins, 1993, p. 148.
12. For a particularly colourful account of this fractured relationship, see W. Sydney Robinson, *The Last Victorians: A Daring Reassessment of Four Twentieth Century Eccentrics*, London, The Robson Press, 2014.
13. Reith, *Into the Wind*, p. 132.
14. McIntyre, *Expense of Glory*, p. 197.
15. Reith, *Into the Wind*, p. 156.
16. Ibid.
17. H. Matheson, *Broadcasting*, London, Thornton Butterworth, 1933, p. 52.
18. L. Fielden, *The Natural Bent*, London, Andre Deutsch, 1960, pp. 56–7, particularly p. 97.
19. Reith, *Broadcast over Britain*, p. 23.
20. Fielden, *Natural Bent*, p. 104.

21 BBC Oral History interview: Cecil Lewis, 1978, p. 10 of transcript.
22 A. Briggs, *The History of Broadcasting, in the United Kingdom: Volume II: The Golden Age of Wireless*, London, Oxford University Press, 1965, p. 120.
23 M. Carney, *Stoker: The Life of Hilda Matheson OBE 1988–1940*, author, 1999, pp. 71–2.
24 Ibid., pp. 75–6.
25 Ibid., p. 63.
26 J. Payne, *Signature Tune*, London, Hammond, 1943, p. 39. See also Briggs, *The History of Broadcasting Vol. 2*, p. 14.
27 Briggs, *The History of Broadcasting, Vol. 2*, p. 11.
28 BBC Oral History interview: Charles Siepmann, p. 4 of transcript.
29 Ibid., pp. 4–14.
30 Ibid., p. 19.
31 J. Seaton, *Pinkoes and Traitors: The BBC and the Nation 1974–1987* (revised edition), London, Profile Books, 2017, p. 300.
32 BBC, Siepmann, p. 10.
33 The letters exchanged are among the Churchill College, Cambridge; CHAR2/198. See also Briggs, *A History of Broadcasting*, Vol. 2, pp. 135–6.
34 Reith, *Into the Wind*, p. 158.
35 BBC, Siepmann, pp. 15–20.
36 Stuart, *Reith Diaries*, pp. 153, 164.
37 Reith, *Into the Wind*, p. 197.
38 Ibid., pp. 181–2.
39 Stuart, *Reith Diaries*, p. 164.
40 Reith, *Into the Wind*, p. 210.
41 Stuart, *Reith Diaries*, p. 164.
42 Reith, *Into the Wind*, p. 212.

11 'Equal partners in a great enterprise': Experiencing radio in Yorkshire in the time of J.H. Whitley

Christine Verguson

> Broadcasters and listeners should be equal partners in a great enterprise. Theirs is the opportunity of harnessing the wireless waves to the best service of man. Happily our British system lends itself to the ideas of partnership.[1]

Why did J.H. Whitley, despite failing health, accept the job of BBC Chairman? Writing to his brother Alfred in June 1928 regarding his resignation from the Speakership Whitley, using words that he later used in Parliament to announce his retirement, felt that he might be capable of 'further service in a quieter sphere',[2] although there was nothing in the short history of the BBC to suggest that this might be an apt description of its chairman's role. But as the *Yorkshire Post* commented at the time of his death, 'He was, it might be said, born into public service.'[3] And if, as his son Oliver claimed, 'the personal qualities, the experience and the public reputation' all pointed him towards the Speakership[4] then it is not surprising that he believed he might be able to contribute to an institution which was committed not only to informing and educating as well as to entertaining but to reaching people within their own home. In a tribute to Whitley at the time of his death the *BBC Year Book* pointed out that 'his association with the BBC covered years in which a gradual but marked extension of the controversial range of the broadcast programmes took place'.[5] Rather than focus on the BBC as an institution and the controversy that Whitley faced, particularly concerning access to the microphone, which has been discussed by David Hendy in Chapter 9,[6] this chapter will consider how sound broadcasting was experienced within the Yorkshire region before Whitley's death in 1935 and the extent to which this reflected Whitley's own understanding of the BBC's aims and achievements.

Radio did not begin with the BBC – the magazine *Wireless World* in 1921 listed eight stations in Yorkshire including 6KD transmitting from Wainhouse Tower in Halifax.[7] The call sign belonged to Percy Denison, a radio operator in the Merchant Navy during World War One, whose father and fellow enthusiast would certainly have been known to Whitley. W.E. Denison, chairman of the *Halifax Courier*, was listed as an 'assenter' to Whitley's nomination as Liberal parliamentary candidate in 1900.[8] But in 1922 the interests of the 'Big Six' radio equipment manufacturers were brought together to form the British Broadcasting Company. In Manchester Metro-Vickers had begun broadcasting as 2ZY in May 1922 and in October it became the BBC's second station. However, concerns about the poor quality of reception, especially in some major cities for those using crystal sets, were recognised by the 1923 Sykes Committee which reported that 'indeed, even with expensive valve apparatus, there are places like Sheffield and Brighton which have difficulty in obtaining a satisfactory service from any of the existing stations'. The committee considered who might run smaller relay stations, whether it be local companies, municipalities, wireless societies and 'other bodies that may undertake the work'.[9] Just a few weeks later on 16 November 1923 the BBC officially launched its first local relay station (6FL) in Sheffield, followed in Yorkshire by the Leeds/Bradford (2LS, 8 July 1924) and Hull (6KH, 15 August 1924) stations. In 1926, referring to the coverage of the Leeds Centenary Celebrations, the *Yorkshire Evening News* declared that Leeds had found 'a mouth, so to speak, through which the city can speak to the world'.[10] But this begs the question whose 'mouth', whose voice? And who was it that wanted a local relay station in the first place?

Whitley identified with the BBC because he judged it to be a great public service, but little is known about his own listening habits either before or after he became the Corporation's Chairman. He did, however, have some advice for listeners. Addressing a summer school of wireless listening group leaders in Oxford in 1932, Whitley said that the work of broadcasting as the BBC saw it was to provide listeners with the best in both speech and music by bringing 'leading figures' into the home. However, his advice was not to listen too much: 'Listening that was done at the expense of reading was not a benefit. The BBC, he said, sent out some 14 hours of broadcasting each weekday, but he did not advise any individual to listen for more than two hours a day.'[11] Instead they should reach for a book when programmes failed to interest them. Forty years earlier, a correspondent to the *Halifax Courier* who was almost certainly J.H. Whitley, wrote: 'The first duty of government, says Ruskin, is to educate . . . The time is not far distant when the prosperity of a town or a nation will depend more on education and intelligence and less on natural advantages of trade.'[12] The documentary film-maker John Grierson said of the BBC's first Director-General, 'Reith talked of an informed and reasonable public opinion as an essential part of the political process in a mass democratic society'[13] but this was a view that was shared by Liberals and Nonconformists like Whitley.

The form that the new local relay stations took was not inevitable but was largely determined by events in Sheffield. In 1922 Frederick Lloyd, a tool maker, inventor and founder of the Sheffield Wireless Society, set up a radio station in his home. An effective self-publicist, Lloyd's account of the 'strenuous fight . . . for Sheffield to obtain even a small place in the sun' of wireless broadcasting was serialised in the local press in 1929.[14] The BBC's monopoly meant that licences for experimental broadcasting between stations could only be granted by the Postmaster General so Lloyd obtained a licence to transmit to the city's university. According to Lloyd's own account, 'The next thing was to see how Sheffield's interests could be secured and safeguarded.' He wrote to Sir William Clegg, leader of the city council and Pro-Chancellor of the university, pointing out the educational benefits of radio. It was Clegg's suggestion to broadcast a lecture from Lloyd's house to teachers assembled in the university's Mappin Hall, which resulted in a conversation by wireless between Clegg, John Reith (then the BBC's General Manager) and Peter Eckersley, the BBC's Chief Engineer. Eckersley was sent to Sheffield to investigate.[15] In addition to Clegg, Lloyd could count on wider support from the university which he had involved in several of his demonstrations. The university's Vice-Chancellor, Sir William Henry Hadow,[16] was to make his own contribution to the development of broadcasting as a member of the Crawford committee which led to the establishment of the BBC as a public corporation by royal charter[17] as well as producing a report for the BBC on the use of broadcasting in adult education.[18]

Initially the purpose of a local relay system was to do nothing more than relay broadcasts from a main station, but Lloyd was still not satisfied; he argued that the city's listeners did not want Birmingham's local news or somebody from that city telling Sheffield how steel was manufactured. But while the BBC's local relay stations were established to improve audibility they also provided an opportunity for local broadcasting. As a temporary measure the new station 6FL was located at Lloyd's home managed by his son Harry who was instructed by the BBC to keep programmes as light as possible given that this was predominantly an industrial area.[19] By the end of 1923 the BBC had appointed its own 'representative', but transmissions to schools were still being managed by Frederick Lloyd in 1926.[20]

Welcoming the imminent arrival of the Leeds–Bradford station (2LS) in July 1924, the *Colne Valley Guardian*, published in Slaithwaite a few miles west of Huddersfield, commented: 'Save for a few enthusiasts who have made a study of electricity and people with long purses, the listening habit has not caught on in this district' – although only 20 miles from Manchester, 'all sorts of impediments' were in the way.[21] An advertisement in the same issue of the newspaper stated that electricity would shortly be available in Slaithwaite. The official opening of the Leeds–Bradford station by the Lord Mayors of both cities was broadcast from Leeds Town Hall and simultaneously relayed to a crystal set equipped with loudspeakers outside Bradford Town Hall, attracting a large crowd.[22] A later Lord Mayor of Bradford, Horace Hird, remembered that the opening of the relay station 'led to a demand for thousands of receiving sets by people who wished to sample this new entertainment in their home', crystal sets costing 7/6d with F.W. Woolworth sometimes selling them for 6d.[23] By 1925 radio sets were still enough of a novelty to be listed in some detail when a Dewsbury company went into receivership.[24]

In the Leeds–Bradford station's opening broadcast Reith, perhaps with the potential audience in mind, stressed the importance of local concerts, as did the newly appointed Station Director Philip Fox. Professor Whiddrington, Cavendish Professor of Physics at Leeds University, told the *Yorkshire Post* that listeners-in would now be able to compare local and metropolitan talent.

The paper revealed that a group of wireless enthusiasts at the university had applied to the Postmaster General for a licence to use radio to 'further its extra-mural activities' but this had been refused because of the agreement restricting such licences to the BBC and there was concern that scientific ideas could be over-simplified in broadcasts. Whiddrington, who was also a past president of the Leeds Radio Society and Advisory Editor of the journal *Modern Wireless*, suggested that some broadcasts could be accompanied by talks to bring out their 'inner meaning' and that the university might be usefully involved in broadcast talks and lectures.[25]

Musical recitals, programmes for women and children, broadcasts for schools and local talks were the daily fare of the local relay stations which entered into both formal and informal relationships with local organisations. The universities in Leeds and Sheffield both provided speakers for talks and local advisory committees were set up to advise on religious affairs and schools broadcasting. In Leeds in 1925 the station's broadcasts to schools in the autumn term included a series of thirty-minute talks from speakers at the university including S.J. Curtis on 'Incidents in the development of an Empire'.[26] Although there were no broadcasts from Park Road Congregational Church in Halifax with its strong Whitley family connections, members of the family may have occasionally listened to services broadcast regularly from Horton Lane Congregational Church in Bradford and Queen Street Congregational Chapel in Leeds. The Hull station broadcast regular talks from the boy scouts and from Hull Wireless Society.[27] 6FL first featured 'Sheffield Education Week' in 1924 but the more extensive wireless coverage given to the city's Education Week in 1927 included a religious service from the studio, talks from councillors and the university Vice-Chancellor, as well as an afternoon concert from local schoolchildren.[28] Programmes for children were given priority – Philip Fox in Leeds later claimed he had £20 a week to spend on programmes with more than a half going to the *Children's Hour* programmes.[29] Young listeners were encouraged to send for badges so they could further identify with the station – according to Lloyd the call sign for Sheffield should have been 6SL but '6FL' was printed in error on badges ordered for the children's Radio Circle. In Halifax the Board of Guardians purchased wireless licences for its children's homes.[30]

Despite occasional guidance in the form of memorandums from London, the BBC local stations were left very much to themselves when it came to organising their own programmes. But after visiting Hull in 1926, J.C. Stobart, the BBC's Director of Education, suggested that without a university to provide speakers, perhaps the station should be closed down.[31] He made a series of such visits to the local relay stations, focusing in his reports on religious and educational provision. In Sheffield he noted that the rota for Sunday services provided for members of the city's Anglican and Free churches but the Religious Advisory Committee believed that it wasn't yet possible to obtain co-operation from Roman Catholics.[32] While he found the Leeds–Bradford station's output to be generally satisfactory he noted that on occasions the need to focus on both cities meant that Bradford had been ignored.[33] When Stobart died in 1933, J.H.

Whitley attended his memorial service[34] and Helen Whitley later officiated at the dedication of a cot in Stobart's memory at Charing Cross Hospital.[35]

The presence of BBC stations across the country meant that the broadcaster played a significant role in the discovery and nurturing of local talent. Dialect writer James Gregson, who had started his working life as a half-timer in a mill, had taken a prominent part in the founding of amateur theatre companies in Leeds, Huddersfield and Bradford before giving his first radio talk in 1924.[36] His 'humorous north country' play, *Devil A Saint*, was performed in the Leeds studio for radio listeners in between matinee and evening performances at the Leeds Civic Playhouse. He would bring his own company, the Yorkshire Players, into the Leeds studio on many occasions and in 1946, by this time a BBC staff member, Gregson was sent back to Leeds to launch the BBC North Region's sound drama department.[37] But, then as now, those who hoped to appear on the radio had to spend time making themselves known to BBC staff. The diaries of Halifax 'professor of music' Herman Van Dyk, who may have been acquainted with the Whitley family, detail his attempts to both get work and have his compositions performed and his approaches to BBC stations across the country – 2LS claimed to be 'full' while Nottingham informed him that it only used local performers, but he had more success with both London and Manchester.[38] The Leeds station seem to have quickly responded to complaints from Huddersfield radio dealers who were critical of the station's Friday night music programmes: 'The official reply was "Can you do any better?" The challenge was immediately accepted, and the BBC were told that they could do better without going out of Huddersfield for the talent.'[39] The *Huddersfield Night* was the first of several Huddersfield Concert Party broadcasts, most of which came from Manchester with the Leeds–Bradford station opting instead to broadcast the London programme.[40]

In her study of *The Week's Good Cause* programme strand, Eve Colpus relates new modes of cultural interventionism to older messages about philanthropy suggesting that by 1928 charity appeals had become a central concern of the BBC. However, such appeals had been a regular Sunday feature on the local stations. In October 1926 2LS transmitted an appeal on behalf of the Bradford Council of Social Service and City Guild of Help[41] – J.H. Whitley had been a founding member of the Halifax Citizens' Guild of Help in 1905.[42] The new opportunities provided by radio occasionally resulted in informal temporary partnerships – an appeal for the Leeds Poor Children's Holiday Fund was dubbed 'charity-by-wireless' by the *Yorkshire Evening Post* who had joined with the city's Scala Theatre and with Fox, the Leeds–Bradford station's Director, in organising the event.[43] Typically, the appeals were made by voluntary activists – Georgina Kitson Clark appealed for the Leeds University Development Fund[44] as well as the Leeds Babies' Welcome Association[45] – and civic dignitaries.

Civic weeks also provided opportunities for relay stations to identify with their audiences, although in 1927 the Liverpool station hosted a studio debate asking if civic weeks were worthwhile.[46] The Leeds Tercentenary Celebrations in 1926 were used not just to boost the city, but the radio station linked it to its own anniversary – it too was a symbol of how far the city had travelled in 300 years. Station Director Philip Fox, son of former Town Clerk Sir Robert Fox, was well placed to serve on the tercentenary celebration executive committee and it may be that the *Yorkshire Evening News*'s depiction of radio providing a voice for the city may have been prompted by the BBC agreeing to broadcast nightly hour-long concerts from the newspaper's 'Modern Leeds' exhibition. While, as far as it is possible to tell at a time when most programmes were transmitted live and scripts were not kept, controversy was usually avoided in the BBC's local stations, the broadcasting of the Special Tercentenary Service also gave listeners the opportunity to hear the Archbishop of York say, referring to slum clearance, 'Leeds has not been wholly praiseworthy in its development'.[47]

But the BBC had only seen local relay stations as a temporary way of dealing with reception problems and in the north of England their closure was made possible by the opening of a new high-powered twin transmitter station at Moorside Edge near Slaithwaite, designed to carry both the national and regional channels, in July 1931. Six years to the day after the Leeds–Bradford station opened, the *Yorkshire Evening Post* reported on the 'sacrifice' of the local relay stations 'on the sacred altar of progress'.[48] In Sheffield, as early as 1926, Frederick Lloyd was suggesting publicly that the BBC intended to close the station and his concerns were shared by the city's Council and Chamber of Commerce. Reith's response was that while the transmitter would close eventually, in Sheffield it would be likely to stay open because of the educational, musical and other talent to be found in the city.[49] This seemed to be confirmed by a meeting between the BBC and the Sheffield Wireless Advisory Committee on 29 February 1932 when the Corporation's delegates were reported as saying:

> that the pioneer work done by Sheffield in the early days of broadcasting was recognised, and it was not at present intended to sever connections with the city. The meaning of this is that the Sheffield studio will be resumed for local artists, but the transmitter will not be used again and will shortly be dismantled.[50]

The BBC's Board of Governors, with Whitley in the chair, had resolved in December 1931 that the transmitters at Liverpool, Stoke, Hull and Sheffield be abandoned.[51] Despite representations from Sheffield's Town Clerk and Chamber of Commerce, by the time of Whitley's death the BBC had no studio or representative in Sheffield.

The extent to which the Yorkshire stations were missed by the region's audience is not clear. Mark Pegg has commented: 'The "giant transmitter" was capable of a much superior quality and choice of broadcasting when compared with the old fashioned local stations and their loss was mourned barely at all.'[52] But, while for the duration of Whitley's chairmanship, new technical problems as a result of the new transmitter network were still being identified, the BBC had by 1935 become sufficiently aware that there were problems between its centre and regions to commission a report from Charles Siepmann, its Director of Regional Relations.⁵³ Siepmann pointed to problems of over-centralisation not only in the Corporation as a whole but within the BBC Northern Region.⁵⁴ However, more homes were now in reception distance of a transmitter and could choose between the National and Regional Programmes. It has been estimated that 33 per cent of households in Yorkshire and North Derbyshire had licences by 1931 and 73 per cent by 1938,⁵⁵ while E.D. Smithies suggests that in Halifax in the mid-1930s there was one radio licence for every twenty-seven people.⁵⁶

And while the BBC may have closed its studios in Sheffield and Hull, it opened a new studio in Leeds in 1933, declared to be the most modern in the country, where James Gregson continued to bring his plays – the *Radio Times* notes that his play on Captain Cook transmitted on the Northern Region on 2 November 1934 was a recording of a production devised for and originally recorded on the Empire Service.⁵⁷ Even some of those involved in the first Huddersfield Concert Party would continue to make occasional radio appearances. Sheffield teacher and music hall comedian 'Stainless Stephen' (Arthur Clifford Baynes) used the presence of the relay station in Sheffield to launch a successful radio career – in a *Who's Who* of 'the leading personalities of the microphone' published in 1933, the entertainer was given considerably more space than J.H. Whitley⁵⁸ – but he moved to London in 1935 so he could be closer to the BBC. The disappearance of the relay stations meant there was less broadcasting time to provide coverage of local events but in 1931 when Bradford held a Historical Pageant to accompany the Imperial Wool Industries Fair taking place in the city in an attempt to boost its textile industry, the opening speeches were relayed not only to the region but to the nation.⁵⁹ For diarist Dorothea Turner, growing up in 1930s Huddersfield, the radio put her in touch with both national artists and events; on 17 May 1933 she reports a visit to the town's Palace Theatre, 'They were all BBC artists that were on', while on 11 November 'We went home at 9.30. It was Armistice Day. We heard the service on the radio.'⁶⁰ Thomas Hajkowski, in his study of the role the BBC played in the creation of national identity before 1953, suggests that many commentators have underestimated the extent to which the BBC provided a platform for listeners across the nation to hear regional voices and dialects: 'The BBC made British national identity more flexible and accommodating of the diversity of the peoples of the British Isles.'⁶¹

The activity of listening-in was not confined to the home or school. Beginning with the opening of the Empire exhibition in 1924, loudspeakers were installed in public places, not only for national events such as Cup Finals but even for the relaying of music programmes by wireless retailers.⁶² But group listening could be used as the basis for group discussion – the BBC estimated that the number of 'wireless listening and discussion groups' had risen from fifty in 1927–28 to 1,000 in 1930–31.⁶³ In 1924 Stobart had written in the *Radio Times* suggesting that broadcast talks could lead to collaboration with other organisations such as public libraries⁶⁴ and, for the BBC, the setting up of listening groups in response to Hadow's 1928 report into adult education and broadcasting, would be based on such partnerships.⁶⁵ The first meeting of the Yorkshire Area Council for Broadcast Adult Education took place in November 1929, presided over by Sir Percy Jackson, chairman of the West Riding Education Committee.[66] The National Council for Social Service, the successor to the Guild of Help movement which Whitley had helped to launch in Halifax in 1905, was one of the organisations which helped to fund sets for the listening groups as part of its role in co-ordinating voluntary schemes to assist the unemployed in the use of their time.[67] Addressing the first annual conference of the Central Council for Broadcast Adult Education in January 1931, Reith told delegates, 'broadcasting is the integrating element to which democracy looks to secure the cohesion and unity of the body politic more effectively than anything which has yet come on the scene',[68] a notion which would have surely appealed to Whitley. In the following year the BBC Chairman was present both at the second conference of the Council and at its summer school for group leaders. Whitley told the conference that:

> The BBC wanted them to feel themselves partners in the great trust of making that wonderful discovery [radio] minister to the great bulk of the people in the way they needed. They had great difficulty sometimes in keeping the balance between entertainment and education, but people would rapidly respond to every endeavour to give them what was really good, and he thought that they must realise already that it was the intention of the BBC to make that the guiding principle of their work.[69]

In practice both the content and mode of delivery of the work of the listening groups was frequently contested; the Central Council of Broadcast Adult Education was wound up in 1934,[70] although the BBC continued to transmit series it believed would be suitable for voluntary groups, including the unemployed.

In Sheffield, Library Listening Groups had been started by the City Librarian at the suggestion of the BBC in 1929. Speaking at the 1931 conference, J.N. Reedman, leader of the listening group at the city's Hillsborough library, 'emphasised' that the talks should be aimed at either 'elementary students' or at those who required more specialised study. He described his own group as consisting of around twenty-five people, most of whom were working-class men. 'For such a group', he suggested, 'academic lectures, where the discussion was a particularly valuable feature, were unsuitable'.[71] In a report on the Discussion Groups at Walkley and Hillsborough for the Autumn Session 1930, the City Librarian J.P. Lamb commented that there was standing room only for Professor A. Carr-Saunders' talks on eugenics. And in Walkley, he judged, 'interest and liveliness in discussion has been well maintained'.[72] But correspondence between Lamb and George Gibson, the Secretary to the North Eastern Area Council for Group Listening, based at the BBC Leeds office, shows Lamb's increasing reluctance to continue the discussion groups. When Gibson proposed a visit to the Walkley Group in January 1932, Lamb advised against it, given that the group was 'composed largely of vociferous young men who claim to hold communist views. They suspect a deep and sinister capitalist purpose', some believing that the intended visit was because the BBC intended to limit their freedom of discussion. In September 1933 he went as far as to tell Gibson: 'Frankly I think your programmes get more ghastly every year. This, of course, is a private view. Officially there may be something in the talks business although I have very serious doubts.' In December he told Gibson that he would not be reintroducing the wireless talks because with 'book talks and discussions' the groups could choose their own subjects while 'I myself have long felt that the work of the BBC is too obviously educational'.[73] Gibson continued to support the groups as part of his role as a BBC Adult Education Officer; 'The listening group', he told a Nottingham conference in 1940 'is the symbol of the democratic spirit for which our country stands.'[74]

When Whitley became chairman of the BBC in 1930 sound broadcasting was just a few years old and not only were broadcasting practices being invented but audiences were also being created. Looking back, Clifford Stephenson, who opened his radio dealership in Huddersfield in 1924, commented: 'Wireless was a national obsession, the craze which swept the country, a hobby, a cult and a passion cutting across class and creed but especially attractive to those on limited income as it offered near continuous entertainment at comparatively small cost.'[75] Whitley's own recommendation that people should restrict their listening time suggests that he did not really understand the ways that people made use of this new medium. From 1933, if listeners were not interested in what the BBC had to offer and did not want to pick up a book then they could always tune in to Radio Luxembourg. A 1939 survey, commissioned by the BBC, pointed to the different ways that people used radio even within the same household.[76] The history of sound broadcasting in J.H. Whitley's Yorkshire reflected the pragmatism with which the BBC continued to approach its regional and local broadcasting, but the 1939 survey also concluded that when many people were listening to the same programme then they might feel they were part of the same nation.[77] *Have a Go!*, presented by Wilfred Pickles from Halifax,[78] would be the most listened to programme on the radio between 1946 and 1957, perhaps helping to provide at least for a moment some of 'the happiness and comfort' that his fellow-townsman J.H. Whitley had hoped for when he became the first Halifax man to broadcast to the Empire.

Notes

1 J.H. Whitley, 'Partners in a great enterprise', *The Times*, 14 August 1934.
2 J.H. Whitley to Alfred Whitley, 1 June 1928, JHW/4/2/7. See also, *Hansard*, Vol. 1419, 18 June 1928.
3 *Yorkshire Post*, 4 February 1935.
4 Oliver Whitley, 25 June 1969, JHW/1/1/4.
5 Extract from *BBC Year Book 1934*, JHW/2/7/33.
6 See, for example, A. Briggs, *The History of Broadcasting in the United Kingdom: Volume II: The Golden Age of Wireless*, London, Oxford University Press, 1965; P. Scannell, 'Broadcasting and the politics of unemployment 1930–1935', in R.E. Collins, J. Curran, N. Garnham and P. Scannell (eds), *Media, Culture and Society: a critical reader*, London, Sage, 1986, pp. 214–27, at p. 217; 'History of the BBC: the Hashagen Affair 1932' [http://www.bbc.co.uk/historyofthebbc/research/culture/bbc-and-gov/hashagen, accessed 10 January 2017].

7 'Directory of Experimental Wireless Stations in the United Kingdom', *Wireless World*, 20 August 1921, pp. 325–31.
8 *Halifax Courier*, 29 September 1900.
9 *The Broadcasting Committee Report* (the Sykes Committee), Cmd. 1951 (1923).
10 *Yorkshire Evening News*, 2 July 1926.
11 *The Times*, 1 August 1932.
12 JHW/2/1/11, nd. The inclusion of the letter in the scrapbook and the marking of the cutting with the letter 'H' suggests that the anonymous correspondent was Whitley and it may have been written c.1890. See also Chapter 4 of this volume for references to Ruskin.
13 F. Hardu (ed.), *Grierson On Documentary*, London, Collins, 1946, p. 78.
14 F. Lloyd, *Wireless Reminiscences*, April–May 1929, typescript of articles published in the *Yorkshire Telegraph and Star*, Sheffield Local Studies Library, 384.5SQ.
15 Lloyd's account is largely confirmed by Eckersley in P. Eckersley, *The Power Behind the Microphone*, London, Jonathan Cape, 1941, p. 68.
16 Hadow was Vice Chancellor of Sheffield University between 1919 and 1930.
17 Cmd. 2559 (1926) *The Broadcasting Committee Report* (the Crawford Committee).
18 W.H. Hadow, *New Ventures in Broadcasting*, London, BBC, 1928.
19 BBC Written Archives Centre (WAC) R13/365/1, 19 November 1923.
20 Ibid., 20 October 1926.
21 *Colne Valley Guardian*, 27 June 1924.
22 *Yorkshire Post*, 9 July 1924.
23 H. Hird, *How a city grows: historical notes on the city of Bradford*, Bradford, Horace Hird, 1966.
24 Valuation of wireless set re TH Wood (bankruptcy), WYAS Kirklees, Holroyd Sons, WYK1139/3/1/77.
25 *Yorkshire Post*, 9 July 1924.
26 *Talk to Local Schools*, 2LS, 2 October 1925, BBC Genome [http://genome.ch.bbc.co.uk/17345f043f264a35ad93b79657b1cbb3), accessed 8 January 2017].
27 BBC Genome: *Radio Times* 1923–2009 [http://genome.ch.bbc.co.uk/, accessed 8 January 2017].
28 Lloyd, *Wireless Reminiscences*.
39 *Yorkshire Post*, 5 January 1952.
30 Halifax Board of Guardians, Wireless licences for properties under the Halifax Union 1928–1929, WYAS Calderdale, PL:25.
31 BBC WAC R13/358.
32 BBC WAC R13/365.
33 BBC WAC R13/358.
34 *The Times*, 20 May 1933.
35 cutting, n.d., JHW/2/8/89.
36 B.D. Smith (ed.), *The Autobiography of James Gregson*, Brighouse, E.R. Smith Publications, 2011, p. 195.
37 C.J. Verguson, '"Opting Out"? Nation, Region and Locality: the BBC in Yorkshire 1945–1990', PhD thesis, University of Huddersfield, 2014, pp. 64–5.
38 Herman Van Dyk, pianist, conductor and composer, diaries, WYAS Calderdale, WYAS1249/65; his diary entry for 6 November 1925 simply states 'Mrs J.H. Whitley died during the night'.
39 *Huddersfield Daily Examiner*, 12 June 1925.
40 C. Verguson, '"All Huddersfield": our town on the wireless in the 1920s', *Huddersfield Local History Society Journal*, 2015, 20–9.
41 *Appeal*, 2LS, 3 October 1926.
42 K. Laybourn, 'The New Philanthropy of the Edwardian Age: The Guild of Help and the Halifax Citizens' Guild 1905–1918', *The Transactions of the Halifax Antiquarian Society*, 23 (2015), 73–94, particularly 73.
43 *Yorkshire Evening Post*, 25 July 1925.

44 *Appeal*, 2LS, 21 August 1927.
45 *The Work and Aims of the Leeds' Babies Welcome Association*, 2LS, 18 June 1926.
46 *Is Civic Week Worthwhile*, 2LV, 1 October 1927.
47 Leeds Tercentenary Celebrations, WYAS Leeds, LA2705/3/23; Leeds Tercentenary Cuttings, WYAS Leeds, LA2705/3/22.
48 *Yorkshire Evening Post*, 8 July 1930.
49 BBC WAC R13/365/1, 15 January 1926.
50 *Manchester Guardian*, 2 March 1932.
51 BBC WAC R1/2/1, 11 November 1931.
52 M. Pegg, *Broadcasting and Society 1918–1939*, Beckenham, Croom Helm, 1983, pp. 29–30.
53 Ibid, pp. 31–3; Briggs, *The Golden Age of Wireless*, pp. 331–4.
54 Ibid., p. 333.
55 Pegg, *Broadcasting and Society 1918–1939*, p. 12. Pegg's analysis is based on figures included in the BBC's Year Books.
56 E.D. Smithies, 'The Contrast between North and South in England 1918–1939: a study of economic, social and political problems with particular reference to the experience of Burnley, Halifax, Ipswich and Luton', PhD thesis, University of Leeds, 1974, p. 146; this was higher than any of the other towns in his comparative study.
57 *Radio Times*, 26 October 1934, p. 72.
58 *Who's Who in Broadcasting: a biographical record of the leading personalities of the microphone*, London, Pitman, 1933.
59 *The Historical Pageant of Bradford*, BBC National Programme, 17 July 1931; Bradford Borough Council, Town Clerk, papers concerning Bradford Historical Pageant, WYAS Bradford, 39D81.
60 Diaries of Dorothea Turner, Huddersfield, 1929–1936, WYAS Kirklees, WYK1469.
61 Thomas Hajkowski, *The BBC and National Identity in Britain, 1922–1953*, Manchester, Manchester University Press, 2010, p. 237.
62 *Huddersfield Examiner* 31 October 1932.
63 *The Times*, 4 January 1932.
64 *Radio Times* 13 June 1924.
65 Hadow, *New Ventures in Broadcasting*.
66 *Sheffield Independent*, 16 November 1929.
67 M. Bailey, 'Broadcasting and the Problem of Enforced Leisure during the 1930s', *Leisure Studies*, 26/4 (2007), 463–77, 468.
68 *The Observer*, 4 January 1931.
69 *The Times*, 4 January 1932.
70 Pegg, *Broadcasting and Society 1918–1939*, pp. 166–8.
71 *Sheffield Independent* 5 January 1931.
72 Sheffield City Council, Wireless Discussion Groups, Sheffield City Archives, CA990/7; The Carr-Saunders series was entitled *Standing Room Only*.
73 Ibid.
74 *Nottingham Evening Post*, 12 October 1940.
75 Jennifer Stead collection, Cuttings scrapbook: Clifford Stephenson, WYAS Kirklees, WYK1487/1/2.
76 H. Jennings and W. Gill, *Broadcasting in Everyday Life: A Survey of the Social Effects of the Coming of Broadcasting*, London, British Broadcasting Corporation, 1939.
77 Ibid., p. 12.
78 Wilfred Pickles made his radio debut on *Children's Hour* on the Leeds–Bradford relay station, 2LS, in 1927.

12 Self-government

J.H. Whitley's worlds in context

Keith Robbins

'Democracy has arrived at a gallop in England,' wrote Stanley Baldwin, Conservative Prime Minister, in 1928 'and I feel all the time that it is a race for life; can we educate them before the crash comes?' He was writing to Edward Wood, son of Viscount Halifax, and a man frequently in the saddle. Wood, as Lord Irwin, had been Viceroy of India, since 1926. As a Conservative MP he had had some brief experience as President of the Board of Education, a post whose occupancy still made it possible to go hunting twice a week. Could India, – another 'them' – also be educated before the crash came? Field Marshal Sir William Birdwood, Commander-in-Chief in India had welcomed Irwin's appointment, writing that he seemed to be 'a really first-class English gentleman, and as such, seems to be exactly what we want'. Birdwood had but some 57,000 British troops at his command. Indians outnumbered Britons in the sub-continent by two thousand to one. Irwin found a scramble for power amidst the endemic problems of poverty and illiteracy. Notwithstanding the impression of permanence created by the new Viceroy's House in New Delhi, into which the Irwins were shortly to move, the British would surely one day withdraw from India. The Viceroy himself concluded that in time India should acquire full Dominion status and be on a par with the 'White Dominions'. In 1929 he wrote that it had to be made perfectly plain to India that 'the ultimate purpose for her is not one of perpetual subordination in a white Empire'.[1] The Simon Commission of 1928, solely British in composition, had been set up to report on whether or to what extent it was desirable to establish the principle of 'responsible government'. It had rejected Dominion Status, but Irwin, with a new Labour government in London, steered his own course. When the ultimate would become actual, however, was not revealed. It would be determined by the volatile politics both of Britain and of India.

Words were being used on all sides which were grand but opaque in their precise meanings: self-government, popular government, commonwealth, empire, Dominion Status. At the provincial level, the British Montagu–Chelmsford reform of 1919 had already given a mild degree of 'Home Rule' in permitting Indians at a provincial level to head certain ministries, though not ones which touched upon security. Looking to the future, what might be the balance between a central government and provincial governments? Would the princely states have 'self-government'? Did the depth of Moslem–Hindu animosity mean that 'self-government' would in fact produce some kind of partition? How could it be determined what 'the people' wanted?

It was into this sub-continent in flux that J.H. Whitley came as Chairman of the Royal Commission on Indian Labour. Together with a separate Royal Commission on Indian Agriculture, such investigations constituted a kind of demonstration of and perhaps justification for British imperial 'stewardship'. Their findings in themselves would be unlikely to affect the momentum towards self-government but would clarify the scale of the tasks confronting any government in India. Unlike the Simon Commission, Whitley had many Indian fellow-commissioners drawn from different backgrounds. Beryl Power was the solitary woman among the men.[2] She sometimes sported a pince-nez and was forensically formidable. The work of the Commission is examined in Chapter 9 of this volume but Whitley's appointment was announced by the India Office. It was in certain respects a strange appointment in so far as Whitley, now 62, had resigned the Speakership of the House of Commons on grounds of ill-health after seven strenuous years in office.[3] It could not be supposed that lengthy travels, and interviews with many people in many places across the sub-continent, however well-appointed on voyage, would constitute an undemanding recuperation. Following the death of his first wife in 1925, he had recently remarried. However, on resignation the Speakership, he had not accepted a peerage and therefore did not contemplate a continuing role, as a member of the House of Lords, in national politics. He would be a free agent. It would be for the government of the day, of whatever colour, to decide how far the Commission's recommendations should be implemented. His involvement at the end of the First World War in establishing the formal machinery of mediation between Capital and Labour, the eponymous Whitley Councils which are considered in Chapter 6 by Greg Patmore, had enhanced his reputation.[4] His reputation made him an obvious candidate to head the investigation of Labour in India. On the other hand, he had no direct personal experience of India and his awareness of India's problems stemmed very largely from the extent to which they were debated in the House of Commons. England's cotton spinners, however, had known for decades of the challenge presented by India's mills. His appointment made possible a novel adventure to visit exotic sights and encounter 'the Orient'. Acceptance of the role implied that he had no root and branch objection to the British *Raj*. The Commission might see much poverty and suggest specific suggestions but it had no brief, nor did it desire one, to pronounce on the future self-government of India.

There was a certain piquancy in the position of these two Yorkshiremen – Viceroy and Commission Chairman – at this critical period both in the history of India and of the wider history of Britain and the British Empire. Irwin's tenure ended in 1931, the year in which the Commission's report was published. Both men at this juncture found in the BBC a place for their talents and their eminence. Irwin (to become better known as Lord Halifax) paid tribute to Whitley on the latter's death in 1935.[5] The two men do not seem to have been intimate in their earlier political careers. Yorkshire men they both were, but their pedigrees did not suggest a likely intimacy. The Woods were landed aristocracy in all the ridings of Yorkshire. Edward's grandfather, the first Viscount Halifax had married the daughter of Earl Grey, the Whig Prime Minister, and rose to become Chancellor of the Exchequer and Secretary of State for India.[6] The second viscount was rather feudal in his general politics. His devotion was to the English Church Union. After Eton, Edward took a first in History at Oxford, gained a Fellowship at All Souls and, sharing his father's High Anglicanism, wrote a book on John Keble. At the age of 29, he slipped comfortably into the Commons as Conservative MP for Ripon in January 1910 and was successful again in December. No one bothered to stand against him thereafter.

J.H. Whitley came from a different England. Fifteen years older than Wood, he had entered Parliament as a Liberal MP for Halifax in 1900. He had not been to Eton or Oxford. He did not therefore directly absorb that strongly Anglican historical scholarship, which, in the form of Stubbs's *Select Charters* and his *Constitutional History*, imprinted a conception of the English genius on eager minds in the new School of Modern History.[7] He did gain a BA as an external student of the University of London in 1885. It may or may not have included the study of history. He did not ride to hounds. He did not have landed estates. He would not be seen, when in London, worshipping, alongside the Woods, at St Mary's, Bourne St. At home in Halifax he was a Congregationalist, no enthusiast for a State Church nor admirer of 'ritualism'. Dissent, however, was shifting from the negative tone of Nonconformity to the positive 'Free Church'. He was a man of business working for his uncle and father in the family firm of Samuel Whitley & Co. cotton spinners of Skircoat, Halifax.[8] No history of the firm exists. It appears to have occupied a solid place among the many mills of the town but did not dominate. Cotton, on the wrong side of the Pennines, was not in fact king in the major textile world of Halifax. The Whitleys saw themselves as responsible employers, though no more capable than anyone else of avoiding economic downturns. They clearly weathered the 'Cotton Famine' of the years immediately before the birth of J.H. The firm did not avoid appearing in an 1899 list of Halifax employers reprimanded by the Factory Inspectorate for failing to provide adequate means of fire escape.[9] The business gave J.H. Whitley a comfortable income and an ample but not ostentatious town house. He occupied a significant place in the town's commercial elite, though the plateau was occupied by the Crossleys. Halifax was an 'old' town with a sixteenth-century, but currently struggling, grammar school and other long-established institutions but it was its new men, native or incoming, who set its tone. It was mature in the sense that in 1901 it reached its maximum population (in the period before 1914). In 1881 it was listed among the towns which gave no rate support to its library.[10] A return of 1886 reported that Halifax had no large or particularly noticeable ground owners (unlike Huddersfield).[11] The Whitleys seem men who were impelled into business enterprise by a desire for social advancement and for whom success was measured by reaching goals which were locally and reasonably available. Success was not to be measured against a scale of landed status 'that for most was unimaginably remote'.[12] Richard Cobden in 1863 had lamented that manufacturers and merchants 'as a rule' seemed only to desire riches 'that they may be enabled to prostrate themselves at the feet of feudalism'.[13]

The Whitleys did not acknowledge this rule. They did not prostrate themselves. Their trajectory illustrates the weakness of any view of the 'middle class' which posits straightforward dichotomies, such as North/South or making goods/making money, Nonconformist/Anglican.[14] They immersed themselves in the life of Halifax as we have seen in earlier essays in Chapters 2, 4 and 5. J.H. Whitley's father Nathan became Mayor in 1877, 1882 and 1883. This was the world of 'local government', a term first used in English in the mid-nineteenth century and receiving its first statutory mention in the Local Government Act of 1858. As is often pointed out 'the most direct experience of most people of government was of local government; it affected their lives more visibly than did central government'.[15] It was of course the Municipal Corporations Act of 1835 which introduced representative local government through elected councils in 178 places. The Local Government Act of 1888 applied the same principle to the countryside (and this Act designated Halifax as a county borough). An Act of 1894 established elected parish councils. England was frequently described as 'the home of local self-government'. G.C. Brodrick, writing in 1875, was among those who still saw its origins in 'the primitive but well-ordered communities of our Saxon forefathers'. Local policy-making initiatives could be influenced by what was happening in other localities. Of course, there were those who saw 'local self-government as cheap government, more concerned with keeping the rates down than with uplifting a community'. The counter-position was that local energies were sapped if subjected to legislation of 'national' scope in an ever more centralising state. There was, however, an inescapable fiscal reality. In 1868 the state was contributing 5 per cent of the costs of local government through grants-in-aid. By 1914 a quarter of local authority revenue came from this source. It might seem that 'self-government', in a fundamental sense, was dying.[16] As Keith Laybourn notes in his discussion in Chapter 5, Whitley continued as a local Liberal councillor until well after being returned to the House of Commons.

Individual enterprise mattered. Edward Akroyd of Halifax was behind the establishment of the West Riding Penny Savings Bank in 1859, which, after many changes, became the Yorkshire Bank a century later. Founded in 1853, the Halifax was the largest building society in the United Kingdom by 1913, but it was not until 1924 that it opened its first office in London. New entrepreneurs started up without 'national' backing. John Mackintosh began his working life in Halifax in a mill at the age of 10 in 1878. He later turned his energy and initiative into what became 'Mackintosh's Toffee' and turned Halifax into 'Toffee Town'. An ardent advertiser, he himself travelled widely in Europe and America. Native Strolling Players on the Nile and lady missionaries on the Tibetan frontier displayed the Mackintosh toffee tin. American magazine readers were asked to sing a charming ditty: 'Oh do you know the Toffee Kings that live in Halifax?' Apparently a good many Americans did. Mackintosh served on the Town

Council, could have been Mayor and could have entered Parliament, so it was said. His Methodism remained ardent. He declared that he was determined 'to bring London to our way of thinking'.[17]

Yet the simple image of Whitley as another northern man of business, Dissenting to the core, will not do. As we have seen in C.S. Knighton's essay in Chapter 3, he was sent by his father to the newly founded Clifton College in Bristol. Visiting Bristol Grammar School in 1867, one of the commissioners of the Taunton Commission thought that it should develop on lines 'essentially different from that of the great Public Schools for the richer classes, of which Clifton College is so successful an example'.[18] The College did seek to recruit in the Yorkshire press but it is not known why the choice fell upon Clifton. As C.S. Knighton has indicated in Chapter 3, its Anglican ethos was broadly Liberal Evangelical under the guidance of its initial clerical headmaster, the Westmorland-based John Percival, who came from schoolmastering at Rugby. There were some Dissenting schools which might have been considered, but were not chosen. It is likely that it was the early death of his mother which prompted the decision to send him away as a boarder. Bristol was easily accessible by train. Clifton was salubriously aloof, but Bristol itself was a commercial and industrial city, at this time the only city of the largest nine in England – leaving London aside – to be in the South. So the raw world was very much present, even if largely out of sight. Moreover, leading Bristol commercial families, most notably the Wills brothers, were Congregationalists and were distributing their largesse to schools, chapels and other cultural developments.[19] So Whitley's experience as a schoolboy blended North and South, Dissent and the Church and reinforced an already powerful sense of citizenship. Congregational polity was itself a form of self-government. Its members recognised no hierarchy and did not promise obedience to a bishop. At its best, the inner life of chapels teemed with mutually sustaining lives. There could be no better example of this than Redland Park, the Congregational chapel nearest Clifton College.[20] The ethos of Clifton penetrated in other ways, and remained with him for the rest of his life. He remained active in its affairs until the end. Sir William Birdwood in India, recognising in Lord Irwin a first-class English gentleman, might almost have accorded Whitley the same accolade. After all, he and Whitley had overlapped at Clifton College, though not in the same House!

Whitley's indubitable Englishness nevertheless had an unexpected European element. Samuel Whitley & Co surely had commercial links with the continent, but Whitley himself does not appear to have travelled widely there. He had visited the United States on a fact finding mission to learn about trams – lessons that might be applied in Halifax. However, his first wife, while born in Putney, was the daughter of Giulio Marchetti, a Garibaldino of 1859. Marchetti had observed and participated in the mid-century decades from which an 'Italy' emerged. Giulio then settled in England, married Anne Crossley in Halifax in 1871 (some six months after Italian troops had occupied the Rome of his birth and made it Italy's capital). He had joined the Crossley carpet business in England – not a normal career path, one imagines, for Garibaldi's followers.[21]

It was impossible to ignore the drama in Garibaldi's life. Here was the compelling call of national self-determination. Liberals believed in it. In this respect a glance at the map of Europe showed that there was still scope for more 'self-government'.

Whitley as a schoolboy and young man inherited the continent's 'new realities' – the Prussian defeat of Austria, the Prussian defeat of France, the creation of an Austro-Hungarian dual monarchy, the achievement of Italian unity – had all taken shape in the late 1860s and early 1870s. Whitley was born in 1866. A 'Concert of Europe' of a kind existed but major states did not subordinate their particular interests to the 'common good'. Their alliances and alignments were designed to ensure their individual security. Whether they did so was arguable. States might be one thing, however, and nations another. The formal political map disguised unresolved but potentially explosive issues. Within the German, Russian and Habsburg empires, Finns, Poles, Latvians, Czechs, Slovaks, Croats, Estonians, Lithuanians and other 'nationalities' all had grievances. However, whether such peoples aspired, realistically or not, to 'Home Rule' or perhaps to 'Independence' was far from clear. Norway, united with Denmark until 1814 had retained its own Parliament under the subsequent union with Sweden but in 1905 that Parliament resolved to end the union, a decision confirmed by plebiscite and accepted by Sweden.

It could not be assumed, however, that full independence for 'subject nationalities' was in the offing. Meeting Count Apponyi in Budapest in 1906, the Scottish historian Robert Seton-Watson was firmly told that the Magyars would not countenance local government on the basis of nationality. 'As much individual freedom as you like: it is all untrue that we desire to deprive the Roumanian or Slovak of his language, but there can be only one state and one state idea.'[22] In the Balkans there was clearly much unfinished business. Liberals supposed that Turkey remained the last great blot on the face of Europe and a challenge to what European civilisation was believed to have achieved in the nineteenth century. Back in 1876 Gladstone's pamphlet 'The Bulgarian Horrors and the Question of the East' sold 200,000 copies in its first month. Whether the Whitley household was among the purchasers is not known, but Congregationalists stood out at the time for the weight and quality of the leadership they provided in the agitation and their sympathy with Gladstone's tirade may be presumed.[23]

English historians of a sympathetic disposition kept the vision of self-determination alive. In July 1904, having been given Garibaldi's *Autobiography* as a wedding present, G.M. Trevelyan settled down to writing about the great liberator. It was 'far and away the best fun I have ever had in writing,' he declared.[24] The writing matured into a trilogy and made his name. The publication of the final volume in 1911 coincided with the celebrations to mark the fiftieth anniversary of the foundation of the Italian kingdom.[25] The trilogy was a Risorgimento romance, not a work which probed the nature of the Italian nation. Garibaldi, the great liberator of 'Italy', had in fact grown up speaking a Ligurian dialect. The second tongue of the neighbourhood was French. Later, while he set himself to speak Italian, his accent, grammar and spelling betrayed that it did not come quite naturally.[26]

In a Preface, Trevelyan thanked Giulio Marchetti for the help he had given him. It seems highly likely, therefore, that the epic of Italy was a real presence in the Whitley household. However, Whitley does not seem to have been deeply involved in the questions of foreign policy. He is not found to be prominent alongside those Liberal backbenchers critical of Sir Edward Grey's foreign policy.[27] When criticism of the Foreign Secretary from such quarters was at its height in 1911 Whitley had just been promoted to the Chairmanship of the Committee of Ways and Means, not an office designed to encourage a partisan mentality. Indeed, it appears also that in other aspects of policy Whitley saw himself primarily as having a skill in handling the business of Parliament.

G.M. Trevelyan was not coming cold to the question of Italy. His father, George Otto Trevelyan, had gone out to Italy in 1867 in the hope of joining the Red Shirts in their attack on Rome, believing that Liberals should support nations rightly struggling to be free, particularly when the Papacy could be identified as an oppressor. He later regarded his adventure as the 'greatest romance' of his life. The magic words '*Sono Deputato Inglese*' apparently opened all doors. Garibaldi the man surpassed Trevelyan's expectations.[28] The Trevelyans, father and son, disliked the notion that one country should wield domination over another. The year 1911, in which the fiftieth anniversary of the Italian kingdom was celebrated, was also the year in which Italy seized Tripoli and Rhodes. Italy, Trevelyan thought, had thereby thrown away the 'one inestimable advantage that she had hitherto had over the other Great Powers', namely that she had conquered no other race.[29] National self-determination, after all, could become arrogant and aggressive.

And how, in such a context, did J.H. think about his own country, conqueror of many races? While he was English by ancestry and upbringing, the state to which he belonged was the United Kingdom of Great Britain and Ireland. (often shortened by foreigners and some natives to 'England'). As a state, it looked more convincing than the new 'Italy' that his father-in-law had heroically helped to cobble together. Two Acts of Union had brought 'Great Britain' into existence at different dates and in different circumstances. It seemed, on the whole, to work.[30] If full *Italianita*, in constitutional and political terms, remained a work in progress, 'Britishness' appeared largely unproblematic.[31] Great Britain was certainly not uniform but it operated with one Parliament, one government and one monarch. Its party system functioned across its entire territory, though parties had different levels of support within it. In 1906, for example, the Liberals and their allies won every seat in the Principality but if the election had been held under a system of proportional representation Wales would have been represented by eleven Unionist and nineteen Liberal MPs.[32] The 1707 Act of Union, of course, had preserved certain administrative, educational, legal and ecclesiastical distinctiveness in Scotland. Scotland had been a state. A Scottish Secretary had come to have a particular place in British government. A trickle of legislation applying to Wales alone had emerged by the end of the century and, on another front, libraries, museums and a university were promoted as Welsh institutions. Wales had a language. In short, in a kingdom under the Edwardian franchise and with no vote for women, general elections in its proto-democracy produced results which hid the extent to which, within a different constitutional structure with national or regional devolution, 'self-determination' would have produced outcomes significantly different from an overall United Kingdom result. As things were, however, the distinct preferences of different parts of the country did not unduly matter, so long as difference, whether of interest or identity, remained within a sufficiently cohesive sense of 'belongingness'. In politics and many other walks of life individuals straddled the boundaries and borders of the United Kingdom without undue discomfort – as they would continue to do, as Paul Ward has shown, for many decades to come.[33]

In the case of Ireland, however, 'Integration and Diversity' would have to be put very differently. In the two decades before Whitley entered the House of Commons the 'Irish Question' dominated politics for considerable periods and fractured the Liberal Party. As a schoolboy at Clifton he had indicated his support for Irish Home Rule, which became a life-long commitment, as explained in Chapters 4 and 5. In 1882, on the assassination of Lord Frederick Cavendish in Dublin, Gladstone sent that very same admirer of Garibaldi, George Otto Trevelyan, to be Chief Secretary. Was he there to quell Irish national aspirations? As a six-year-old in Dublin, his son G.M. felt unconsciously a sense of the drama of English and Irish history (as he later recalled). Emotions ran high, Gladstone was converted to Home Rule in 1885. The Nonconformist ministers of Bristol lamented the neglect of 'the constitutionally expressed desire of the Irish people for Local Self-Government'. Mr Gladstone agreed and was gratified that Nonconformists supported the determination of the Irish people 'to maintain their civil rights, and to do justice to their national and perfectly constitutional aspirations'.[34] However, Gladstone's zeal in the cause wrecked his last two ministries, in 1886 and 1893–94. In 1885 Irish Nationalists gained a strong majority at Westminster for the first time and while that fluctuated in size in the remaining nineteenth-century elections it could lay claim to represent most Irish voters. Gladstone's two Home Rule Bills could not succeed because the House of Lords would inevitably block their passage. The bills illustrated, in their different drafts, just how difficult it was to put flesh on the slogan 'Home Rule'.[35] Not the least of these difficulties was the question of continued voting by Irish members at Westminster. The proposed 'Legislative Body' of 1886 became the proposed 'Parliament' of 1893. In the last House of Commons to be elected before the First World War Ireland sent eighty-three Nationalists to Westminster, most of whom were followers of Redmond, one Liberal, sixteen Unionists and three Liberal Unionists. The Irish vote therefore supplied the Liberals with a necessary pro-government vote. The issue of self-government moved again to the fore.

It was a question with many dimensions because it touched raw nerves within Ireland, within Britain, between Britain and Ireland, and within the British Empire. The wonderful thing about 'Home Rule' was that it could mean whatever one wanted it to mean. The Nonconformist ministers of Bristol seemed to think that what the Irish wanted was 'Local Self Government'. But was it? Did the Irish know what they wanted? Home Rule, for Lord Hugh Cecil, was a 'sordid, silly and degrading dream'. The Irish should feel 'a real pride of true citizenship in the great nation to which we and they belong'. The notion of Irish nationality was 'dangerous to the whole Empire'.[36] George Wyndham, too, had another surge of Tory optimism, suggesting that remedial land legislation would do the trick. They, the Irish, would believe in the Empire because they believed in him. By 'they' he meant 'the whole lot – Unionist, Nationalist, Celt, Norman, Elizabethan, Cromwellian, Williamite, agriculturalist, educationalist and folk-lorist'.[37] It was his clear implication that if his legislation failed and Home Rule followed, the aforementioned would identify different expressions of 'home'.

So, did 'Home Rule' in the United Kingdom, in various European states, in the British Empire offer a solution to the vexed questions surrounding statehood and identity, or was it a mirage? 'Home Rule' might provide a solution 'all round' – that is to say it could mean that in multi-national or multi-regional states constitutional and administrative arrangements could be found which not only safeguarded their integrity but also allowed 'self-government': the best of all worlds. However, though such a separation of powers might be theoretically possible it would nevertheless lead to a never-ending financial and legal wrangle. Authority and accountability would become muddled. Centralised states might indeed oppress minorities (however defined) either mildly or severely but they did preserve order and gave clarity to decision-making. Multi-layered states were too complex and their decision-making too cumbersome. 'Home Rule', of course, was a slogan not a template. In these years Europe was a continent of imperial states, nation-states and stateless-nations. The existing states, whether themselves 'new' or 'old' (in terms of European history) all asserted their legitimacy but they had never been primordial. Norman Davies has brilliantly uncovered the 'Vanished Kingdoms' of Europe, their borders and institutions now known only to historians, and perhaps only dimly to most of them.

In October 1901 the new Conservative MP for Oldham, Winston Churchill, a man who knew the British Empire at first hand, complained that the existing structures of government at Westminster were inadequate. He wrote to a senior civil servant to talk about a scheme he had been discussing with his friend Lord Hugh Cecil. Churchill felt that 'the reputation and efficiency of Parliament almost entirely depends upon its being cleared of the over-press of minor duties on which so much time is wasted, and which prevents any detailed criticism being brought to bear on the affairs of a world-wide Empire'. One solution would be the creation of Provincial Councils in England to deal with local matters. The civil servant, however, was sceptical. The production of Northeastern or Southwestern Provincial Councils would be 'the work of centuries'. Besides he suspected that new Provincial Councillors might be little better than County Councillors since the attractions of Parliament for 'the best men' would and should remain.[38] Changing some cumbersome parliamentary procedures would be a better way forward. When Asquith in 1908 suggested that the now Liberal Churchill should enter the Cabinet as President of the Local Government Board, Churchill demurred, explaining 'There is no place in the Government more laborious, more anxious, more thankless, more choked with petty & even squalid detail, more full of hopeless and insoluble difficulties.'[39] His plea was heard. The MP for Dundee was not let loose on English local government, but his early concern as an MP that the 'management' of Empire was not being effectively done at Westminster remained with him.

The number of colonies of British settlement enjoying 'responsible government' had been steadily growing. The Canadian Confederation of 1867 had been subsequently enlarged. The Australian Commonwealth was formed in 1901. Such statements read simply, but behind them lay long debate and complex identity transfer. Both countries were federal, but their respective arrangements between their provinces/states and 'the Dominion' differed. New Zealand and Newfoundland were unitary and post-war South Africa became a Union. The Colonial Conference of 1907 conferred the title of Dominion on all of them: it sounded impressive. They possessed the common characteristic of fully representative legislatures and fully responsible executives: self-government. Their constitutional development had been chosen by the colonies themselves. In that same year they were allowed to negotiate but not yet conclude separate treaties. On both sides, few politicians could have supposed that a permanent set of constitutional settlements had been put in place. It was no easy task to describe what the whole of this 'Britain overseas' amounted to. They were not 'independent' states. They acknowledged the Crown for whom the Governor-General did duty. They had 'Home Rule' but could not be said to have 'taken control' of their foreign relations and did not possesses diplomatic services which would be required for such a task. They were all 'British' although, leaving aside indigenous inhabitants who stood outside the political process, in Canada and South Africa respectively, French and Afrikaans speakers were participants. Perhaps that augured well, but it might be too early to tell whether in Australia and Canada provincial/state/Dominion powers and competences would prove enduring and acceptable.

The Imperial Federation League, founded in 1884, had advocated the systematic organisation of the empire. The book on the subject by the Canadian G.R. Parkin referred to the 'Problem of National Unity' – and by national unity he did not mean Canadian unity.[40] In 1893 he had published 'The British Empire Map of the World based on Mercator's Projection', which aimed to show how modern communications made it possible to turn the scattered British Empire into an organic unity. He and another Canadian, a man virulently anti-American, George T. Denison, continued to press the case. As Canadians, they took pride in the fact that the small provinces had been merged into a great Dominion, Canada, which would be one of the dominant powers of the world. Such consolidation, they believed, complemented rather than undermined 'Imperial Unity'. However, the League dissolved in 1893 in some acrimony.[41] Nevertheless, into the twentieth century, from the lips of Joseph Chamberlain and Alfred Milner, among others, Whitley would have been very familiar with the argument that the future of the world lay with great empires and not little states (and the United Kingdom on its own was a little state which would find it hard to retain its place 'amongst the foremost nations of the world').[42] The difficulty lay in getting people to 'learn to think imperially'.[43] It may now appear that 'the permanent Unity of the Empire' in which local self-government would be preserved but where all its members would be 'better together' was always a mirage. Was it ever realistic to envisage 'the deliberate adoption of the Empire as distinguished from the United Kingdom as the basis for public policy' as the economist W.A.S. Hewins advocated in 1899? Individuals and groups, however, continued to offer 'solutions'. For Lionel Curtis, whether the Dominions were to become independent republics, or whether a world-wide Commonwealth was destined to stand more closely united as the 'noblest of all political achievements', was the question of the hour. He wanted to see a separate Cabinet and a separate Parliament responsible to the electorate of the United Kingdom for its own domestic affairs, and an Imperial Cabinet responsible to an Imperial Parliament governing the whole. The question, for him, was whether England could 'bear to lose her life, as she knows it, to find in a Commonwealth, wide as the world itself, a life greater and nobler than before'.[44]

In the years immediately before 1914 it was at least conceivable that a multi-layered solution would emerge which would simultaneously deal with the 'United Kingdom question' and the 'Empire/Commonwealth question'. 'Internal' affairs and 'external affairs' could supposedly be clearly separated. An Imperial Parliament would have nothing to do with the domestic affairs of the United Kingdom and in turn a United Kingdom Parliament would not concern itself with the 'local' affairs of its several constituent parts. Writing in 1912, Lord Selborne, a Unionist peer and former MP for Edinburgh West, thought only a single United Kingdom Parliament was necessary, but Parliaments in England, Scotland, Wales and two in Ireland would not be disastrous.[45] If that happened, in a United Kingdom abounding in 'Home Rule', Ireland would cease to be a 'special case'. The state would be a explicitly multi-national, one in which decision-making was appropriately tiered.[46] All parts – call them nations if you wished – would have their particular needs catered for but in turn 'big issues' were for the United Kingdom Parliament. However, that Parliament would also be part of an imperial system, within which, over time, decision-making, would become multi-lateral. In the event, of course no such multi-layered structure emerged. What would have been the longer-term consequences of such a restructured United Kingdom, invites intriguing counter-factual speculation.[47]

It was of course the outcome of the First World War and the break-up of Europe's three empires – German, Austrian, Russian – which made the consideration of new statehoods possible. That same war to led to the partial break-up of the United Kingdom as the Irish Free State emerged as a reluctant and restless Dominion and a Northern Ireland emerged with a 'Home Rule' Parliament which was unique within the United Kingdom, one which Unionists had never originally wanted.[48] There was no Imperial Parliament. There were no Parliaments in England, Scotland or Wales to consider 'local issues'. It was a new European order whose broad contours were decided by the three victorious great states: Britain, France and, somewhat oddly, the United States, with Italy 'standing by'. The bargaining of the great post-war conferences cannot detain us here, but even when most central difficulties had been apparently agreed intractable issues remained. Who should decide boundaries and borders? What mechanism should be employed? Should 'the people' decide who they were and where they belonged? But did 'the people' know who they really were? And what if what they wanted, in any given instance, might be at loggerheads with economic sense and, more generally, render European order unstable. Philosophers could ask what was the 'self' that was doing the 'determining'? National coherence, thought of in terms of language, religion, culture, even race, ran up against fault lines of class, education and the urban/rural divide. Almost all old or new 'nation-states' had 'minorities', cast adrift, as they might feel, from their fellow 'nationals' in other states, contiguous or distant. Sizeable minorities, often formerly culturally dominant, now found themselves excluded from the new hegemonic 'national communities'. The classic case here was the new state of Czechoslovakia. But these issues did not only arise at what might be called the German/Slav interface. What should be the capital city of new Lithuania? Vilnius, the capital of contemporary Lithuania had a Polish majority and there were few Lithuanians around. The city became, eventually, part of the new Poland but continued to be seen by Lithuanians, for historical reasons, as Lithuanian. One could give many more examples. In some cases plebiscites were held, but their outcome left the losing side still feeling that its 'homeland' was elsewhere. 'Minority' issues thus became part and parcel of inter-war European politics in many countries. The international organisation created to buttress the new order – The League of Nations – was itself shot through with ambiguity. It wasn't really a 'League', as diplomacy had understood that term in European history, and it was a League of States not of Nations. So, taken in the round, the settlement of 1919 had not in fact solved 'self-government' in Europe.

The 'British Empire' question too had moved on. With accelerating speed through the period of Whitley's Speakership, and then in the years immediately afterwards, the kind of scenario sketched by Curtis and others, admittedly in some desperation, ceased to be a plausible picture. Of course it had been the British Empire which had fought the Central Powers and there had indeed been a kind of Imperial War Cabinet, but 'self-government', as conceived before the war, dropped away. The 1926 Imperial Conference presided over by Lord Balfour took matters a stage further. The 1931 Statute of Westminster demonstrated that a half-way house was no longer feasible. To most intents and purposes, the Dominions were 'independent', no longer directed in their external relations by the 'mother country'. When Lord Irwin in 1929 held out the prospect of 'Dominion status' to India it was already a term whose meaning was changing rapidly. That is not to say that all of the Dominions wished to assert themselves at the same speed or that they ostentatiously chose to set out on contrary paths. The Crown remained a symbol of a kind of unity, though not always and everywhere one acknowledged with enthusiasm.

Back in 1879, in one of his Midlothian speeches, Gladstone had declared that no wise statesman or 'right-minded Briton' would want to weaken the authority of the Imperial Parliament (Westminster) but, subject to that limitation, if a way could be found whereby Ireland, Scotland, Wales and portions of England could deal with questions of local and special interest to themselves more efficiently than Parliament could, that would be 'a great national good'.[49] He never found the way.

Whitley's lifetime happened to coincide almost precisely with the passing of legislation which marked the transition of the United Kingdom from a constitutional state to a democracy. Born in the year before the 1867 Reform Act significantly extended the parliamentary franchise (for men) Whitley left the House of Commons in 1928, the year in which, with the further extension of the vote to women, the parliamentary system in the United Kingdom became based upon a universal franchise. His departure from Parliament therefore could be taken to confirm that the accelerating journey which had lasted the half-century of his life had reached its true destination. 'Parliamentary democracy' had just arrived. Moreover, the end of the journey, if it was the end, seemed, in general, satisfactory and desirable. It was broadly, though not universally, agreed that the country's political and judicial institutions were class-neutral.[50] When Walter Bagehot, the celebrated writer of *The English Constitution* (as he called it) turned in its second edition in 1872 to considering the Reform Act of 1867 he was cautious. A new world had certainly arisen but it was still too early to judge its effect. The people enfranchised under it did not yet know their own power. The great change of politics was a change of generation. The grave question, as he put it, was whether the peculiar old system before its passage would survive. Only time would tell. Similarly Whitley's generation had brought the peculiar old system into a 'democratic era' but its practical meaning remained obscure. Whitley knew, by the time of his death, that 'democratic Europe' had quickly crumbled. 'Merely representative government is not democracy,' wrote J.A. Hobson in completing a study of the working of democracy in Switzerland begun in 1901–02 by the American Henry Demarest Lloyd, 'however wide the franchise, however proportionate the representation, because it embodies no provision fastening a conscious continuous responsibility upon the minds of the citizen-voters. Government by the people could only be secured by giving the people an effective veto on the acts of those to whom they have accorded a general power of agency . . .'[51]

This chapter has been written in 2016, the year when 'the British people' voted in favour of leaving the European Union by 51.9 per cent to 48.1 per cent and a new course has been set for the future. It has not been its purpose to comment explicitly on this outcome. Nobody can know with any certainty what that future will be, either for the structure of the United Kingdom itself, for its external relations, or for 'Europe' more generally. It has also been written a century after the Easter Rising in Dublin in 1916, and also in the wake of the Referendum on Scottish independence. In all these contexts, in one way or another, it would seem that 'we' have been asked to declare whether we are 'Better Together' or 'Better Apart'. 'We' have been asked to weigh participation in a larger entity/ community/commonwealth/union (with whatever limitation of sovereignty that may entail) against an independence, a sovereignty, which is in principle absolute. By taking 'Self-Government' and 'Home Rule' as a theme, some of the similarities (and dissimilarities) between the worlds of J.H. Whitley and the uncertain present have been noted. We have seen that J.H. Whitley might have come to be Speaker of a House of Commons with United Kingdom 'local issues' as its remit. He might have been Speaker of a House of Commons with English 'local issues' as its remit. He could even conceivably have become Speaker of an Imperial Federal or quasi-federal Parliament. In the event he became none of these things. Playing a role in a European Parliament never entered the picture. In fact, he became 'just' the Speaker of a House of Commons in which, Northern Irish Unionist MPs apart, members came from Great Britain. He lived with a Parliament and Prime Minister in Northern Ireland. Parliaments/Assemblies in Edinburgh and Cardiff, however, seemed in 1928 to be both unlooked for and unlikely. However, in his era the Imperial Conferences of 1921, 1923 and 1926 wrestled again with 'imperial unity' and 'local issues' as members of the 'family' began, though only slowly, to conduct their own external affairs. The 'British' Commonwealth of self-governing 'Dominions' which Whitley knew has passed. It may now be a 'Commonwealth' but it is not a Union.

Suddenly, however, in 2016, assumptions about 'the course of history' have been jolted and perhaps destroyed. Matters which appeared to have been settled have become unsettled: politics, economics and culture could go in many directions. Anybody seeking to discover what 'History teaches' in these circumstances would only have found distinguished groups of historians reaching opposing conclusions and firing heavy weapons at their opponents. Reason and emotion have all been jumbled up. 'We Europeans' wrote one German historian, himself familiar with Britain, in a book which appeared in English, French, German, Italian and Spanish 'have grown used to our ancient states and nations; they will still be with us for a long time to come and we shall still need them. But they have constantly changed in the past, and they will go on changing in the future, they may gradually fade away and recede into the background to make way for one united Europe, the shape of which we can at present only dimly discern.'[52] Now, the shape of the future may be discerned even more dimly.[53]

Notes

1 Andrew Roberts, *'The Holy Fox'*, *A Biography of Lord Halifax*, London, Weidenfeld & Nicolson, 1991, p. 30.
2 A Cambridge history graduate, she was the sister of the historian Eileen Power.
3 The great increase in legislative activity and the pressure on parliamentary time had enhanced the role and rulings of the Speaker. W.H. Greenleaf, *The British Political Tradition, Volume Three, A Much Governed Nation, Part 2*, London, Methuen, 1987, p. 802.
4 W.H. Greenleaf, *The British Political Tradition, Volume One, The Rise of Collectivism*, London, Methuen, 1983, p. 90.
5 In his autobiography, Lord Halifax, *Fullness of Days*, London, Collins, 1957, p. 106, Halifax paid tribute to Whitley's success, as Speaker, in getting members to listen to opinions with which they sharply disagreed.

6 Sir Charles Wood (Viscount Halifax) was a Whig and his grandson was not a 'true Blue'. R.J. Moore, *Sir Charles Wood's Indian Policy 1853–66*, Manchester, Manchester University Press, 1966.
7 James Vernon, 'Narrating the Constitution: the discourse of "the real" and the fantasies of nineteenth-century constitutional history' in the volume he edited, *Re-reading the Constitution: new narratives in the political history of England's in nineteenth century*, Cambridge, Cambridge University Press, 1996, pp. 204–238: James Kirby, *Historians and the Church of England: Religion and Historical Scholarship, 1870–1920*, Oxford, Oxford University Press, 2016.
8 In general see Jane Garnett, 'Evangelicalism and Business in Mid-Victorian Britain', in John Wolffe, (ed.), *Evangelical Faith and Public Zeal*, London, S.P.C.K., 1995, pp. 59–80.
9 Halifax. A list of works visited by H.M. Inspector of Factories where the means of escape in case of fire were considered defective.
10 P.J. Waller, *Town City & Nation: England 1850–1914*, Oxford, Oxford University Press, 1983, pp. 125, 313.
11 F.M.L. Thompson 'Town and City', in F.M.L. Thompson, (ed.), *The Cambridge Social History of Britain 1750–1950, Volume 1: Regions and Communities*, Cambridge, Cambridge University Press, 1990, p. 38.
12 F.M.L. Thompson, *Gentrification and the Enterprise Culture: Britain 1780–1980*, Oxford, Oxford University Press, 2001, p. 17.
13 John Morley, *The Life of John Morley*, London, T. Fisher Unwin, 1903, p. 946.
14 Alan Kidd and David Nicholls (eds), *The Making of the British Middle Class? Studies of Regional and Cultural Diversity since the Eighteenth Century*, Stroud, Sutton, 1998, p. xxxi.
15 Pat Thane, 'Government and Society in England and Wales, 1750–1914', in F.M.L. Thompson (ed.), *The Cambridge Social History of Britain 1750–1950, Volume 3: Social Agencies and Institutions*, Cambridge, Cambridge University Press, 1990, p. 3.
16 This paragraph is indebted to Asa Briggs, 'Local, regional, national: the historical dimension of public authority', in Adolf M. Birke and Magnus Breckten (eds), *Kommunale Selbstverwatlug Geschickle und Gegerwart im deutschbritisches Vergleich*, Prinz-Albert-Studies 13, Munich, K.G. Saur, 1996, pp. 13–24; see also Keith Robbins, 'Local Self-Government in Britain since 1945: Inexorable Decline?', in A.M. Birke and Magnus Brechtgen (eds), *Kommunale Selbstverwaltung/Local Self-Government*, Munich, Saur, 1996, pp. 13–24 and pp. 97–104.
17 G.W. Crutchley, *John Mackintosh, A Biography*, London, Hodder & Stoughton, 1921, p. 47.
18 Keith Robbins, *Pride of Place: A Modern History of Bristol Grammar School*, Andover, Phillimore, 2010, p. 13. Clifton's representation in the House of Commons found a place for itself in the 'Other Public Schools' set alongside the 32 Etonians, 13 Harrovians and 17 Rugbeians sitting on the Liberal benches in 1906. J A. Thomas, *The House of Commons 1906–1911*, Cardiff, University of Wales Press, 1958, p. 38.
19 On Bristol see Helen Meller, *Leisure and the Changing City 1870–1914*, London, Routledge and Paul, 1976.
20 Its vast and varied activity under its minister can be seen in David Morgan Thomas, *Urijah Rees Thomas: His Life and Work*, London, Hodder & Stoughton, 1902.
21 Note the essays by D. George Boyce and Derek Beales on 'Gladstone and Ireland' and 'Gladstone and Garibaldi' respectively in Peter J. Jagger (ed.), *Gladstone*, London, Hambledon Press, 1998, pp. 105–22 and pp. 137–56.
22 Hugh and Christopher Seton-Watson, *The Making of a New Europe: R.W. Seton-Watson and the last years of Austria–Hungary*, London, Methuen, 1981, p. 32: In his book *The Nation State and National Self-Determination*, London, Collins, 1969, first published in 1945, Alfred Cobban, the historian of France, cited with apparent approval the 1913 observation of the French historian Seignobos that little nations, oppressed by foreigners, had no hope of winning independence by force of arms (p. 48).
23 R.T. Shannon, *Gladstone and the Bulgarian Agitation 1876*, London, Nelson, 1963, pp. 166–8.

24 Peter Raina, *George Macaulay Trevelyan: A Portrait in Letters*, Bishop Auckland, Pentland Books, 2001, p. 61.
25 David Cannadine, *G.M. Trevelyan: A Life in History*, London, HarperCollins, 1992, pp. 68–9. Trevelyan in his *British History in the Nineteenth Century*, London, Longmans, 1922, made his support for Irish Home Rule plain.
26 Denis Mack Smith, *Garibaldi*, London, Hutchinson, 1957, p. 11.
27 Keith Robbins, *Sir Edward Grey: A Biography of Lord Grey of Fallodon*, London, Cassell, 1971. One of Grey's two brothers at Clifton College was killed in Africa by a lion. Another, not a Cliftonian, died at the hands of a buffalo. The Foreign Secretary restricted himself to contact with birds, ducks and fishes. Keith Robbins, 'The Foreign Secretary, the Cabinet, Parliament and the Parties' and 'Public Opinion, the Press and Pressure Groups', in F.H. Hinsley (ed.), *British Foreign Policy under Sir Edward Grey*, Cambridge, Cambridge University Press, 1977, pp. 3–21 and pp. 70–88; Michael Hughes, 'Nonconformity and Foreign Policy', in Keith Robbins and John Fisher (eds), *Religion and Diplomacy: Religion and British Foreign Policy, 1815 to 1941*, Dordrecht, Republic of Letters Publishing, 2010, pp. 33–60.
28 George Macaulay Trevelyan, *George Otto Trevelyan: A Memoir*, London, Longmans, 1932, pp. 80–4.
29 Cited in John Pemble, *The Mediterranean Passion: Victorians and Edwardians in the South*, Oxford, Oxford University Press, 1987, p. 240.
30 Keith Robbins, *Nineteenth-Century Britain: Integration and Diversity*, Oxford, Oxford University Press, 1988.
31 Paul Ward, *Britishness since 1870*, London, Routledge, 2004, Keith Robbins, *Great Britain: Identities, Institutions and the Idea of Britishness*, London, Longman, 1998: Helen Brocklehurst and Robert Phillips (eds), *History, Identity and the Question of Britain*, Basingstoke, Palgrave Macmillan, 2004.
32 Thomas, *House of Commons*, pp. 6–7.
33 Paul Ward, *Unionism in the United Kingdom, 1918–1974*, Basingstoke, Palgrave Macmillan, 2005.
34 W.E. Gladstone to Urijah Rees Thomas, 7 December 1887, and surrounding material, in Thomas, *Urijah Rees Thomas*, pp. 267–70.
35 Alvin Jackson, *Home Rule: An Irish History 1800–2000*, Oxford, Oxford University Press, 2004.
36 Arthur Mejia, 'Lord Hugh Cecil', in J.A. Thompson and Arthur Mejia (eds), *Edwardian Conservatism: Five Studies in Adaptation*, Beckenham, Croom Helm, 1988, p. 29.
37 J.A. Thompson 'George Wyndham: Toryism and Imperialism', in Thompson and Mejia, *Edwardian Conservatism*, p. 114.
38 Winston S. Churchill to Sir Thomas Elliott, 22 October 1901: Sir Thomas Elliott to Winston Churchill 28 October 1901. The late Sir Hugh Elliott made these letters available to me.
39 Martin Gilbert, *Churchill: A Life*, London, Heinemann, 1991, p. 19.
40 George R. Parkin, *Imperial Federation: The Problem of National Unity*, London, Macmillan, 1892.
41 George T. Denison, *The Struggle for Imperial Unity*, London, Macmillan, 1909.
42 E.H.H. Green, 'The Political Economy of Empire, 1880–1914', in Andrew Porter (ed.), *The Oxford History of the British Empire: The Nineteenth Century*, Oxford, Oxford University Press, 1999, pp. 347–9.
43 Carl Bridge and Kent Fedorowich (eds), *The British World: Diaspora, Culture and Identity*, London, Routledge, 2003.
44 Lionel Curtis, *The Problem of the Commonwealth*, London, Macmillan, 1916 pp. vii and 216–20. The Round Table had started its reflections on these matters in 1910.
45 D. George Boyce (ed.), *The Crisis of British Unionism: The Domestic Political Papers of the Second Earl of Selborne, 1885–1922*, London, The Historian's Press, 1987, p. 91.
46 The condition of Ireland was perceived and felt differently, on the one hand 'oppressed colony' and on the other as 'Imperial partner'. See Kevin Kenny (ed.), *Ireland and the British*

Empire, Oxford, Oxford University Press, 2004 and, in particular, the contribution by Alvin Jackson, 'Ireland, the Union the Empire, 1800–1960', pp. 123–53: Stephen Howe, *Ireland and Empire: Colonial Legacies in Irish History and Culture*, Oxford, Oxford University Press, 2000: Keith Jeffrey (ed.), *'An Irish Empire'? Aspects of Ireland and the British Empire*, Manchester, Manchester University Press, 2006.

47 J.E. Kendle, *Federal Britain: A History*, London, Routledge, 1997: Patricia Jalland, 'United Kingdom Devolution 1910–14: Political Panacea or Tactical Diversion', *Economic History Review*, 4 (1979), 757–85: Alvin Jackson, 'British Ireland: What if Home Rule had been enacted in 1912?', in Niall Ferguson (ed.), *Virtual History: Alternatives and Counterfactuals*, London, Papermac, 1997.

48 D.W. Harkness, *The Restless Dominion: The Irish Free State and the British Commonwealth of Nations 1921–31*, London, Macmillan, 1969.

49 Gladstone at Dalkeith 26 November 1879 cited in David Marquand, 'Regional Devolution', in Jeffrey Jowell and Dawn Oliver (eds), *The Changing Constitution*, Oxford, The Clarendon Press, 1989, p. 385.

50 Ross McKibbin, *Classes and Cultures England 1918–1951*, Oxford, Oxford University Press, 1998, p. v and *Parties and People: England 1914–1951*, Oxford, Oxford University Press, 2010, p. vi.

51 Henry Demerest Lloyd, (ed.) J.A. Hobson, *The Swiss Democracy: The study of a Sovereign People*, London, Fisher Unwin, 1908, pp. 243–4. If it was, as it was sometimes said, that democracy could only work in small countries, Lloyd thought that it was up to Americans to turn themselves into a country in which the centre was not out of reach of those on the circumference.

52 Hagen Schulze, *States, Nations and Nationalism: From the Middle Ages to the Present* (Oxford, Wiley-Blackwell, 1996), p. 326.

53 Brendan Simms, *Britain's Europe: A Thousand Years of Conflict and Cooperation*, London, Allen Lane, 2016, offers a long view on these matters.

13 J.H. Whitley's 'first draft of history'

A study of the obituaries and personal tributes

John Barrett

> If I can, I will prevent my death from saying anything not first said by my life.[1]

The above declaration is taken from Michel Montaigne's 'That the intention is judge of our actions', and with the rather prescient nature of such things, was written just before his death in 1595. Montaigne wanted his death to be 'morally at one with his life'; broadly speaking his assertion attempts to take into account a person's moral worth at the point of death. Similarly, this chapter will consider its significance and relationship as part of an appraisal of the 'first draft of history' upon the death of J.H. Whitley.

Unfortunately, and unlike Montaigne who wrote a great deal about himself and others, there is no existing memoir written by Whitley, so we are left with what others thought of him. Can what was said of Whitley in anyway confirm the declaration of Montaigne and suggest that Whitley was himself morally at one with 'his' own life? In as much as there is a lack of a self-written memoir, we should consider the immediate responses to Whitley's death in 1935, primarily the obituaries and later material gathered from the tributes, memoirs and recollections in the years following his death.

A published obituary can be a curious thing. It can reveal a range of interesting facts and expose a number of revelations, none of which are generally scandalous, but sometimes these facts can elicit enough attention to warrant further research. To some the ultimate posthumous acknowledgment might be to have an obituary published in one of the major newspapers, as this might signal to those envious readers who spot our demise, that one has led a full and valuable life. They may not readily agree, but there is still a certain cachet in having one's trumpet blown in serious column inches. The newspaper obituary itself has changed little in style and content over the years; after all, obituaries tend not to write ill of the dead. In the 1930s it was rare that an obituary told the reader what the deceased died of, or their age, though today death-details are more relaxed. Obituaries will say someone left their job, but not usually why, and a divorce may be mentioned – but not who threw what at whom! What interests us as readers is the culture of curiosity, and an interest in the lives of others, customarily those much more famous than ourselves, means that we engage in a form of social voyeurism. Today the newspapers record the obituaries of a wide range of people, many of whom may be unknown to us, but typically they have all been influential in their own particular way. Of course the obituary is not the sole domain of the national papers; many regional and local papers record the passing of 'their' local notables and were we to miss the printed obituary, the internet and social media are more than capable of both soliciting and satisfying our need to know. And yet, the ephemeral nature of the majority of obituaries, in their many forms and formats, means that this fleeting snap-shot of a life is often soon forgotten. Ultimately we have little or no control over our 'first draft of history'. In order to avert such a startling predicament we should ensure that at the point of death, our deeds in life say everything about us. What did Whitley's deeds say about him and his life?

Whitley's obituaries

By looking at the possible transient nature of the many obituaries dedicated to J.H. Whitley, one can see how these early sources offer a rather ordinary account of his life. Although they tend to be somewhat repetitive, particularly around the biographical details, there are a select few which offer interesting insight, but little revelation. In order to get close to the spirit of Whitley one should examine the more personalised memories and tributes, these tend to capture the essence of the man and give this initial draft of history a realistic structure – from such sources, Whitley takes shape.

When J.H. Whitley died on 3 February 1935, *The Daily Telegraph* reported that he had died in a London nursing home at the age of sixty nine (Whitley was actually 68).[2] The *Telegraph* hints at certain milestones in his political career, dealing in the main with his time as Speaker, which the paper describes as 'unusually short'. This is rather misleading as Whitley had been Deputy Speaker since 1911 and Speaker from 1921 to 1928, and during his tenure as Deputy Speaker he had the onerous task of filling in for the often absent Speaker, James Lowther.[3] The paper records that during Whitley's Speakership there were frequent outbursts 'of a kind unprecedented in the House of Commons', and where 'a hot tempered Speaker might have quelled their interruptions more rapidly than Mr Whitley', who, we learn, 'adopted an attitude of patient counsel, which in the long run proved thoroughly effective'.[4] These frequent outbursts came from the benches of the Labour Party, which the paper refers to as the 'Socialist Party', and which by 1922 had 'brought a new type of politician to Westminster; [where] defiance of the Speaker and impatience with Parliamentary procedure characterised their methods'.[5] *The Times*, equally fascinated by Whitley's Speakership, reports that 'Like Manners-Sutton, he rode the House on a snaffle, gentling it as a high spirited horse is gentled.'[6]

Apart from his tenure as Speaker, it is Whitley's northern origins that have an equal attraction for the papers. This was largely due to the fact that Whitley was considered something of an enigma in political circles, and, as such, his northern roots and industrialist background are picked up by *The Times* – which notes that he was the first Speaker 'to sit for a great industrial constituency and he was the first Speaker to be engaged in trade, thus breaking the long tradition which associated the office with the Bar or with the landed gentry'.[7] It is useful to compare these comments in the *Times* with a much later piece quoted from the *Trading and Educational News*, by Whitley's son Oliver in 1969. Marking the fiftieth anniversary of the 'Whitley Councils' the article gives a personal account of the man behind *Whitleyism*. Oliver Whitley considers his father's northern roots and the qualities required of an even-handed Speaker, whilst at the same time promoting his father's benevolence as a younger man – 'Here for once and at last, was a businessman, a cotton spinner from the industrial north, a conciliator, a fervent believer in participation, consultation, [and] delegated shared discipline, who had practised these precepts in his boy's camps and co-partnership schemes in the mill.'[8]

By and large *The Times* obituary offers little in the way of a true 'first impression' of Whitley, yet there is some clearer insight offered from those who worked alongside him. The recollections of Sir Alexander Mackenzie Livingstone and Mr Edward Miles are particularly apposite. Quoted in *The Times* on 5 February 1935, in consideration of the obituary reported the day before, Livingstone recalls that 'When I first met him on entering the House of Commons as a young member in 1923 I knew at once that I had found a friend, an hour or less spent with him was a liberal education – his private appraisement of the personality of the individual member was always illuminating, but ever gentle and generous.' Edward Miles, Whitley's butler when Speaker, recalls that he had 'the greatest respect and admiration' for him, and that 'to me he was more than an employer – he was a generous and appreciative friend', 'a very great and modest Englishman'.[9] A similar appreciative, though much later recollection from the former Prime Minister Harold Macmillan, recalls the fondness he had for the 'genial' Whitley.

> Presiding over this House of Commons, with the mixture of individuals and groupings that I have described, was our genial 'headmaster', Mr. Speaker Whitley. I have sat under five Speakers. Capt. Fitzroy ruled the House with a severe discipline which was accepted because he was absolutely fair. But he was rather frightening. [As] for Whitley, my first Speaker, I had the affectionate regard which any young member feels for a Speaker who treats him with sympathy and understanding. He seemed always to enter into the anxieties of unimportant back-benchers sitting through long hours of debate waiting hopefully to be called. If, at last, five or ten minutes could be spared during the dinner hour, with not more than a dozen Members in the House, Whitley, whether in the chair himself or perhaps later on his return, would somehow make one feel that he had been glad to help. Some said he was a weak Speaker. But all government whips say that about Speakers, who very properly protect the opposition and the minorities in the House. Whitley was a kindly Speaker.[10]

Similar sentiments are expressed by the *Manchester Guardian*, a paper which was traditionally affiliated with the centre-left Liberal Party, and had a strong northern Nonconformist circulation. It recalled two occasions from Whitley's Speakership which reveal something of his character.[11] The first was what the paper described as a particularly 'fair hearing of Mr Saklatvala', the second, an allegation of 'counterpoising Cromwellianism', which Whitley received from the benches after granting closure to a debate on the 1925 Finance Bill. In the case of Saklatvala, who was an MP representing the Communist Party of Great Britain in Battersea, Whitley insisted upon a fair hearing for the somewhat 'unpopular member' and called upon him in equal rotation with the more numerous parties, a practice which gave that 'loquacious propagandist' more than his share of the House's time. This was a typical Whitley trait and one which he also showed towards the Labour Party.[12] Such sympathies are supported by Sir Ralph Verney, Whitley's secretary during his Speakership. Verney, in a letter to Lord Hemingford in 1945, recalled that the Speaker's treatment of the Labour Party was deliberate, and that he (Whitley) was never 'diverted by any hostile criticism', though he would never allow them to 'transgress the rules of order or to act contrary to recognised procedure'. 'If a member did transgress, Whitley would often put the responsible party right in the privacy of his library and out of earshot of any opponents.'[13] The allegation of counterpoising Cromwellianism was as a result of Whitley granting closure to the Conservative government at 11.45 pm on the first day's debate of the motion for the second reading of the 1925 Finance Bill. The MP for Swansea Walter Runciman and others had risen to catch his eye, but had been supposedly ignored by the Speaker. As a result, Lloyd George, Sir John Simon, Runciman, Sir Alfred Mond and Captain Wedgwood Benn spoke in support of a motion of censure upon the Speaker for his alleged conduct on this occasion – only the Liberals voted for the motion, but were roundly rejected by a majority of 279 votes against. On such issues *The Guardian*'s summing up of Whitley's term as Speaker was – 'although he showed excessive amiability against those critical of his high-mindedness, it may be that in reality he steered a carefully pondered and shrewdly judged course'.[14]

The Halifax obituaries and tributes

As one might expect the tributes from Halifax were extensive. There was, like the nationals, a reflective account of Whitley's life printed in the Monday edition, whilst on the following weekend, the *Halifax Weekly Courier and Guardian* went into much more detail under the laudable title 'Death of an illustrious son of Halifax'.[15] The double-page spread accounted for every major milestone in Whitley's life. By and large the various articles praised Whitley for his long and continued association with Halifax and, with a sense of pride, the *Courier* named other local and regional papers that had carried the news of his death. The opening paragraph of *The Halifax Courier and Guardian*'s tribute on the 4 February initiated the feelings of much later commentary, when the paper exclaimed that men of Whitley's ilk are 'by instinct and training destined for a life in public service'. Whitley's independent spirit and early service towards those in need in his home town during the 1880s, plus his experience in municipal politics, polished his instinct in readiness for national politics; though his objections to the government's proposals for the future of state education were a significant driver towards his decision to finally accept the Liberal Party's nomination in 1900. Following the trend of many of the papers that week, and according to the *Courier*, his true character, was reflected in his Speakership

> He did not allow his exhaustive knowledge of Parliamentary rules and usages, [and] his deep respect for tradition, to shackle his adaptability to circumstances – tempering stern justice with kindly conciliation – by the end of his term he had earned the respect and appreciation of old as well as new parties.[16]

These latter comments are enforced when the paper reports a tribute from Mr George Lansbury: 'No one who was a member of the House of Commons during Mr Whitley's term of office will fail to receive the news of his death with very profound regret and I wish to put on record appreciation of his very great public service.'[17] There was further praise from the Labour ranks under the title 'From a Fellow Worker – An appreciation by Mr James Parker'. The former Halifax Labour MP had known Whitley since 1897, when they had both served on the council; their association was continued when Parker was an MP for Halifax between 1906 and 1918. Said Parker:

> I cannot say that we were close friends though we were always friendly. Whitley was somewhat reserved; he did not gush nor was he demonstrative. I have to confess that I never was able to get close to him. I do not think it was pride or stiffness – he was of a retiring disposition. He could be angry and severe but his anger was usually aroused by injustice and his severity tempered by a kindly disposition. Whitley was a true commoner, he desired no title, the gilded hereditary chamber had no attractions for him. Many persons blamed him for declining a peerage and, what was much more the monetary advantage that went with it. He was not mercenary. He held himself in iron discipline. He could not slack. Duty to him was the first object and no effort was too great to perform it with full efficiency.[18]

The Halifax papers also reported the various tributes from groups and individuals associated with the town. One of many tributes from the various church groups was reported as taking place at the Park Congregational Church. The memorial service was conducted by the Rev. G.V. Jones, who, in the eulogy, referred to Whitley as 'A Christian gentleman who left his mark in the spheres of religion, social service and political activity . . . Forty years ago he taught young men in this church and continued to do so when busy with affairs of the nation.'[19] From his fellow Liberals there were tributes and messages of condolence, the association of Halifax Liberals resolved to send a message of condolence to Mrs Whitley and the Halifax Women's Liberal Association, under the auspices of Lady Fisher-Smith JP, recognised the contribution Whitley had made to both local and national politics.[20] The local Conservatives also paid their ritual tribute, as did the Labour Party.

Whitley's links to local education and public service were also applauded; Heath Grammar school, paid tribute to Whitley on the Thursday following his death. The Headmaster Mr Owen Byrde praised the Whitley family and Whitley himself for the efforts he and the family had made towards the benefit of the school. In particular he recognised the recreational evening school and the poor boys' camps at Filey, he said – 'there was no stronger conviction in his soul, than that it was the duty and privilege of all to help those less fortunate than themselves and that camp and gym became the training ground in public spirit and good citizenship of dozens of young men'. Byrde also recalled the usefulness of the 'Whitley Scheme' which, with the assistance of many manufacturers in the town and charitable subscriptions of £60, enabled many boys to make the most of a university education.[21] The final cutting from the *Courier* under the sub-heading 'Yorkshire Speakers and Not Disenfranchised', raises a rather important point, that of a Speaker's effectiveness as an MP when he is in the chair. Indeed, the *Courier* posed just such a dilemma facing the public of Halifax during Whitley's Speakership – 'There were of course, certain sections of the Halifax public which inclined to the view that during Whitley's Speakership the borough was largely disenfranchised as the Speaker took no part in debates.' The paper reports that a Sheffield paper note writer discussed this very point with Whitley, who replied:

> Halifax is probably as well looked after as any constituency in the country – for members of all parties are particularly kind to me as Speaker and if I mention that I should like to see something done for the benefit of Halifax they unite to do it as quickly as possible.[22]

The Clifton obituary

In a similar vein there were tributes from Whitley's old school, Clifton. The *Cliftonian* magazine recorded the death of their past president and former pupil and from the obituary we learn that the 'Whitley' boys had occupied the school from 1878–92, and that it was their father's choice, as it was a school 'in which differences of opinion were tolerated and a boy had to make his way by character and industry'.[23] One of Whitley's Clifton contemporaries said of him, 'I have never seen a boy who looked more high-minded', 'but he was no prig – he was a great promoter of diverse education, mixing the old with the new – in manner he was direct, sometimes blunt'.[24]

Whilst there is within these tributes from the local press a sense of loss and wholehearted praise for one of its own, there is also a subliminal message aimed at the readers, one which advocates a commitment to public duty towards one's community and, if that should lead towards duty to the nation, the path best followed is no better represented than the life of this 'illustrious son of Halifax'. As a young man Whitley had set out to improve the lives of young men and boys in Halifax; he did so by entering into a well organised philanthropic culture, one which required proof of moral worth and commitment towards Christian care and compassion. By participating in these ideals, opportunities of advancement opened up for him.

Personal tributes

Perhaps the most telling and important, though often uncritical, tributes regarding Whitley come to us by those who knew him best, particularly members of his family, primarily his son Oliver, and those who worked alongside him, most notably Whitley's secretary when Speaker, Sir Ralph Verney. The Whitley family recorded the following observations of Verney, in a memoir by Oliver Whitley where he compares his father's first secretary when he was elected as the MP for Halifax in 1900 with Verney. He says that his father's first secretary resembled 'a cross between Eddie Waring and Michael Parkinson', whereas Verney couldn't have been more different. He was establishment personified. 'He had a slight patrician stoop and had an ancestor who had been a standard bearer for Charles I.'[25] Verney's memories of Whitley are particularly detailed. In a letter to 'Dennis' (believed to be Dennis Herbert) written on 5 January 1945, he states that Whitley was never keen on occupying the Speaker's chair, but agreed to do so on two conditions agreed to by Austen Chamberlain, 'firstly, that he should be committed to tenure of not less than two years and thereafter was free to resign, and secondly he would not be pressed into receiving a peerage at the end of his term'.[26] According to Verney his reasons for refusing a peerage at the end of his term were that he did not want his son to inherit a title, and furthermore he thought a peerage might adversely affect the family business and his first wife did not want the burden of a title. However, and with the future in mind, Whitley did not want his actions on this matter to prejudice future Speakers who might want to succeed to a title.[27] On matters of entertainment and social etiquette Verney states that Whitley was 'un-attracted by, and ignorant of London society'. Due to interruptions during the war, Speakers' dinners had been severely curtailed, but Whitley was more than happy to resurrect these dinners, and despite being 'a poor man, as far as personal fortune was concerned, he never grudged the money spent on entertainments'.[28] It is clear that Whitley was less inclined to involve himself with the social and ceremonial aspects of his Speakership and more inclined to immerse himself in the political and administrative functions of the role.

Perhaps surprisingly it is the relationship with the Director-General of the BBC, John Reith, that provides us with some of the most enlightening memories of Whitley; theirs was a relationship that originated from rather obscure and uncertain beginnings, as Reith was notoriously difficult to get along with and his relationship with Whitley's predecessor Lord Clarendon, had for some time been strained. With the announcement on 7 February 1930 that Clarendon was to be appointed the next Governor General of South Africa, Reith was summoned to No. 10 by Ramsay MacDonald who had it in mind to release Clarendon as Chairman of the Board of Governors. In a heart-beat Reith agreed.[29] The sense of relief is palpable from Reith; he notes in his diary, 'We could not contain ourselves and did not know what to do to show our delight.'[30] Reith's suggestion that Clarendon's replacement might be Lord Gainford was probably made out of past loyalties, as he had been the Chairman of the Board of Directors of the old British Broadcasting Company Ltd (1922–26).[31] Gainford's appointment was vetoed by Ramsay MacDonald on the grounds of his age, so Reith suggested he might be allowed to take on a dual role as Chairman of Governors and Director-General, a suggestion he pursued vigorously, setting out his argument in writing to the Prime Minister, the Postmaster General Lees-Smith and the Lord Chancellor Lord Sankey, all to no avail. By the middle of May Reith had heard that Whitley was to be appointed. Lees-Smith told Reith he had racked his brain for a suitable appointment and had poured over a list of Privy Counsellors only arriving at Whitley at the end of the list. On the evening of the announcement of Whitley's appointment, Lord Burnham visited Reith and made clear his dissatisfaction regarding Whitley. The root of Burnham's displeasure was that Whitley was a 'Liberal and a Non-conformist'.[32]

At their first meeting on 11 June, Reith described Whitley as 'impressive in appearance; quiet and courteous; of a natural dignity; a man whom one could trust; who would be utterly sincere'.[33] Such a summary of human qualities gained from an initial meeting seem a little far-fetched, and was probably the result of their five-year partnership, as 'trust and sincerity' were the apparent hallmarks of Whitley's tenure as Chair of Governors. Over time, Reith grew to appreciate Whitley's candour and calm exterior, especially on those occasions when Reith was 'publicly outspoken'. Often expecting a stern rebuke, Reith frequently found his Chairman in good humour over such incidents, describing him as 'a man of surprises, for all the wisdom and dignity of seventy years, the heart and spirit of a boy'.[34]

However, their working relationship was a short one and it is towards the end of Whitley's life that the two of them became quite close friends. In September 1934, Reith left for South Africa at the invitation of the Prime Minister, General Hertzog, to advise on how radio might develop in the Union. Returning in mid-November he stopped off in Portugal where he heard that Whitley was seriously ill 'but his doctors had, they believed, got to the root of the problem'. At this point, Whitley had been in poor health for over a year.[35] On 18 January 1935, and back in England, Reith visited Whitley in a nursing home in London. Whitley told Reith that he was sure that he would not live much longer and believed that his doctors had been 'bluffing him' and although he was able to rest at night 'he hoped some morning he would not wake up'.[36]

On 3 February Reith received a phone call from Whitley's son Oliver to say that his father had died at 11.30 am that morning. Reith's diary reveals his thoughts on hearing of Whitley's passing:

> Of course I am glad that he has gone because he was so anxious to be off and was so tired of it all. Apart from this, however, I am very sad indeed and can never be grateful to him enough for all that he has done for me. It began when he arrived bringing peace and comparative happiness again in place of our so miserable state under the 'lord' and the 'Red Woman'.[37] It seemed that one of his main objects was to make me happy, and if he did not succeed I suppose it was because nothing would make me happy, but he certainly removed completely the major cause for my unhappiness in the two or three years preceding 1930. He was a great comfort officially as he was never the least worried about the machinations of our enemies and one felt certain of his backing in everything.[38]

Whitley's death was quite a severe blow for Reith, and according to Ian McIntyre 'Reith felt Whitley's death almost as keenly as that of his own father . . . and the tribute which he broadcast had all the sonority of a funeral oration in the high Roman style.'[39] Three days later the *Listener* published Reith's tribute to the late Chairman:

> He came to us by no means willingly, for his service had been long and arduous; he had hoped to spend his remaining years largely in foreign travel. Whatever he may have lost in this respect he and we gained far more. . . . in his own words he was so very happy and privileged at the end of his career to have had the experience and interests of this service; we because he was all to us that a chairman could be. To an immense enthusiasm for the work were joined the decision and strength, the calm and impartial judgement, of a statesman and man of affairs. For all this, for the Christian and absolute integrity of his character, and for his kindliness, we bear him high, very high, in honour and in love.[40]

The broadcast ended with the following elegy –

> Hail and farewell. The laurels with the dust
> are levelled, but thou hast thy surer crown
> Peace, and immortal calm, the victory won.
> Somewhere serene thy watchful power inspires;
> Thou art a living purpose, being dead,
> A fruit of nobleness in lesser lives,
> A guardian and a guide; hail and farewell.[41]

On 6 February, Viscount Halifax (Lord Irwin) paid tribute to Whitley in a broadcast from a regional transmitter.[42] Irwin's tribute gets to the heart of the matter, and is a carefully crafted acknowledgment of both Whitley's deeds and character. Irwin rightly mentions Whitley's social work 'among the boys and young people of his native town'; unlike any other tributes, Irwin draws on the comparison between Yorkshire's moorland and its wild places amongst the natural surroundings as a source for Whitley's 'simplicity of character', which he believed marked the way he conducted himself, both publicly and privately. Adept at summing up his fellow man and possessing 'imperturbable good temper and patience, coupled with a shrewd sense of humour' made Whitley a natural peacemaker and considerate respecter of the other point of view. Irwin admits that his first intimate contact with Whitley first occurred in India and that:

> The work that Mr. Whitley did on that Commission is likely to influence, more than the work of any other single man, the future of Indian industrial development. And I have no doubt that the sympathy which he showed through the whole enquiry with the lot of women and children in that great sub-continent was prompted by his early experience of human needs in his native town of Halifax.

Irwin concludes his tribute by casting Whitley with 'characteristic modesty' and

> were he still here, he would disclaim praise as he disclaimed the customary recognition of a retiring Speaker's services. Yet of him, as of few others, it may be said in the words of Pope:
>
> A scorn of wrangling, yet a zeal for truth;
> A generous faith, from superstition free:
> A love to peace, and hate of tyranny:
> Such a man was this.[43]

It is quite fitting perhaps that some of the last words on Whitley be left to those who knew him best, his family. In this section from a personal memoir of his father written in 1969, Oliver Whitley shares his opinions of his father's character and the importance of family history.[44] He states that he believed that 'privilege should be earned and not inherited or conferred, and that everyone should have an equal chance to earn such benefits'. As to his father's legacy and the topic of greatness, he states that he would have laughingly 'discounted any suggestion that he was a great man. He was a good man, very good. The good he did was enormous always . . . and whenever possible anonymous, if he had any enemies it must have been a very uphill task for them.'[45] We learn that as well as Whitley's apparent 'simplicity of character', there was a unconventional side to his nature. Two particular memories bear witness to this. Whitley was a pipe smoker and to the apparent amusement of his family would often put his pipe in his pocket, forgetting to tap-out the burning element and, in a similar precarious vein, on the occasions when he drove the family car he didn't like to look behind, in the apparent belief that 'obstacles were either inconsiderable or moveable, occasionally they were neither'.[46]

Though with any life considered there are opinions to the contrary, and opinion is clearly divided on some aspects of Whitley's personality. He could be direct and blunt at times and he could be angry, though any anger he showed was usually aroused by some injustice, and any severity was often tempered by a kindly disposition. At times he could be hesitant and wavering, and this might explain his reluctance to take on the various positions throughout his years in Parliament and beyond. And yet the opposing argument should take into account the fact that he was a good judge of his abilities, he possessed an 'iron discipline' and was resolute in performing every task he undertook to the best of his ability. According to Lord Irwin's assessment of Whitley's 'simplicity of character', his straightforwardness, if you will, is best illustrated by Whitley himself. In a letter written to his brother Alfred around the time of his resignation from the role of Speaker, he states that he 'is happy that a plain Yorkshireman can do a big job in a simple way without pretending to be an aristocrat'; he goes on, 'will you say to Halifax folk that I prefer to remain Mr Whitley to acquaintances and Harry Whitley to my friends'.[47] Perhaps the sentiment supported by his Labour rival James Parker, accurately describes Whitley as he would have like to have been characterised, a 'true commoner'.[48] On 22 June 1988, Oliver Whitley gave an address at the Percival Whitley College in Halifax. The address, entitled 'Percival Whitley and his forbears' ran with the theme of the 'ignorance of the possibilities' for young people in education.[49] Using his family as an example for the students present, Oliver Whitley believed that 'character' was mostly due to inheritance and if his father and the Whitley family had an unspoken rubric, it might be along the lines of:

> Respect and trust your fellow men and women. They should be weighed rather than counted. They will be weighed eventually, but not by you. Consult them constantly. You will learn from them. Cultivate the art of entering quickly into another person's thoughts and of indicating assent or dissent in graduated terms. Wealth beyond moderate personal needs is an offence unless used for the community's benefit. Privilege inherited should be justified anew in each generation. Any healthy society must provide opportunities for the top to be renewed from the bottom. Tradition is fine unless it stifles innovation. Good government may be fine but it is no substitute for self-government. Don't seek preferment or bother about recognition. Just get on with the job. Oh yes, and be able to laugh at yourself.[50]

Conclusion

Taking into account the obituaries, what do they make of Whitley's life and what major characteristics emerge as a result of them? Clearly they suggest that, as Speaker, Whitley adopted an attitude of patient counsel and that such a characteristic proved effective, especially with regard to the emerging Labour Party, towards whom he adopted a fair and conciliatory attitude. Such an attitude towards minorities throughout his political career endeared him to parties old and new. The Halifax papers believed that he was a man who by instinct and training was destined to a life of public service, and contemporaries of his from his old school at Clifton admired his high-mindedness and the fact that he was a great promoter of diverse education.

Of course obituaries are not inclined to write ill of the dead, though as Voltaire once said: 'To the living we owe respect, to the dead we owe the truth' and once the obituary is written and the dust has settled, sometimes revelations can emerge; long gone are the days of the *de mortuis nil nisi bonum* convention, not speaking ill of the dead. From the material considered here we can say that with the exception of a few minor eccentricities in character and a mild tendency to waver over political and public appointments, Whitley's posthumous account of himself passes reasonably unscathed, and on the whole the responses to Whitley's moral well-being stand up to scrutiny. Of course the selection of evidence, through obituaries and tributes here, is in the main deliberate, enabling us to try and draw out such material that will illustrate some of the moral attributes which Whitley displayed throughout his life. A more accurate assessment in such an area would be better completed over many more pages and with much greater evidence. But here, it is hoped, is a glimpse of the immediate and thoughtful responses to a life, which it appears, was dedicated to a strict set of principles based around high-minded values and an inheritance of familial integrity. By these general principles we might assume that 'in life' as at the point of death, Whitley writes his own 'first draft of history' and from the partial evidence here he might appear to be 'morally at one with his life'. This collection of essays rather endorses the view of a modest man, of some ability and much honest morality. Proud of his Halifax roots, Yorkshireness and Radical roots, Whitley's life dictated the fair judgement of his obituary writers, although the detailed analysis of his life had to await many years for analysis to avoid merely being interred in the cemetery of print.

Notes

1. Michel de Montaigne, *Michel de Montagne: The Complete Essays*, London, Allen Lane, 199, p. 29.
2. *The Daily Telegraph*, 4 February 1935, JHW6/1/4, from the J.H. Whitley Archive in the Heritage Centre of the University of Huddersfield.
3. James Lowther, 1st Viscount Ullswater, Speaker elect, 1905–21.
4. JHW6/1/4
5. Ibid. Jon Lawrence and Richard Toye have both written about the conflict between radical MPs and the more civilised and ordered style of most Parliamentarians; see Jon Lawrence, 'The transformation of British Public Politics after the First World War', *Past & Present*, 190 (2006), 185–216 and Richard Toye, 'The Rhetorical Culture of the House of Commons after 1918', *History*, 99 (2014), 270–98.
6. Charles Manners-Sutton, 1st Viscount Canterbury (1780–1845), Tory Speaker 1817–35 in *The Times*, 5 February 1935.

7 Ibid.
8 O.J. Whitley, article in *The Trading and Educational News*, issue 5 (1969), JHW/7/7.
9 *The Times*, 5 February, 1935. Sir Alexander Mackenzie Livingstone (1880–1950), Liberal MP for the Western Isles (1923–1930), defecting to Labour in 1930.
10 H. Macmillan, *Winds of Change 1914–1939*, London, Macmillan, 1966, p. 179.
11 *Manchester Guardian*, 4 February 1935, JHW/2/7/11.
12 Shapjuri Saklatvala (1874–1932) Communist Party MP for North Battersea.
13 Sir Ralph Verney, letter to Dennis Henry Herbert, 1st Baron Hemingford, (1869–1947), 5 January 1945, JHW/4/3/15.
14 *The Manchester Guardian*, 4 February 1935, JHW/2/7/11.
15 *The Halifax Weekly Courier and Guardian*, 9 February 1935, JHW/2/7/18.
16 *The Halifax Weekly Courier and Guardian*, 9 February 1935, JHW/2/7/2.
17 George Lansbury (1859–1940), Labour leader 1932–35.
18 *The Halifax Weekly Courier and Guardian*, 9 February 1935, –James Parker (1863–1948), JHW/2/7/4.
19 'Memorial Service at Park Congregational Church'. Park church, Francis Street, Halifax, was, during Whitley's lifetime a Congregational Church, JHW/2/7/19.
20 Lady Hattie Fisher-Smith (1857–1938).
21 *The Halifax Weekly Courier and Guardian*, 9 February 1935, JHW/2/7/6. Owen Richard Augustus Byrde (Oscar), Headmaster 1916–35.
22 *The Weekly Courier and Guardian*, 9 February 1935, JHW/2/7/4.
23 Attributed to the Headmaster at Clifton, Mr Whatley in his eulogy, *Bristol Evening World*, 7 February 1935.
24 *The Cliftonian Magazine*, February 1935, 394, JHW/10/6.
25 Hand written notes made by O.J. Whitley, 13 January 1981, JHW/1/1/6.
26 Letter from Sir Ralph Verney to 'Dennis', 5 January 1945, JHW4/3/15. Dennis Henry Herbert, Deputy- Deputy Speaker 1928–29 and Deputy Speaker 1931–43, later 1st Baron Hemingford – see p. 6.
27 As a Liberal Councillor in Halifax in the 1890s, Whitley had been a stern critic of the House of Lords and had wished to see it abolished. Also, as Keith Laybourn indicates in Chapter 5 of this volume, Whitley was strongly opposed to the undemocratic House of Lords in his youth.
28 JHW/4/3/15.
29 George Herbert Hyde Villiers, 6th Earl Clarendon (1877–1955).
30 C. Stuart (ed.) *The Reith Diaries*, London, 1975, p. 151.
31 Joseph Albert Pease, 1st Baron Gainford (1860–1943).
32 J.C.W. Reith, *Into the Wind*, London, Hodder & Stoughton, 1949, p. 132.
33 Ibid.
34 Ibid, p. 176.
35 Ibid., p. 205.
36 Ibid., p. 211.
37 The 'Lord' was the previous governor Clarendon and the 'Red Woman' was Mrs Snowden, later Viscountess Snowden, wife of Philip Snowden, Labour Chancellor of the Exchequer (1924 and 1929–31).
38 Stuart, *The Reith Diaries*, p. 164.
39 I. McIntyre, *The Expense of Glory, A Life of John Reith*, London, Harper Collins, 1993, p. 213.
40 *The Listener*, 6 February 1935, JHW/2/7/13.
41 McIntyre, *The Expense of Glory*, p. 421 – Reith was quoting from an elegy on the death of Sir Stanley Maude, the British army commander in Mesopotamia, who died of cholera at Baghdad in 1917. According to McIntyre the poet was James Griffyth Fairfax, a Lieutenant in the Army Service Corps.
42 Edward Frederick Lindley Wood (Lord Irwin), 1st Earl of Halifax, 1881–1959.
43 A. Pope, 'Epitaphs on Sir William Trumbull', 1716.

44 O. J. Whitley, 'John Henry Whitley 1866–1935', 25/6/1969, JHW/1/1/4.
45 JHW/1/1/4.
46 Ibid.
47 Letter to Alfred Whitley, 21 June 1928, JHW/4/2/7.
48 *The Halifax Weekly Courier and Guardian*, 9 February 1935.
49 O. J. Whitley, *Percival Whitley and his forbears: and their Concern for Education*, 22 June 1988, JHW/1/1/7.
50 Ibid.

Index

Abbey, E.A. 115
Abbey School 58
Acts and Regulations: 'Balfour' Education Act 2; Education Act 1902 11, 81; Finance Bill 1925 186; Government of India Act 1919 132; Local Government Act 1858 169; Local Government Act 1888 169; Reform Act 1867 178; Representation of the People (Equal Franchise) Act (1928) 1; Representation of the People Act (1918) 1; Third Reform Act (1884) 1; Town Planning Act 24; Trade Union Act 1929 129
Advisory Committees 115
AFL 93–94; *see also* American Federation of Labor
AJICIRC 90–91; *see also* Association of Joint Industrial Councils and Interim Reconstruction Committees
Akroyd, Edward 20
All-India Muslim League 132
All-India Trade Union Congress 129, 133
Amalgamated Society of Engineers 73, 89
American Federation of Labor 93–94
Anglo-Indians 136–37
Anglo-Irish Treaty 105
Arnold, Alfred 30, 72, 74–75, 79
artists 63, 116–17, 119, 122–23, 148
ASE 73, 89; *see also* Amalgamated Society of Engineers
ASLEF 91; *see also* Associated Society of Locomotive Engineers and Firemen
Associated Society of Locomotive Engineers and Firemen 91
Association of Joint Industrial Councils and Interim Reconstruction Committees (AJICIRC) 90–91
Australia 3, 18, 99, 131, 147, 175; industrial relations 97; and the influence of the Whitley Reports 86; and interest in the labour question during and immediately after the First World War 96
awards 35–36, 97

Bagehot, Walter 178
Baird, John 117, 120
Baldwin, Stanley 2, 20, 39, 103, 124, 132, 166
'Balfour' Education Act 2
Banbury, Sir Frederick 106
Barrett, John 5, 183–94
Barry, Charles 113–14
BBC 1, 4, 8, 51, 62, 139, 143–53, 155–63, 167, 189; blurred lines of accountability at the top 146; and the Board of Governors 160; and the Chairman 143–44, 150, 155, 162; and news programmes 145, 147–48, 152, 156–61, 163; and the politicians 151; programmes for women and children 4, 134, 138, 158, 192; staff members 159; stations 4, 159
BBC Corporation *see* BBC
Beeby, George 96–99
Beever, James 73–74, 77–78
Beyer, Otto 93–94
Billson, Alfred 56, 71, 77–82
Binfield, Clyde 3, 24, 50–64, 69
Bingham, Francis 106
Birdwood, Sir William 36, 38, 166
bishops 32, 39, 51, 170
Blatchford, Robert 74
boards 39, 87–88, 96, 105, 145; joint conciliation 90; statutory 89; united 150
Boer War 2, 18, 79, 81, 131
Bombay 129, 132–33
Bombay cotton mills 131

Bonar Law 103–4, 108
Booth, Charles 69, 74, 79
Boothroyd, Betty 8
boys 7, 9, 22–23, 26, 30, 33–36, 57, 59, 188–90, 192; in Halifax 189; poor 10, 13, 26, 188; working-class 69
Bradford 60, 69–70, 74, 156–59, 161
Bradford Council 159
Bradford Guild 23
Bradford station 157
Bradlaugh, Charles 34
Briggs, Asa 9, 149
Bristol 3, 9, 12–13, 30, 32–33, 36–37, 68, 170, 173
Bristol Grammar School 170
Britain 2–5, 81, 92–93, 95, 97–98, 115–16, 118–21, 123–24, 129–31, 172–73; growth of embryonic socialism in 67; growth of workplace rank-and-file movements in 98; industrial conflict in 3; and Ireland 173; moves from constitutional government to democracy 5; national policies of 72; and the productivity needed to trade in the post-war world 88; social structure of 5
British Empire 4–5, 8, 119, 124, 129–32, 139, 158, 163, 166–67, 173–79; see also Empire
British Government 96, 129, 132, 172
British industrial relations 88
British politicians 129, 132–33, 135–36, 138
British society 1, 3, 71, 87
broadcasting 145, 147–48, 156–57, 160–162; and adult education 161; development of 156–57; early days of 160; experimental 156; hours of 156; and music 145; policy 144; practices 163; public service 152; to schools 158; services 148, 153; sound 155, 163; technology of 145; wireless 156
Broadcasting House 149, 153
broadcasts 139, 150–152, 157–60, 163, 191; inaugural BBC radio 8; and the relay system 157; for schools 158
Brown, James 121
Brunswick Mills 10, 20
Building of Britain scheme 113, 115–16, 118–21, 123–24
'The Bulgarian Horrors and the Question of the East' (Gladstone's pamphlet) 171
The Burial of the Unknown Warrior in Westminster Abbey (Frank Salisbury) 114
burials 59, 114, 120

Burma 133–35
Burton, Antoinette 129–30
Buxton, Sydney 35–36
Byrde, Owen 188

Cabinet 35, 95, 174, 176
Cambridge 9, 14, 30, 58–59; dons 34; philosophers 32; Union 34
Canada 18, 86, 94–96, 99, 131, 147, 175; geographical dispersion of industry in 95; and India 147; self-government for 18; and South Africa 175; workers in 95
Canadian Federal Government 94, 96
Canadian government 95
candidates 19, 56, 74, 77–78, 82, 104, 106, 167; Labour Party 80–81; Liberal 77–78, 131
capital 2–3, 35, 57–58, 93, 95, 167, 177; and labour 2–3, 167; representative of 95; surplus 16
Catholic schools 2
'Cawnpore Conspiracy case' 129
Chamberlain, Austen 106, 150, 189
Chamberlain, Joseph 2, 81, 175
Chapel, Clifton 37
Charles, (King) 63
children 4, 15–16, 27, 69, 134, 138–39, 158, 192; teaching of 11; and women 4, 134, 138, 158, 192; and young people in Halifax 27, 69
Churchill, Winston 150–151, 174
Civil Service Whitley Councils 90
Clare Hall 22
Clarendon, Lord 145, 152, 190
Clarke, J.A. 13, 19
Clarke, P.F. 2, 71
classes 22, 82, 163, 170, 177; evening education 69; gymnastic 22, 57, 63; labouring 134, 140; maternity 24; municipal 56; parliamentary 55; winter evening 22; working 19, 68, 71, 73, 77, 119
Clayton, Murgatroyd Silk Spinners 73
Cliff, John 132, 135
Clifton College 3, 9–10, 13–14, 30–39, 51, 58–59, 170, 173, 188, 194
Clyde Workers' Committee, Glasgow 86
Coalition Government 105
Cobden, Richard 169
collective bargaining 87, 89, 94, 98; machinery 92; processes 89; rights of unions 86
Colpus, Eve 159

Commissions 170; Indian Labour Commission 26; Indian Statutory Commission 132; Royal Commission on Labour in India 4, 62, 86, 129–40, 147; Simon Commission 132–33, 166–67
committees 15–18, 33, 38, 69, 74, 86–88, 91–92, 94, 97–98, 114–15; ancillary 87; co-operative 94; colliery 92; executive 160; formal 114–15; union-management 94
commonwealth 5, 89, 166, 176, 178–79; *see also* empire
Congregationalists 3, 50, 56, 59–60, 68–69, 168, 170–171; and Cliftonians 60; local 22; Yorkshire 57
Conservative and Unionist government 81
Conservative and Unionist Party 72
Conservative candidates 74–75, 79
Conservative government 186
Conservative voters 74, 80
Conservatives 19, 53, 72–74, 77–79, 82, 103–4, 107–8, 149–50; and Bonar Law 107; critical of Whitley for excessive laxity towards Labour MPs 103; local 188
Conservatives/Unionists 104
cotton mills 131
Craig, David M. 104
Cromwell, Oliver 11, 50, 113
Crossley, Sir Francis 7–8, 15–16, 19–20, 22, 24, 56, 72, 80–81, 168
Crossley, Sir Savile Brinton 72, 79, 81
Crossley and Porter Orphanage School 56
Crossley Schools 13
Curtis, Lionel 158, 176–77

'The Danger of the Whitley Scheme' 97
Davies, Norman 174
Dawson, Pat 19, 72–73
deacons 11, 51, 59–60, 62
democracy 5, 72, 76, 162, 166, 178; and community 72; local political 72; Parliamentary 178
Denison, George T. 155, 175
Denison, Percy 155
Deputy Speaker 9, 53, 61, 104, 184
design awards (for architectural excellence) 24
Director-General of the BBC 143–48, 150, 155, 162, 189–90 *see also* John Reith
Disraeli, Benjamin 1
Dissenting schools 170
donors 37, 115–16, 123; *see also* fundraising
Dumas, Alexandre 33

Earle, Sir Lionel 115
Eckersley, Peter 157
education 3, 7, 10–11, 14–17, 56, 58, 60, 156, 158, 193–94; adult 157, 161; issues 13, 17, 26; liberal 185; local 188; public school 22; and religion 3; state 187; technical 82, 87; university 188; women's 9, 58
Education Act 1902 11, 81
elections 17, 19–20, 25, 38–39, 53, 55, 77–80, 103, 105–6, 172–73; *see also* parliamentary by-elections
Electricity and Tramways Committees 56
Empire 4–5, 8, 119, 124, 129–32, 139, 158, 163, 166–67, 173–79
Employee Representation Plans 93–96
employees 20, 68, 86, 88, 91–92, 94, 96–98; encouraged to join trade unions 92; of non-unionised plants 95; from rural areas 138
employers 1, 14, 58, 81, 86–90, 92–98, 138–39, 185; list of Halifax 168; organisation of 88, 95; responsible 168; in staple industries 89; and unions 97–98; unorganised 90
England 79, 117, 121, 160, 166, 168–70, 172, 174, 176, 178; and competition faced by the cotton spinners from India 167; the home of "local self-government" 169, 173, 176; and local government 175; and the role of historians keeping the vision of self-determination alive 171
English Church Union 168
ERPs 93–96; *see also* Employee Representation Plans
Eton 53, 55, 168
Europe 50, 169, 171, 174, 176–78; and inter-war politics 177; and the post-war break-up of the three empires 176
European civilisation 171
European history 174, 177
European order 176–77
European Parliament 179
European Union 178
evening schools 17, 22

factories in India 134, 136, 138; and conditions viewed as inadequate 4, 138; and workers 130, 134–35, 138, 140
Federal Government 95–97
female enfranchisement, partial 105
Fielden, Lionel 147

Finance Bill 1925 186
First Commissioner of Works 114–15, 117, 120–121
First World War 2–3, 21, 23, 51–52, 73–74, 86–87, 92–93, 95–96, 114, 129–31
Fisher-Smith, Sir George 61
FitzRoy, Edward 53, 104, 185
Flight of the Five Members 114
Fox, Philip 158–59
Fox, Sir Robert 160
Fry, Roger 33–34
fundraising 37, 115–16, 123
Furst, Herbert 123

General Election 1895 72, 74–75, 77, 79
General Election 1900 71–72, 82
General Election 1906 18, 82
General Election 1900 3, 82
General Election 1918 104
General Election 1922 103
General Strike 1926 4, 8, 20, 53, 97, 103, 122, 145, 151
George V, (King) 63, 115, 124
Gibson, George 162–63
Girni Kamgar Union 133
Gladstone, W. E. 1–2, 35, 130, 173, 177; death of 130; government weakened by the failure to save Gordon 34; tirade of 171; zeal in proposing two Home Rule Bills 173
Glasgow 86–87
Gompers, Samuel 93
Gorman, Daniel 130
government 4–5, 17–18, 34, 86, 88, 90, 92, 105–6, 167, 174; central 166, 169; constitutional 5; contracts 94; departments 92; and employer interest in Whitleyism 98; in India 133, 167; of India 5, 132; interference 150; official 151; parliamentary 107, 109, 118; popular 5, 166; provincial 96, 166; regulations 87; representative 178; responsible 166, 175; whips 36, 53, 185; workshops 90
Government of India Act 1919 132
governorships 8, 15–16, 32, 38, 56–57, 62, 143–46, 150, 152, 190
Great Britain *see* Britain
Grey, Alexander 36
Grey, George 36
grievances 97, 107, 171; exacerbated nationalist 131; and the role of collective agreements 88
guilds 23, 57, 69, 162

Haig, Earl 13, 36–38, 60
Hajkowski, Thomas 161
Halifax 1, 7–20, 22–27, 54–59, 67–69, 71–82, 158–59, 161–63, 168–70, 186–89; growing problem of poverty in 23, 69; and the Halifax Independent Labour Party 67; and the Halifax Labour Union 73–74; and the Halifax Labour Union/ILP 73; and the Halifax Trades and Labour Council 73–74; and the Municipal Election Committee 73; strike action in the 1890s 73; Viscount 26, 166, 191; and The Workers' Election Committee 73
Halifax Citizens' Guild of Help 23–24, 69, 159
Halifax Council 73–74
Halifax Courier 12, 21, 75, 78, 82, 131, 155–56
The Halifax Courier and Guardian 186
Halifax Guardian 79
Halifax Guild of Help 9, 57
Halifax High School for Girls 15
Halifax House 26
Halifax ILP (formally called the Halifax Labour Union) 74, 77–79
Halifax Industrial Society 16
Halifax Labour Union 73–74
Halifax Liberal Party 71, 79, 188
Halifax Liberalism 74, 77
Halifax Mechanics Institute 15, 19
Halifax politics 3, 67, 69, 71, 73, 75, 77, 79, 81, 83
Halifax Poor Boys' Camps 22, 24
Halifax Trades and Labour Council 73–74, 81
Halifax Weekly Courier and Guardian 186
Halifax Women's Liberal Association 13, 188
Halifax Workers' Council 81
Halifax Workers' Election Committee 73–74
Hanson Lane Mills 15, 20–21, 68
Harcourt, Lewis 114–15, 119
Hargreaves, John A. 1–5, 7–27, 69
Harris, Jose 131
headmasters 30, 33, 37, 39, 51, 59, 185, 188
Heath Grammar School 15–16, 22, 56, 188
Henderson, Arthur 106
Hendy, David 4, 143–53, 155
Herbert, Dennis (Lord Hemingford) 108–9, 189

Hessel, Hannah 12
Hichens, Robert 32
Hird, Horace 157
historians 2, 32, 117, 119, 145, 174, 179; deprived by Whitley of formal and accessible written records of the decoration of St Stephen's Hall 115; English 171; modern 67; pioneer 59; regular 117
Home Rule for Ireland 2, 5, 18, 71–72, 77, 82, 166, 171, 173–76, 179
Hore-Belisha, Leslie 35
Horne, C. S. 60–61
House of Commons 1–4, 7–9, 16–18, 25–26, 31–34, 52–53, 71–72, 103–9, 121–23, 184–85
House of Commons' Chamber 63
House of Lords 25, 67, 71–72, 76, 77
Huddersfield 10, 21, 27, 58, 60, 157, 159, 161, 163, 168; card makers in 58; commission agent in 10
Huddersfield Examiner 20

Illingworth, Percy 62
ILO 92; *see also* International Labour Organisation
ILP 3, 67, 70, 72, 74–79, 81; *see also* Independent Labour Party
The Imperial Federation League 175
Imperial Parliament 176–77
imperialism 5, 130–131
Independent Labour Party 3, 67, 70, 72, 74–79, 81
India 4–5, 8, 34–37, 59, 62, 129–40, 147, 150–151, 166–68, 170; factories 136, 139; factory workers 130, 134–35, 138, 140; labour unrest in 129, 139; problems of 167; trade unions 138
Indian Labour Commission 26
Indian Legislative Council 132
Indian members of the Commission 132
Indian people 4, 131–32, 136, 140
Indian Statutory Commission 132
Indians 121, 132–34, 138–39, 166, 192
Industrial Commission of Employers 92–93
industrial conflict 3–5, 73; in Britain 4; potential 97
industrial councils 61, 95, 97–98
industrial relations 4, 7, 10, 20, 26, 87, 92–93, 97, 130; and addressing poor factory conditions 4; arrangements 95; Australian 97; British 88; and business 10; experience of 7, 20, 26; in India 139; and joint industrial councils 86–99; processes 89

industrial tribunals 97–98
industrial unrest 53, 61, 86, 94–95, 98, 130
industries 3, 30, 87–89, 91–92, 95–99, 129–30, 133–34, 138, 188; coal mining 92; cotton 103; of India 138; local 58; munitions 86; organised 89, 132
International Labour Organisation 92
Irish Free State 2, 173–74, 176
Irish Nationalists 173
Irish voters 173
Irwin, Lord (Viceroy of India) 32, 132, 139, 166–67, 170, 177, 191–93

JICs 2–3, 8, 86–93, 95–99, 129; *see also* Joint Industrial Councils
Johnson, Matthew 12
Johnston, Thomas 121–22
joint committees 87, 93, 97
joint conciliation boards 90
Joint Industrial Councils 2–3, 8, 86–93, 95–99, 129
Joyce, James 148

Keble, John 168
King, Horace 103
King John at Runnymede, 1215 122
Knighton, C.S. 3, 30–40, 170

labour 2–4, 19–20, 73–74, 80, 86–87, 89–92, 95–97, 104–5, 129–33, 137–39; compulsory 131; conditions 133; delegates 95; exploitation 97; militancy 98; organisation as a central reform 138; and organised co-operation with management 93, 95, 99; shortages 93; solidarity 94; unrest in India 129, 139
Labour Party 4, 67, 70–71, 81, 104, 107–9, 184, 186–88; candidates 19, 56, 104; challenges at the municipal and parliamentary levels 72; emerging 194; fledgling organisation 70; in government 20, 103, 119, 148, 166; and the Labour Church movement 74; leader Ramsay MacDonald 20, 107; members moving endless amendments 36, 108; movement 73; movement, emergent political 3; movement, emerging local political 82; MPs 3, 5, 19–20, 55, 82, 103, 107–9, 121, 145; Prime Minister Ramsay MacDonald in July 67, 92; representation in House of Commons 26; resurgent 19; supporters 78; and a tactical ploy with the Conservatives 74; voters 74, 78, 80; youthful 2

labour relations 86, 98
Labour Representation Committee 81
land taxation 18, 70
land values 3, 18, 70
landed estates 168
Lansbury, George 187
Laybourn, Keith 1–5, 23–24, 67–83, 169
leadership 23–24, 171
lectures 19, 25, 73, 157–58
Leeds-Bradford station (2LS) 157, 159
Leeds Poor Children's Holiday Fund 159
legacy 26, 35, 192
legislation 5, 87, 90, 92, 97–98, 139, 169, 172, 174, 178; industrial arbitration 99; intended 17; remedial land 174
letters 37–38, 51–52, 75, 78–79, 108–9, 115, 118–19, 123–24, 186, 189; animated 118; of apology 109; to Edward Marsden 75; to John Reith 148; joint 150; long 52; to Lord Hemingford 186; private 75, 108, 115; of support 13
Lewis, Cecil 147
Liberal Party 2, 19, 25, 35, 71–72, 74–78, 80–81, 104, 106, 111; and accusations by the Conservative Party of indifference (and even hostility) to Empire and imperialism 130; backbenchers 172; candidates 17, 77–78, 131; centre-left 186; chances of challenging their own candidate 80; clubs in Halifax 75; commitment to the 'progressive alliance' with the youthful Labour Party 2; grassroot members 19, 73, 104; in Halifax 72–73, 79; ideology 110; intellectuals encourage Lloyd George to introduce a synthesis of Liberal and Socialist policies 71; and Labour 104; landslide in 1906 56; and leader Lloyd George regrets the retirement of John Henry Whitley 20; millowners 71; MPs 60, 63, 74, 77, 79, 86, 106, 168, 172; opinion split on the Sudan crisis 34, 82; opponents of the South African War described as pro-Boer 131; and political representation 73; radicalism represented by Whitley 76; and the relationship with the Labour Party 19, 80, 82; values 2, 4; voters 74, 77, 80; and Winston Churchill 174
Liberal Unionists 72, 79, 81, 173
Liberalism 16, 19, 53, 71, 75, 78, 82, 104, 110, 130; and the approach to industrial relations 130; Edwardian 71; growth in Halifax 19, 75; growth of 16, 19; international 18; progressive municipal 14; Whitley's conception of 104
Liberals 17, 19, 53–56, 67, 70–71, 74–81, 104, 110, 130–131, 171–73
Library Listening Groups 162–63
Lincoln College, Oxford 52
listeners 134–35, 148–49, 155–56, 158, 160–161, 163, 191; and broadcasters 155; platform for 161; radio 159; and their habits 156–57
listening groups 161–63
Lister, John 73–75, 77, 79
Lloyd, Frederick 156–58, 160
Lloyd George, David 18, 20, 35, 71, 87, 90, 103–7, 122, 150, 186
local government 169, 171
Local Government Act 1858 169
Local Government Act 1888 169
Local Government Board 174
London Missionary Society 60, 62
Lord, Mary 10
Lowther, James 103, 184

MacDonald, Ramsay 20, 92, 103, 107, 109, 122, 190
Mackintosh, John 169
management 14–15, 17, 88–89, 92–94, 97–98, 175; Beyer Plan for union representatives and 94; local 88; and union co-operation 93–94, 99
Manchester Guardian 186
Mann, Tom 78–79
Marchetti, Ernest 24, 31, 170
Marsden, Edward 68, 74–75, 77–78
Marshall, Earl 25
Marx, Karl 73
Master Builders' Association 98
Mathers Royal Commission (Canada) 94, 99
Matheson, Hilda 147–49
MBA 98; *see also* Master Builders' Association
McCarthy, Helen 136
McCormick, Cyrus 93
McIntyre, Ian 147, 191
McNamara, Michael 129, 139
McNeill, Ronald 106
McTaggart, John 32, 34
members 11–12, 15–17, 23–24, 76–77, 106–9, 121, 132–33, 138–39, 157–58, 185–89; employee 94; fee-paying 74; founding 159; private 38, 106; rank-and-file 86; recalcitrant 20; senior 61;

socialist 77; unpopular 186; wealthy 77; young 22, 185
mills 8, 21, 26, 133–34, 159, 168–69, 185; cotton 93, 131; and the employment of children 69
Milner, Alfred 175
Miners' Reform Committees 87
Monnington, W. T. 121, 123
Montagu, Edwin 35
Montaigne, Michel 183
Montreal Gazette 95
Morality in Public Schools and its Relation to Religion 30
Municipal Election Committee 73
municipal politics 7–8, 10, 15–16, 26–27, 68, 72–73, 77, 187

National Council of Social Service 23, 57, 162
nationalisation of key industries 87, 89
Nationalist Federal Government, Australia 96–97
New Liberalism 67–68, 72; national perspective of 72; progressive policies of 72
Newbolt, Sir Francis 36, 38
newspapers: *Halifax Courier* 12, 21, 75, 78, 82, 131, 155–56; *Halifax Guardian* 79; *Halifax Weekly Courier and Guardian* 186; *Huddersfield Examiner* 20; *Manchester Guardian* 186; *Montreal Gazette* 95; *Radio Times* 161; *The Record* 74; *The Times* 185; *Trading and Educational News* 185; *Yorkshire Evening Post* 159–60; *Yorkshire Post* 13, 155, 157
Nicolson, Harold 148
Nightingale, Florence 63
Northern Ireland 18, 176, 179; Unionist MPs 179

obituaries 5, 51, 183–85, 188, 193–94; national 5; newspaper 183; praising Whitley for his impartiality and ability to mediate discussions 139; of Whitley 184
office committees 90–91
Old Cliftonians 35–38
Old Liberalism 67, 71; and New Liberalism 67; and the vision of Whitley to unite with New Liberalism 68
Oman, C. W. C. 122–23
Oxford 30, 37, 39, 52, 58–59, 156, 168; and Cambridge Unions 34; colleges 51; heads of house 32; historians 122

paintings 113–14, 118, 120–124; *The Burial of the Unknown Warrior in Westminster Abbey* 114; *Flight of the Five Members* 114; *King John at Runnymede, 1215* 122; *Richard the Lionheart* 123
Palace of Westminster 4, 7, 39, 53, 62, 113–17, 119–21, 123, 125, 129
pamphlets 97, 171; 'The Bulgarian Horrors and the Question of the East' 171; 'The Danger of the Whitley Scheme' 97
Panesar, Amerdeep 129–40
Parker, James 3, 5, 19, 56, 61, 68, 78–79, 81–82, 187, 193
Parkinson, Michael 189
Parliament 17–18, 20, 52–53, 55–56, 58, 106–7, 109, 171–74, 176, 178–79; and by-elections 74, 77–78, 105; and Cabinet 35, 95, 174, 176; history of 63, 113
parliament, and seats 17, 34, 69–70, 74, 77, 79, 105, 107, 172
Parliament, *see also* British Parliament
Parliamentary Labour Party *see* Labour Party
Parliamentary Union of England and Scotland 121
parties 2, 4, 70, 72, 75–78, 88–89, 107–9, 119, 121, 186; mayoral 16; new 187; parliamentary 36; progressive 77, 82; responsible 186
party politics 68, 70
Patmore, Greg 86–99, 167
Pauzé, Frank 95
Pearce, Senator George 98
Peel, Robert 115, 117, 119–20, 122–23
peerages 24–25, 53, 58, 62, 69, 106, 167, 187, 189
Percival, John 30, 37, 39, 51, 59, 170
Percival Whitley College, Halifax 193
Phillips, E.I.A. 37
Pickles, Wilfred 163
policy 18, 68, 82, 110, 130, 146, 149; foreign 172; and John Henry Whitley 172; Liberal Party 70, 72; national 72
political candidates 19, 56, 74, 77–78, 80, 82, 104, 106, 167
political figures 3, 67, 70, 73; dominant 2; transitional 68
politicians 1, 67–68, 109, 147–48, 150–151, 175, 184
politics 1, 3, 19, 58, 67, 71, 110, 168, 173, 178–79; caucus 16; civic 1; community 82; early twentieth-century 5; extra-parliamentary 104; Halifax 3, 67, 69, 71,

73, 75, 77, 79, 81, 83; Indian 133; local 19, 72, 76, 81; municipal 7–8, 10, 15–16, 26–27, 68, 72–73, 77, 187; national 67, 69, 131, 167, 187–88; parliamentary 17, 24, 68, 74; party 68, 70; progressive 76; radical 3, 30; two-seat constituency 68; volatile 166; Westminster 104
Poor Boys' Camps 9, 22, 69
Porter Orphanage 15–16
post-war years 87, 89, 96, 98
poverty 23, 67–70, 72, 131, 138, 166–67; endemic problems of 23, 166; extremes of 23; urban 69
Power, Beryl 134, 136, 167
Prentice, Herbert 35
press 75, 106–7, 120, 122, 146, 175; *see also* newspapers
Price, Richard 80
Prime Ministers 36, 53, 62, 104, 106, 108, 116, 121, 124, 190
Prince Consort 15, 113
Prince of Wales 13, 37
Private Members' Bills 53
privilege 5, 19–20, 67, 76, 188, 192–93; attack on 72; high 152; landed 72; removal of 76
problems 1, 3, 67, 69–72, 108, 138, 143, 149–50, 152, 160–161; chronic 146; contemporary 150; drink 18; economic 138; endemic 166; growing 23; industrial 22, 97; new technical 160
productivity 88, 94, 96, 138–39
progressive education 13; *see also* education
public ownership of the means of production 77
public schools 30–31, 34; great 170; progressive 9; revolution 58
public service broadcasting 152
publications 140, 171; *Morality in Public Schools and its Relation to Religion* 30; *Parliamentary Union of England and Scotland* 121
Pugh, Martin 71
Pugin, Augustus 113

Radicals 55
radio 147, 155, 157, 160–163, 190
radio listeners 159
Radio Times 161
Rae, Norman 61
railways 87–88, 93–94, 97–98
recommendations 4, 30, 90, 95, 129, 138–39, 163; to establish a 'bureau for promoting Industrial Councils' 95; to improve the productivity of Indian factories 139; to reduce factory hours and improve conditions for men, women and children 4; of the Royal Commission 86, 138–39, 167; that there should be an annual cleaning of factories and clean facilities such as toilets and canteens 138; of the Whitley Committee 98, 138; within the voluntarist traditions of British industrial relations 88
The Record 74
Recreative Evening School classes 22, 57
Recreative Evening School Gymnasium 9
Reform Act 1867 178
Reith, John 4, 143–50, 152–53, 156–57, 160, 162, 189–91; character and ability 145; Director-General of the BBC 143–48, 150, 189–90; displays ill temper at the appointment of Whitley to the Chairmanship of the BBC 143; and his biographers 147; and his domineering ego 143; pays tribute to Whitley 191
relay stations 156–61
reports 87–88, 90, 95–96, 98, 132–34, 138, 140, 157–58, 160–162, 187–88; on industrial cooperation 96; Mathers Report 95; Nehru Report 132; Whitley Reports 3, 86–90, 92, 98
The Representation of the People Act (1918) 1
representatives 14, 57, 76, 87, 94–95, 130, 157; elected worker 93; employee 87, 94; existing workplace committee 91; union workplace 94; works committee 92
reputation 8, 11, 16–18, 68, 74, 145, 149, 155, 167, 174; electoral 17; father's 16; growing 56; local 74; parliamentary 18; public 155
Richard the Lionheart (painting) 123
Robbins, Keith 5, 166–79
Robertson, Gideon 19, 96
Rockefeller Jr, John D. 93
Rockefeller scheme 95
Royal Commission on Labour in India 4–5, 20, 62, 86, 95, 129–40, 147, 167
Rugby School 30, 33, 51, 59, 170
Russell, Earl 1

Said, Edward 134
Salisbury, Frank 114, 120–121
Sassoon, Victor 133, 139

Scarborough, John 8, 15
schools 10, 13, 15, 30–33, 35–39, 57–59, 61, 124, 157–58, 188; Bristol Grammar School 170; Catholic 2; Clifton College 3, 9–10, 13–14, 30–39, 51, 58–59, 170, 173, 188, 194; Crossley and Porter Orphanage School 56; Dissenting 170; evening 17, 22; Halifax High School for Girls 15; Heath Grammar School 15–16, 22, 56, 188; Rugby School 30, 33, 51, 59, 170
science 30–31, 33, 35, 96
Scotland 18, 51, 60, 113, 117, 119, 121, 172, 176, 178
Scottish Secretary 172
Scottish Unionists 122
Second Report of the Whitley Committee 90
Seel, Graham E. 113–24
self-government 5, 18, 35, 129, 166–67, 169–71, 173–75, 177, 179, 193; for Canada and Australia 18; of India 167; maintaining liberal ideals of 129; and self-regulation 5; substitute for 193
Seton-Watson, Robert 171
Shaw, George Bernard 148
Shaw, Samuel 61
Sheffield 156–58, 160–162, 188
Sheffield Wireless Advisory Committee 160
Shenstone, W.A. 31, 33
shop committees 86, 90, 92, 97
shop stewards 86, 92
Siepmann, Charles 149–50, 152, 160–161
Sigston, James 12
Simon Commission 132–33, 166–67
Sims, Charles 122–23
Snowden, Philip 145–46
social reform 3, 67, 69, 75–76, 83, 105, 131
social welfare schemes 131
social work 7, 11, 13, 22, 26
socialism 33, 58, 67, 77
socialists 68–70, 74; Sunday schools 74; union movement 92
sound broadcasting 155, 163
Speakers 1–4, 7–10, 25–26, 32–34, 50–55, 107–9, 113–24, 179, 184–86, 188–89; office of 7–8, 13; Edward Fitzroy 53–54, 104, 185; Lenthall 63
Speaker's House 36, 63
St Stephen's Hall 63, 113–25; adornment of 120; decoration of 115, 117; and the painters 114–20

Stansfeld, James 18, 75
state education 187
stations 155–58, 160
statutory boards 89
Stephenson, Clifford 163
Stobart, J. C. 158, 161
Stoddart, Amy 129–40
Stormont Parliament 18
Sunday Schools 11, 13, 26, 61
Sykes Committee 156

Tattersall, James 73, 77–78
Taunton Commission 170
taxation 3, 18, 70
Taylor, Arthur 68
Taylor Society 93
teachers 11, 22, 60, 62, 157
technical education 82, 87
Temple, Frederick 30
The Third Reform Act (1884) 1
The Times 185
Tonks, Henry 32
Toye, Richard 1–5, 103–11
Trade Boards 88–90
Trade Union Act 1929 129
trade unionism 3, 71, 89, 99, 129–30
trade unionists 77, 79
trade unions 3, 20, 73–74, 81, 86, 88, 92, 94, 97; alliance of 81; and collaboration of employers 86; emergent 3; frustration 73; membership of 89; monitoring of 129; and political action 73; restriction on 20; substitute for 88; and wage rates 73; and workers 3, 98
Trades Union Congress 87, 89, 91
Trading and Educational News 185
trams 16–17, 170
Trevelyan, George Otto 172–73
tributes 34–35, 37–39, 155, 167, 183–84, 186–89, 191–92, 194; eloquent 109; and Halifax obituaries 183, 186, 194; personal 183, 189; to Whitley's Speakership 38
TUC Parliamentary Committee 89
Turner, H. H. 32
Turner, James 129–40

union membership 87, 94
union movement 73, 89, 98
union officials 86–87
union representatives 94, 96, 98
Unionism 72, 93; industrial 96; promotion of 94

Unionists 2, 72–73, 89, 104–5, 172–74, 176; backbenchers 106–7; *see also* Conservatives/Unionists; see also Liberal Unionists; see also Scottish Unionists
unions 60, 86–92, 94–98, 113, 119–23, 133–34, 171–72, 175, 178–79, 190; incorporated 122; railway 97; structure of 90; support for the extension of Whitleyism into the Civil Service 90
United Irish League, Halifax Branch 71
United Kingdom 2, 5, 86, 91–92, 95–96, 98, 131, 169, 173–76, 178–79
University of Huddersfield 21, 27, 135–37

Verguson, Christine 4, 155–63
Verney, Sir Ralph 62–63, 105, 108–9, 186, 189
Victoria Hall 60
voluntary social work 7, 11, 13, 22, 26
voters 17, 74, 79, 82; Conservative 74, 80; Irish 173; Labour 80; Liberal 74, 77, 80; working-class 70, 80, 83
votes 15, 17, 19, 34, 38, 70, 74, 78–80, 82, 173; national 80; parliamentary 103; progressive 73–74, 79
votes for women 173, 178

wages 17–18, 71, 73, 86, 90, 94–95, 97; cutting of 96; low 138; minimum 130; and working conditions 94
Wainwright, Richard S. 12
war 2, 23, 36, 51, 79, 89, 105, 129, 147, 176–77
Ward, Paul 129–40
Warren, Sir Herbert 36–39
Wartime Coalition Government 90
Wells, H.G. 148
Wells, Sarah 129–40
Westminster politics 104
Whatley, Norman 37–38
Whiteley, George 10
Whiteley, John 20, 54
Whitley, Ada Rinder 9
Whitley, Alfred (brother of John Henry) 17, 21–24, 57, 60–61, 66, 69
Whitley, Edward 24
Whitley, Helen 159
Whitley, Henry 75
Whitley, John Henry 67–68, 82: accepts the Liberal Party's nomination in 1900 187; and Alfred Billson 56, 71, 77–82; allegation of weakness by Conservative MP Dennis Herbert 108; and Broadcasting House 149, 153; and the *Building of Britain* scheme 113, 115–16, 118–21, 123–24; Chairman of the BBC 143–48, 150, 155, 162, 189–90; and Clifton College 3, 9–10, 13–14, 30–39, 51, 58–59, 170, 173, 188, 194; daughters of 10; death of 13, 15, 24, 27, 155, 160, 178, 183, 186–88, 191; decoration of the New Palace of Westminster 113–16, 118–19, 123; describes St Stephen's Hall as 'one of the most famous shrines of British history' 113–24; elected Liberal Councillor for West Ward in Halifax 69; electoral experience provided by the Halifax School Board 14–15, 22, 74; embraces contemporary Nonconformity 61; and the family 7–8, 10–11, 13, 15, 21–25, 50–56, 62–63, 158–59, 188–89, 192–93; and the family business 10, 20, 68, 189; and family marriages 8, 11–12; fervent Congregationalist 86; the first Halifax man to broadcast to the Empire 163; the first Nonconformist Speaker 8; Free Church Speaker 54; and the General Strike 1926 4, 8, 20, 53, 97, 103, 122, 145, 151; governorships 8, 15–16, 32, 38, 56–57, 62, 143–46, 150, 152, 190; guides Labour into the approved channels of behaviour 103; handling of Labour 108; and his ancestry 10, 172; and his association with John Reith 4, 143, 145–48, 150, 152, 157, 160, 189–91; and his conception of Liberalism 104; and his experience of industrial relations 7, 20, 26; and his Halifax credentials 68; and his legacy 26, 35, 192; and his Liberal Party, convictions as a preparation for a parliamentary career 19; and his maternal ancestry in Leeds 9–12, 58, 60, 70, 156–61; and his reputation 8, 68, 145, 149, 167, 174; and his role as Chairman of Ways and Means 53–54, 104, 106; and Irish Home Rule 9, 18, 76, 104, 173; legacy of 26, 35, 192; MP for Halifax 7, 20, 68, 187, 189; obituaries acknowledge his impartiality and ability to mediate discussions 139; offers himself as a Liberal parliamentary candidate 22; the only Speaker representative of religious dissent since the Restoration 8; and radical nonconformity 10–11; regarded Irish Home Rule as 'a deep political grievance' 18; relationship to India 129; reputation of 8, 11, 16–18, 68, 74, 145,

149, 155, 167, 174; responsible for the adornment in St. Stephen's Hall in the Palace of Westminster 4, 113–14, 120, 124; retirement as Speaker 13, 109, 124; returned as one of the two MPs for Halifax in 1900 3, 72, 74–75; and the Royal Commission on Labour in India 4, 62, 86, 129, 131–40, 147; shaped by his Halifax roots 3, 7, 9, 25–26, 67, 194; as Speaker (1921–28) 1–2, 5, 35, 53, 55–56, 60, 62, 103–4, 184–86, 188; and the Speaker's House 36, 63; and St Stephen's Hall 113, 115, 117, 119, 121, 123, 125; an unusual unifying political figure in Halifax politics 3; welcomes parliamentarians from across the dominions and Empire to the Palace of Westminster 129, 175–77, 179; and the Whitley Reports 3, 86–90, 92, 98

Whitley, Nathan 10, 12, 15–16, 20, 24, 30, 56–57, 68

Whitley, Percival 21, 23, 30–31, 51–52, 59–60, 193

Whitley, Samuel 68, 168, 170

Whitley, Sarah 9

Whitley Committees 3, 87, 90, 97–98; *see also* Whitley Councils

Whitley Councils 20, 22, 26, 62, 71, 96, 98, 110, 167, 185; *see also* Civil Service Whitley Councils

'Whitley Document' 146, 150

Whitley Reports 3, 86–90, 92, 98

Whitley Scheme 89, 91, 95–97, 188

Whitleyism 3, 86, 88–90, 92–93, 95–99, 185; awareness of 98; benefits of 90, 96; in Britain 95; bureaucratic support for 90; introduction of 96–97; legal environment for 99; promoted by George Beeby 97

Wilson, James 30–31, 33–34, 36–37

Winnipeg General Strike 95

wireless broadcasting 156

Wiseman, H.J. 31–33, 35

women 1, 4, 21, 24, 134, 136, 138, 173, 178, 192–93; and children 4, 134, 138, 158, 192; votes for 173, 178

women and children, programmes for 158

Women's Liberal Association 13

Women's Voluntary Service 57

Wood, Edward 152, 166, 168

workers 20–21, 74, 77, 86–89, 91, 93, 95, 97–98, 133–36, 138–39; in Australia 98; in Britain 98; factory 134; gas 17, 73; Indian factory 130, 134–35, 138, 140; in industry 87; radical 87; rank-and-file 86; rural 138; and trade unions 3, 98

workplace 87–90, 92, 94, 97; conditions 95; efficiency 88; organisations 94; rank-and-file movements in Great Britain 98; shop stewards 86, 92

works committees 86, 88, 91–92, 94–95, 98

WVS 57; *see also* Women's Voluntary Service

YMCA 22, 51, 60; *see also* Young Men's Christian Association

Yorkshire Area Council for Broadcast Adult Education 161–62

Yorkshire Evening Post 159–60

Yorkshire Post 13, 155, 157

Young Men's Christian Association 22, 51, 60

Younghusband 38; Sir Francis 32, 36, 38